Writing Spaces

Writing Spaces examines some of the most important discourses in spatial theory of the last four decades, and considers their impact within – as well as beyond – the built environment disciplines. The analysis is situated in the context of the scholarly journal, which, the author argues, has become a pre-eminent, if largely unexamined, context for academic debates. Five influential publications, based in disciplines ranging from architectural history and theory, to urban studies and geography, act as case studies. Drawing on theories of representation, research on globalization, and the sociology and political economy of knowledge, the author explores the interplay between critical theories and the wide range of social and institutional forces that support, and inform, their production.

Writing Spaces argues that scholarly writing influences the priorities and values that inform professional practice, and hence, the built form of cities. The case studies will be a key resource for courses on critical theory in architecture, urban studies, and geography, at both the graduate and advanced undergraduate level. The accessible introduction to current paradigms of critical thought provides a crucial reference for academics conducting research in these areas. The book fosters links between architectural history and theory, geography, and urban studies, placing it at the forefront of interdisciplinary debates in architecture. The innovative critical framework will also be of interest to students, teachers, and researchers in communication and media studies, linguistics, and global cultural studies.

C. Greig Crysler is an Assistant Professor at the Department of Architecture at the University of California at Berkeley.

THE ARCHI*TEXT* SERIES

Edited by Thomas A. Markus and Anthony D. King

Architectural discourse has traditionally represented buildings as art objects or technical objects. Yet buildings are also social objects in that they are invested with social meaning and shape social relations. Recognizing these assumptions, the Archi*text* series aims to bring together recent debates in social and cultural theory and the study and practice of architecture and urban design. Critical, comparative and interdisciplinary, the books in the series will, by theorizing architecture, bring the space of the built environment centrally into the social sciences and humanities, as well as bringing the theoretical insights of the latter into the discourses of architecture and urban design. Particular attention will be paid to issues of gender, race, sexuality and the body, to questions of identity and place, to the cultural politics of representation and language, and to the global and postcolonial contexts in which these are addressed.

Already published:

Framing Places
Mediating power in built form
Kim Dovey

Gender Space Architecture
An interdisciplinary introduction
Edited by Jane Rendell, Barbara Penner and Iain Borden

Behind the Postcolonial
Architecture, urban space and political cultures in Indonesia
Abidin Kusno

The Architecture of Oppression
The SS, forced labor and the Nazi monumental building economy
Paul Jaskot

Words between the Spaces
Building and language
Thomas A. Markus and Deborah Cameron

Embodied Utopias
Gender, social change and the modern metropolis
Rebeccah Zorach, Lise Sanders and Amy Bingaman

Writing Spaces
Discourses of architecture, urbanism, and the built environment, 1960–2000
C. Greig Crysler

Forthcoming titles:

Beyond Description
Space historicity Singapore
Edited by Ryan Bishop, John Phillips and Wei-Wei Yeo

Drift – Migrancy and Architecture
Stephen Cairns

Moderns Abroad
Architecture, cities and Italian imperialism
Mia Fuller

Spaces of Global Cultures
Anthony D. King

C. Greig Crysler

Writing Spaces

Discourses of Architecture, Urbanism, and the Built Environment, 1960–2000

Routledge
Taylor & Francis Group
NEW YORK AND LONDON

First published 2003

by Routledge
29 West 35th Street, New York, NY 10001

Simultaneously published in the UK
by Routledge
11 New Fetter Lane, London EC4P 4EE

Routledge is an imprint of the Taylor & Francis Group

© 2003 C. Greig Crysler

Typeset in Frutiger by Florence Production Ltd, Stoodleigh, Devon
Printed and bound in Great Britain by
TJ International Ltd, Padstow, Cornwall

All rights reserved. No part of this book may be reprinted or reproduced or utilized in any form or by any electronic, mechanical, or other means, now known or hereafter invented, including photocopying and recording, or in any information storage or retrieval system, without permission in writing from the publishers.

British Library Cataloguing in Publication Data
A catalogue record for this book is available from the British Library

Library of Congress Cataloging in Publication Data
Crysler, C. Greig (Christopher Greig)
    Writing spaces: discourses of architecture, urbanism and the built environment 1960–2000/C. Greig Crysler.
        p. cm. – (the Archi*text* series)
    Includes bibliographical references and index.
    1. Communication in architecture. 2. Academic writing.
    3. Architecture – Philosophy. 4. Cities and towns – Philosophy.
    5. Critical theory. I. Title. II. Series.
NA2584.C79 2003
720'.1–dc21
                                                            2002153874

ISBN 0–415–27492–3 (hbk)
ISBN 0–415–27493–1 (pbk)

Contents

List of figures   vi
Preface and acknowledgements   vii

1   **INTRODUCTION**   1

2   **SILENT ITINERARIES: MAKING PLACES IN ARCHITECTURAL HISTORY**   29
The *Journal of the Society of Architectural Historians*

3   **STRATEGIES OF DISTURBANCE AND THE "GENERATION OF THEORY"**   57
Assemblage. A Critical Journal of Architecture and Design Culture

4   **UNSETTLED TRADITIONS AND GLOBAL MODERNITIES**   85
The *Traditional Dwellings and Settlements Review*

5   **ECONOMIES OF REPRESENTATION**   113
The *International Journal of Urban and Regional Research*

6   **BODIES OF THEORY**   153
Environment and Planning D. Society and Space

7   **CONCLUSION**   189
Writing Spaces and the Spaces of Writing

Selected bibliography   205
Index   233

Figures

Chapter Two: Cover of the *Journal of the Society of Architectural Historians*, 59, no. 1 (March 2000) — 30

Chapter Three: Cover of *Assemblage. A Critical Journal of Architecture and Design Culture*, no. 41 (April 2000) — 56

Chapter Four: Cover of the *Traditional Dwellings and Settlements Review*, 12, no. 1 (Fall 2000) — 84

Chapter Five: Cover of the *International Journal of Urban and Regional Research*, 24, no. 1 (March 2000) — 114

Chapter Six: Cover of *Environment and Planning D. Society and Space* 18, no. 1 (February 2000) — 152

Preface and acknowledgements

This book investigates, and attempts to build upon, important developments in theory across the built environment disciplines over the last four decades. I explore arguments and debates in the context of a group of English language scholarly journals that have, in different ways, examined the relationship between buildings, urban spaces and their larger social and historical conditions. As I explain in more detail in the introduction, I believe that there are good reasons to examine theory in the context of scholarly journals. Yet the decision to conduct a study of this breadth in the context of academic publications is nevertheless unusual. What follows is an attempt to briefly explain how I came to write a book like this in the first place.

I became interested in studying theory and journals following my experiences as editor of a small architectural publication called *a/r/c* (architecture/research/criticism) in Toronto in the first half of the 1990s. I had returned to Toronto after living in London through the height of the Thatcher era, with its shifts to privatization. Toronto, like many other large cities in the so-called post-industrial West, was in the midst of an overheated economic boom. There was a good deal of feverish discussion about how to seize the moment and turn Toronto into a "world class city." These rhetorical excesses were accompanied by (to name several of the more prominent examples) bids for a world's fair, the Olympics, and plans for an opera house (still underway as I write). But perhaps the most notable (and for some, notorious) of these examples was the one that was actually built: the Skydome Stadium, a costly sports facility with a retractable roof constructed on unused railroad property between the waterfront and the downtown.

Like other property development "anchors" proposed or constructed during this period, the Skydome was produced through partnerships between various levels of government and local investors. Though everyone claimed the stadium would produce widespread economic benefits, the construction costs were financed in part by shifting government funds away from projects that would would have benefited those caught at the bottom of an expanding urban underclass. The "homes not domes" signs that appeared around the downtown captured the conflicting values and priorities that such mega-projects have come to symbolize. Yet the connection between the Skydome Stadium, rising homelessness and other issues, such as a collapsing healthcare system, was frequently lost in the temporary euphoria of the last economic boom. This was particularly true in local architectural circles, where larger firms benefited from the rapid expansion of investment in speculative property development, but voiced few reservations about what was happening to the collective spaces of the city.

Part of the problem then, as now (not only in Toronto but across North America), was the lack of any forum in which critical issues about the built environment could be debated. (As I discuss in Chapters 2 and 3, the situation has only become worse since the early 1990s). When I worked with a group of academics and critics to found *a/r/c*, there was only one journal exclusively devoted to architecture in Canada, a glossy professional trade journal called *Canadian Architect*. Although this publication has made serious efforts in recent years to discuss the larger social and cultural contexts of architecture and construction, it remains primarily a descriptive venue for new work.

a/r/c attempted to examine how architecture and urbanism shape, and are shaped by, a wide range of social and historical conditions. The journal argued that forces such as the collapse of the Keynesian welfare state, the changing structure of the world economy, and the rapidly changing cultural politics of large cities have all had a profound impact on how buildings are designed, for whom, and for what purpose. In seeking to expand the critical context for architecture, I also hoped that *a/r/c* would help to change (or at the very least raise questions about) what counted as "architecture" and good design. As I discovered, this sort of critical operation (which has much in common with many of the journals in this study) is inherently interdisciplinary. Though my goal was to draw upon debates in critical theory, sociology, political economy, history, and to seek alliances with critics in other built environment disciplines, this was easier said than done. Part of the problem was, in my case at least, the design-oriented education I had received while completing my professional studies in London. Though this had expanded my abilities in many ways, it did not really prepare me to situate architecture in broader social and historical contexts. It was partly the growing realization that my own inability to understand what was going on around me was in some respects institutionally produced, that led me towards writing this book.

It is by now well established that architectural education is as much about teaching through informal mechanisms (such as intense scheduling demands or the tacit practices of the jury system) as it is through the stated agenda of the classroom and design studio. As a consequence, I have become increasingly interested in thinking about how institutional practices (such as the organization of curriculum, the changing relationship between theory and practice, and different forms of bureaucratic/administrative organization) enable or constrain particular forms of knowledge. One of the major goals of this book, therefore, is to show how and why such practices (for instituting knowledge) should become part of an expanded agenda for theory.

My interest in the reciprocal relationship between institutions and critical thought also emerged through my work on *a/r/c*. Though *a/r/c* was not, in the strict sense of the term, a scholarly journal, it quickly became clear that it was becoming an institution of sorts, or to be more precise, a social form concerned with putting knowledge into action (instituting ideas). When working on *a/r/c*, I became (as all editors do) very aware of the way the many processes involved in journal publication shape what appears in print. I mean this less in terms of the role of editors and peer reviewers as "gatekeepers," and more in terms of the many small-scale, routine, and often invisible practices that affect what appears in print and how it does so. I discovered when editing *a/r/c*, for example, the art of developing a theme and list of contributions that might attract the interests of a particular funding agency; I also learned about the difficulty unknown journals (and unknown editors) face when starting a publication.

I left architectural practice and returned to graduate school at Binghamton University in upstate New York, with the idea that I would develop a dissertation project that would examine different theoretical frameworks that might begin to shed light on the interrelationship between buildings and power in a global context, while also taking account of the institutional context in which such knowledge is produced. Scholarly journals became the starting point for this project, because (as I say in more detail in the introduction) they are both institutions in themselves, and part of larger institutions of knowledge and power.

Like all dissertation projects, this one was much larger when I began it. Originally I had intended to examine up to twenty journals in thematic clusters rather than (as is the case now) according to case studies of individual journals. It was probably when I arrived at the library and confronted the sheer volume of research published in the *Journal of the Society of Architectural Historians* (*JSAH*), that I realized the scale of the project, and the need to limit its scope. Indeed, after completing my research on the *JSAH* (founded in 1940), I seriously considered redefining the study to focus on that journal alone. I felt that it, like all the journals I consider in this volume, raised more issues than I could possibly cover in a single chapter, let alone a complete book. But in the end, I continued with the idea of writing a cross-section through critical thought in the built environment disciplines.

If anything, I would have liked to cut my cross-section in more than one direction, so that it could pass through not only the major critical theories in scholarly research in the built environment disciplines since 1960, but also travel in the other direction, connecting theoretical discourses to those in professional trade publications and mass circulation magazines that also deal with buildings and urban space. This would have opened up many additional questions about the changing relationship between theory and practice, and perhaps most significantly, how ideas travel between spheres of knowledge and power (such as the academy and the profession) and change in the process.

However, a study of professional magazines is beyond the scope of this study. The number of such journals is large, and the issues they define are sufficiently complex to require a separate study in itself. The role of the copious illustrations and images in these publications raises significant issues that would require a substantially different study from this one, using different methods.

The reader will discover that much of what I have written is, because of the nature of this project, in the end quite critical. As someone who founded and edited a journal, I know very well how much work they involve and how immensely time consuming they can be. I also understand how quickly and easily they can slip away from the place where they began. Indeed, editing a journal is sometimes like chasing an idea that you never quite catch up with. From my point of view, the best journals are often the most slippery: their assumptions and presuppositions change to accommodate what is happening in the world, and as such they have no fixed beginning or end points. Their conclusions cannot be entirely predicted in advance. If my criticisms seek to achieve anything, it is perhaps to restore the shaky sense of (un)certainty that all the debates I have examined shared when they began.

In the flawed and quixotic tradition of modernist thought, I have struggled towards a form of overview and generalization in this book that is almost absurd. But these dreams of totality are imperfectly realized, and as much as possible, deliberately so: I have tried to represent my generalizations not as truth statements, but as partial reflections of my own quest to understand something bigger than my own experience. The case studies are "wide angle" representations that sometimes become very particular (and peculiar). They are "pragmatically guided" by certain interests, political sentiments, and past experiences.

There is something of the specificity of my condition as a writer in all these accounts, and (not least) the mark of the institutions I have passed through and been shaped by in the process of writing. This book is therefore not only a cross-section through debates in the built environment disciplines; like all books, it is also a cross-section through the author's life. My father died when I started writing this book in earnest, and as I rushed to complete the final manuscript revisions before sending it to Routledge, my mother was hospitalized for several weeks. It is perhaps an indication of the struggle this book has involved that she urged me to finish it rather than return to Canada to visit her when she was very ill. My family, which now includes my mother, my brothers and their families, have been generous and understanding throughout.

Much of my initial work was done while I was a graduate student at the State University of New York at Binghamton, and although the manuscript has been revised considerably since that time, I am deeply indebted to the students and faculty in the Graduate Programs in the History and Theory of Art and Architecture for the support and insight they provided. When I started graduate school I was still quite uncertain of my ability to write and rather terrified of "theory." These fears quickly evaporated in the environment of unpretentious intellectual generosity that has been constructed there.

This project would not have been possible without the financial support of Binghamton University, and a multi-year fellowship from the Social Sciences and Humanities Research Council of Canada. Susan Strehle, an enlightened and visionary Vice Provost at Binghamton, was an invaluable source of encouragement during my student career. I would like to extend particular thanks to my fellow graduate students at the time: Abidin Kusno, who read parts of this manuscript and discussed it with me on numerous occasions, and Shawn Parker, who was also my housemate for much of the difficult time at the start of this project. In his inimitable way, Shawn made the surreal characteristics of the megapolis that is Binghamton into something funny and wonderful. To my other close friends in London, Toronto, Chicago, San Diego, and now Berkeley, thank you for the advice and support I received from all of you as I completed this.

I owe a special debt of gratitude to the members of my dissertation committee, Barbara Abou-el-Haj, Charles Burroughs, and Tony King, who have been steadfast and unwavering in their support of this project and my larger convictions about education and academic life. As the chair of my dissertation committee, Tony King was characteristically generous with his time, exacting in his comments, and enormously encouraging throughout. He suggested that I submit the dissertation manuscript to be published as part of the Archi*text* series that he and Tom Markus founded and edit. Both have been remarkably helpful and rigorous in their comments as I proceeded through the revisions that transformed the dissertation into this book. I am very grateful to the anonymous team of eight scholars in four disciplines who commented on this project as part of an extensive peer review process. Thanks are also due to Caroline Mallinder, the commissioning editor at Routledge, who steered the project through the review process, and more recently Helen Ibbotson who has waited patiently for me to finish it between my other obligations. I would also like to acknowledge the invaluable efforts of my research assistant at Berkeley, Michaeljohn Raftopoulos, particularly in the hectic final stages of completion.

I have carried this project with me as I have moved between institutions, to my current position in the Department of Architecture at UC Berkeley. I completed the latter stages of writing during a stint of adjunct teaching at the University of Illinois at Chicago, where Katerina Rüedi was Director. Her insights on architectural education and the social life of institutions have been a source of inspiration for me. Since I arrived at Berkeley in 1999, I have been surrounded by an amazing group of faculty and students who have kept me on my toes.

Preface and acknowledgements ∎

The purpose of this project became clearer to me after I started teaching at Berkeley, in part because I have been asked (and indeed challenged) it in ways that have always been valuable, constructive, and supportive. The students who have taken my classes, and then read this book will undoubtedly recognize the impact my research has had on my teaching. *Writing Spaces* has changed how I think about education, teaching, and indeed, what education and its relation to various forms of practice might become. I hope the text conveys something of these possibilities to the reader.

Chapter 1: Introduction

Over the last four decades, the immense changes brought about by the reorganization of world financial markets, reductions in travel times, the growth of information technology, and massive increases in world migration have allowed the institutions and forces that create large cities to spread their operations around the globe and greatly expand the extent of interconnected urban networks. It is no longer possible to speak of cities as bounded domains (if it ever was, as scholarship on the colonial city and "systems of cities" reminds us). But it is not just the category the "city" that has been unsettled and reorganized in global time and space: the nation has also become increasingly detached from the formal territory of the nation-state through "long-distance nationalism" and the spaces of "diasporic citizenship." In some cases, new building projects now occupy the space of an entire city (as in recent "mega-projects" in the Pacific Rim), and the process of design and construction by architectural firms (as well as the manufacture of component parts) is now spread across nations around the world. These conditions suggest that the categories of nation, city, architecture, and building cannot be understood as separate entities: they exist as simultaneous and overlapping conditions.

If cities and their spaces now constitute intrinsically interdisciplinary, global conditions, how should theory that reflects critically on the activities of the built environment professions respond? That is the question investigated by this book. Given that disciplines such as architecture, planning, geography, and urban studies continue, for the most part, to be organized around professional training and research that is linked to specific scales of analysis, how should theory be transformed to meet the challenges of the globally interdependent conditions in the twenty-first century metropolis? I suggest that the answer not only requires changes within disciplines. It also requires us to rethink the relationships between them, and indeed, how (and why) disciplines are constituted as such.

That is why this book is about discourse, and the way texts define disciplines and their practices. In the following chapters, I examine a group of influential discourses in the built environment disciplines that have developed since 1960 and that have each, in their various ways, sought to challenge the self-enclosed disciplinary space from which they began. In doing so, they have attempted to relate the analysis of space to wider social and historical conditions.

My discussion is organized around case studies of five influential English language scholarly journals, based in disciplines extending from architectural history to geography. They include the *Journal of the Society of Architectural Historians* (*JSAH*), the oldest journal of architectural history in the United States; *Assemblage*, an important forum for architectural theory, design and criticism; *Traditional Dwellings and Settlements Review* (*TDSR*), which focuses primarily on "traditional environments" in the rapidly industrializing countries of the so-called "third world"; the *International Journal of Urban and Regional Research* (*IJURR*), concerned with the political economy of urban and regional development; and *Environment and Planning D. Society and Space* (subsequently, *Society and Space*), a publication that has played an important role in adapting various forms of social and critical theory to the analysis of geographic space at various scales.

The case studies traverse the four decades between 1960 and 2000. The explosion in specialized scholarly publishing that forms part of the background to my discussion began in the post-Second World War expansion of tertiary education in most "Western" and "non-Western" countries, and intensified from the mid-1970s onwards. The journals I examine here construct a historical sequence that remains fragmented until 1989, when the contents of all five overlap for the last decade of the study. However, with the exception of the *JSAH* (which was founded in 1941), they have emerged in different ways from the social and intellectual transformations associated with what the historian Eric Hobsbawm has called the "crisis decades."[1] Though the extended period of social unrest associated with this period was precipitated by the oil shocks in 1973, the deeper causes can be traced to the early 1960s, when so-called "first world" countries were coming to the end of a long period of unprecedented economic expansion. The crisis decades were marked by the dismantling of Keynesian models of national economic planning and widespread social turmoil that questioned the intellectual foundations and social legitimacy of capitalist modernity. From the 1960s, a growing civil rights movement, feminism, gay rights, left wing, and anti-colonial struggles, among others, raised issues that reverberated, and in some cases originated in student movements within expanding university systems internationally.

Though calls for some form of interdisciplinarity are routine today, they can arguably be traced to concerns about an expanding postwar university system that was, from the perspective of many critics at the time, co-opted to the intentions of a technocratic and imperialist "state apparatus."[2] Seminal critiques of the university as a training ground for a professional–managerial class focused on the ideological separation of knowledge into discrete and instrumental specializations.[3] On one level, therefore, this book is part of the continuing effort to challenge the segmentation of critical thought about cities, urban and architectural space into non-communicating subspecializations. I consider how some of the major discourses in architectural history and theory, and in the social sciences, can contribute to an understanding of the globally interdependent conditions of the contemporary metropolis. At the same time, however, I also undertake an analysis of the silences and limitations of these discourses. It is in the very nature of this task that I have placed emphasis on those aspects that I believe can be seriously questioned, and as a result my discussion and conclusions are at times quite critical.

This does not, however, in any way diminish the very valuable and important contributions that the journals and those who have edited, advised or contributed to them have made, both individually and collectively, to the understanding of the contemporary city and its built environments. Indeed, the very fact that I am able to construct the criticisms I present here is due to the efforts that have been invested in these journals, and the many insights I have gained from reading them. In my analysis, I attempt to locate the contradictions, silences, and reversals in the positions I have examined, not to dismiss them, but to point out ways in which the arguments could be developed more fully. My criticisms often seek to extend what are already valuable debates to another level of development.

All the discourses I discuss here have attempted to move beyond modernist paradigms in which space (whether at the scale of the building or the urban region) is regarded as a thing in itself, and towards the analysis of buildings and urban spaces in relation to wider social and historical conditions. In doing so they have played important roles in changing the terms of critical debate in their respective disciplines. They have introduced fundamentally new questions about everything from how the architectural critic represents what s/he criticizes, to the changing influence of corporate capital in the planning and development of urban infrastructure. This has involved, to borrow a term used in *Assemblage*, the "transcoding" of ideas from other disciplines. The research I examine in this book, to a greater or lesser degree, draws upon discourses and debates from other disciplines (such as philosophy, literary studies, political economy, history, anthropology, geography, and sociology).

Yet, as I ask in the case studies, how, and upon what terms, does this interdisciplinarity operate? Academic discourse makes use of shared terms and ideas that define "boundaries" around what is considered important, and what is not, and indeed, how a discipline's very context of operation will be understood.[4] Interdisciplinary work often combines established blocks of knowledge without questioning how these bounded domains are constituted as such. In doing so, research objects are first granted an independent existence, ignoring the presuppositions that underlie their foundation in distinct areas of knowledge. To move beyond simply rearranging established blocks of knowledge is itself a spatial operation. As Rosalyn Deutsche has argued,

> Radical interdisciplinary work . . . takes account of its own spatial relations. It interrogates the epistemological basis and political stakes of disciplinary authority . . . such work is based on the premise that the objects of study are the effect, rather than ground of disciplinary knowledge.[5]

Discourse produces intellectual territories composed of social and geographic distributions of knowledge and power, fields of disciplinary norms and scholarly representation, and embodied spaces of intellectual identity. It is a space-forming practice. It can either reinforce the boundaries between disciplines and the social worlds they construct, or cut across and link them together. "Technical" interdisciplinarity adds to the terrain controlled by an existing discipline, thereby reinforcing its legitimacy and authority as such. The search for "transdisciplinary" modes of critical operation is a different project. It acknowledges that the disciplines, or specializations of architecture, urban studies and geography are not going to disappear any time soon, and therefore to negate them in the service of some new meta-disciplinary category is naive at best.[6] At the same time, however, transdisciplinary theory insists that the "spatial politics" of contemporary cities can only be fully understood by exploring how these categories are linked together in social practice.

In this book, I argue that journals and their discourses matter: texts have a determinate effect on how we understand, imagine, and act in relation to the world around us. Texts and writing play an instrumental role in shaping the critical and imaginative space in which members of a built environment profession – architecture, planning, urban design – operate. By intervening in the politics of writing we intervene in the politics of built form. Each journal is therefore studied as a space of knowledge, governed by shared methods and practices. It is to the underlying assumptions that inform these textual, institutional, and socio-political "worlds" that my analysis and criticism is directed. What sort of worlds do these discourses construct?[7] Which spaces become visible and which become invisible? Which theories are included and which are excluded? Who speaks and who is silenced? Whose histories, cultures and geographies become important in these representations, and upon what terms?

I suggest that texts and built environments comprise a mutually dependent, rather than opposed, condition, thereby linking the politics of space to the politics of writing. In the first part of this introduction I explore some of the larger theoretical arguments that underpin this book. I describe how the opposition between the real and imaginary (central to the presumed opposition between words and buildings) was first challenged in the text-based humanities disciplines, and explore the significance of these arguments for writing that addresses various scales of space. In the second part, I explain in more detail my decision to focus on academic discourse and in particular the scholarly journal, as the context for my study. One of my central concerns is to treat different forms of writing as situated social practices grounded in specific institutions and the actions of particular agents. I discuss how the double identity of the scholarly journal as text and institution permits such an interpretation.

It will become clear as the reader proceeds through the chapters that the journals I examine are based upon very different assumptions, and expressed through languages that are remarkably distinct from each other. When I began this study with all but the most cursory familiarity with the journals I have selected, I was initially overwhelmed by the variation in how they represent their ideas. As I suggest in the case studies, some of the journals expend more energy on producing a common style, and the journal reads as the work of a collective author, while others have encouraged contradictions in writing styles and research methods, and there is much greater breadth in how ideas are represented.

After having spent a number of years studying these journals, I feel confident in saying that none "add up" to a totally coherent and completely unified position. In each of the case studies, I have tried to represent some of their complexity, and non-linear, sometimes unexpected, development by tracking how arguments emerge in a relational manner, and build upon each other (and changes in cities and the world) over time. However, as I suggest at various points throughout the book, it is clearly impossible to represent all that is written in each of the journals. To those who come to this book as readers of the journals I discuss, or, indeed, their various editors over the years, the members of their editorial boards, and their many contributors, I apologize in advance for any misrepresentations or oversights.

In the third part of this introduction, I describe in further detail my criteria for selecting the journals, and the questions I asked when analyzing them. In doing so, I further define the questions that guided my partial and selective of reading of these journals.

SCHOLARLY WRITING AND LITERARY THEORY

The transformation of built environment theory documented in this book follows in the wake of similar changes in text-based humanities disciplines that began in the 1960s. In much the same way that the critical paradigms examined here question space as a socially transcendent category, so too did the reorientation of literary theory challenge the status of the text as an autonomous formal system of meaning. Post-Second World War Anglo-American literary theory initially developed in tandem with cold war culture. The dominant mode of critical analysis at the time, known as the "New Criticism," was concerned with "close readings" that posited the literary text as a closed system. The sealed boundaries of interpretation reproduced the insulated social and cultural position of the West, then caught within the dichotomies of cold war politics.[8]

It was precisely this disinterested abstraction that came under attack as new social movements entered and transformed the Anglo-American academic system. Campus revolts in the late 1960s, sparked by the civil rights movement, decolonization, the emergence of feminist politics, the growing importance of the gay and lesbian movements, drew attention to the often-unacknowledged Eurocentric and masculinist values embedded in the Western canon. As a result, New Criticism's transcendent critical operations became the subject of vigorous and at times polarizing debate. The "culture wars" in literary studies reached their apogee in the 1980s, with recalcitrant warnings about the "closing of the American mind."[9] Allan Bloom and others argued that the universal values of Enlightenment culture were threatened by minor(ity) scholarship and its basis in an emerging politics of cultural difference. Much of the ensuing debate centered on the political responsibilities of the intellectual: should the professional critic uphold the canon and transmit its core values, or should those values be represented as mutable, biased, and historically contingent?

Similar questions emerged in other disciplines. Yet the attempt to rethink the theoretical presuppositions of disciplines such as history, art history, and anthropology in terms of the social relations of power, arguably began by rethinking academic writing as a form of literary production. Hayden White's 1979 *Tropics of Discourse* is one of the seminal contributions to this debate.[10] In this influential book, White argues that historical inquiry has been traditionally concerned with "mimesis," or the faithful imitation of historical events: the historian's job is to find the "correct" facts and then arrange them in a way that would accurately reproduce a historical event in words.[11] In an argument that was highly controversial at the time, White suggests that such historical narratives are guided less by "the facts" than by the literary structures used to "encode" them into narratives. History, suggests White, is not about constructing an objective mirror of the past in words: it is about constructing the past through the literary conventions of extended metaphors or "tropes." Thus all historical writing can be classified according to their plots, climaxes, and denouements – the building blocks of "master tropes" such as biography, comedy or tragedy.[12]

It is easy to see how this argument might be taken as an affront to the seriousness and truth claims of historical research. Suddenly historians were writing fiction, drawing upon irony, metonymy, metaphor and synecdoche to do so. Yet White's intention was not to abolish the "real," or to cast doubts about the value of historical inquiry. Rather, he sought to show how our understanding of the real must always pass through language and its mediating impact on what we say, and how we say it. White's argument, while important for the way it points to the role of representation in shaping critical thought, is also problematic because it ignores a crucial aspect of discourse: its basis in institutions and particular configurations of social power. White has been criticized for positing classical narrative structure as the given (and only) form of representation when it is in fact the product of a particular culture at a specific time and place.[13] In the end, the narrative trope is the only social context that White discusses in his analysis; as a result discourse is stripped of its relationship with systems of power and rendered as a universal, acultural system.

Attention to the historically and socially situated nature of discourse is central to the writing of Michel Foucault. Unlike White, Foucault suggests that discourse is "productive": every discourse creates a center and a margin. As a result, discourse and its truth claims are the site of social struggle as groups attempt to resist or transform the terms of their (in)visibility. Like White, Foucault does not deny the existence of the real; on the contrary, he asserts that what we perceive to be significant and how we interpret objects and events and set them within systems of meaning is dependent on "discursive structures." These are what make objects appear to us to be real or material. One of Foucault's best-known quotes about the constitution of objects is as follows:

> We must not imagine that the world turns towards us a legible face which we would only have to decipher. The world is not the accomplice of our knowledge . . . there is no prediscursive providence which disposes the world in our favor.[14]

As the literary theorist Sara Mills has noted, this statement suggests that there is no intrinsic order to the world other than the ordering which we impose on it through our linguistic descriptions.[15] The changing boundary line that has been drawn between buildings and architecture exemplifies this point. Prior to the Enlightenment, architecture referred to religious monuments and buildings of absolutist state power; today the term is used in various ways: to designate the products of professional expertise, or buildings designed by architects; to define an organizational process (the practice of architecture); and to function as a term of critical distinction. Indeed, "architecture" now describes the very buildings to which the term was once categorically opposed. "Vernacular architecture" marks out an expanding field of knowledge deemed by certain historians to contain "significant" or important examples of every-day buildings produced by people without "formal" architectural training.

Discourse, in Foucault's terms, not only constructs objects such as particular stylistic groupings of buildings or urban space; it also constructs events and sequences of events into narratives which are recognized by particular social groups as "real" or serious. Thus, in the grand narratives of architectural history, certain buildings are excluded as "real" architecture (vernacular or otherwise), and become invisible. Decades or even centuries later, they are recovered because they are viewed as "important" within a different discursive system. This shows us not only how discursive systems can change over time, but how fundamentally important they are in evaluating architecture. Such groups of discourse make up the structure of an episteme, or the grounds of thought in which, at a particular time, some statements and not others, will count as socially legitimate "knowledge."[16]

As Paul Rabinow has noted, Foucault's approach avoids two common and often opposed tactics in contemporary discourse theory: high interpretive science (as in the internal critiques of the text associated with epistemology critique and the history of ideas) on the one hand, and the turn towards "local authenticity, moralism high and low" (as represented by attempts to speak on behalf of, or "give voice" to, dominated or marginal groups) on the other.[17] Instead, the analyst attempts a "pragmatically guided reading of practices and coherence of particular configurations of knowledge and power."[18] This strategy is at its most effective when it is undertaken by someone who shares the actor's involvement in the context examined, but distances him or herself from it. It is a mode of interpretation based on the concept of the "specific intellectual"[19] – someone who, by virtue of his or her training and specialized knowledge, knows the "inside story" of an institution and its background practices but chooses to "defamiliarize" those practices as "meticulous rituals of power."[20]

TEXTS AND BUILDINGS

Buildings and urban space are often considered to be outside representation, their meanings discovered, rather than produced by the critic. Writing about architecture, particularly in the high modernist tradition, has typically assumed that buildings transmit meaning autonomously to the receiving observer: texts ponder and reflect upon these meanings, but are not their source. Authors such as Foucault and White question this position: their arguments suggest that our understanding of buildings, like our understanding of other aspects of the world, also passes through representation, for which there is no prior, pre-linguistic moment.

The relationship between words and buildings has recently emerged as an important area of critical research. It is a fundamental concern of one of the journals examined in this study (*Assemblage*) and it is also the subject of several books. Adrian Forty's *Words and Buildings* (2000) traces the changing meaning of keywords in architectural modernism and argues that language is not a mere supplement to the reality of buildings but plays an active role in structuring our experience of them.[21] Forty emphasizes that the meaning of critical terms is as important for what they resist through exclusion as for what they denote, thus tying them to power relations within and outside the profession. In *The Words Between the Spaces* (2001), Markus and Cameron also argue that buildings are not autonomous representations:

> They are material objects which enclose and organize space. However . . . buildings often do this (or more exactly, their designers do it) on the basis of texts which are representations.[22]

Buildings, they suggest, are imagined through words and images before they are constructed in bricks in mortar. And once they are complete, the capacity of buildings to communicate remains dependent on a multitude of texts, from the tourist's guidebook to the scholarly text of the architectural historian. Forty and Cameron and Markus suggest that, in order for buildings to be read, they must also be written.

As I have stated at the outset, this book is not only about "writing spaces" as a study of the *textual practice* of writing: it is also about "spaces of writing" as the social and institutional context in which writing takes place. One of the most significant attempts to understand this dual relationship is Paul Rabinow's book, *French Modern, Norms and Forms of the Social Environment* (1989).[23] While maintaining a focus on analyzing the practices of reason as they can be understood through historically specific discourses, Rabinow places his analysis within a social and institutional frame of reference that is global in scale.[24] He examines how the "social technologies" of French urbanism – including the theories and practices of architecture and planning – were developed through experiments in French colonies in the late nineteenth century and then mobilized in France on a national scale during the second half of the twentieth century. The central figures in Rabinow's book operate at the intersection of developments in biology, military planning strategy, and urban and architectural design. As members of an emergent "normative class" they are less concerned with writing "theory" than with considering how to implement it; they are "technicians of general ideas."

While Rabinow was concerned with analyzing the practices of reason as fashioned by "middling modernists," I focus on the activities of specific intellectuals who operate at the upper reaches of scholarly discourse. Their writings are concerned with how to define and analyze the built environment historically, socially, economically, aesthetically and, indeed, politically. While their work rarely extends to the level of direct practical application (in terms of writing public policy, designing buildings, planning regions, engaging in historic preservation projects) it is nonetheless influential in that it is used by others to inform policy. Their students and their readership undertake that task; as also do other writers who translate and transform their ideas into the practical languages of trade journals, newspaper articles, and other media. Their "practice" is at the level of the academy – in the texts they write, the curricula they draw up, the lectures they give, the scholarly articles and books they publish, and the archives they sort through and interpret. Thus, while the focus of this book is on architecture, urbanism and the built environment, the medium of that focus is the administration, institutionalization and representation of scholarly research.

JOURNALS AND ACADEMIC INSTITUTIONS

Throughout this book, I maintain that discourse cannot be analyzed outside the settings in which it is produced and disseminated. Academic discourse does not exist on the head of a pin. It is a result of the interaction between speakers and their audiences in specific settings. There are many "sites" of discourse in higher education: these extend from the seminar classroom and the academic conference hall, to the many books and articles that are published annually. Moreover, these sites are connected through pedagogical practice: class lectures and discussions are informed by written texts, and syllabi are organized around readings from books and journals. Scholars communicate with each through verbal and written representations which are often informed by (or later become) books or journal articles.

Given the plethora of "discursive structures" that shape scholarly research, why focus on scholarly journals, rather than, for example, the conferences of professionals, organizations, or textbooks? Though academic discourse is disseminated in many forms, there are good reasons to believe that journals occupy an important, even pre-eminent role in its production and dissemination. Journals are not only part of a matrix of wider institutional forces, they are also institutional structures in themselves. Hierarchies of success defined by social criteria such as income, influence, and power tend to merge within professions in hierarchies of prestige measured in "peer esteem."[25] The dictum of "publish or perish" now operates as an institutional imperative across all disciplines in the university. Tenure and promotion committees routinely look for evidence of regular publication in "refereed" journals.

Journals not only help to construct the reputation and authority of academics, they also play an important role in helping particular departments or research clusters within departments compete for research dollars, students and new faculty. Schools of architecture in particular have successfully exploited the capacity of journals to simultaneously act as marketing devices for generating new admissions, fundraising tools for alumni, and a means to consolidate an "inner circle" of departments linked together by their capacity to publish the research of students and faculty.[26]

While it has become commonplace to link the tenure and promotion of individual academics and, indeed, the survival and success of entire university departments to the amount of published scholarship, it is inaccurate to suggest that this maxim is entirely quantitative in nature. Scholarly journals define a complex system of "cultural capital"[27] that is linked to the reputation of a journal and the standing it is perceived to hold by its readers within a larger field of related journals. Some journals are clearly more demanding, and hence more desirable than others. Journals, like the scholars who publish in them, have reputations; in this respect a scholar's affiliation with a well-established journal translates into a more substantial form of cultural capital than publication in one that is unknown.

In this context journal editors and their peers, who act as reviewers, are often described as academic gatekeepers: the journals they edit play a significant role not only in determining what is said, but who says it, with clear consequences for those whose research work is included or excluded. Scholarly journals are the primary means by which scholars comment publicly on each other's research. They contribute to the construction of reputations and hence, intellectual authority and power, through book reviews and articles that refer directly or indirectly to the "value" of a scholar's work in the field it addresses.

Scholarly journals also occupy a distinctive role in the temporality of academic research: as knowledge production is increasingly driven by intellectual trends and innovation, the journal offers the fastest and most direct means to publication. Indeed, a significant aspect of scholarly publishing consists of edited collections and "readers" frequently composed, at least in part, of material reprinted from journals. Intrinsic to this recycling process is the relative slowness of book production compared to that of many scholarly journals: in best case scenarios, a scholarly journal article may be published within a matter of months, whereas a book can sometimes take a year or more.

JOURNALS AND COMMUNITIES OF METHOD

Journals are also a valuable resource to understand the shared critical languages that define different forms of "spatial imagination." My goal in this study is to understand collective ways of knowing and understanding. I am less interested in the statements of individual authors than in the groups of ideas those statements define when they are examined together with others.[28] Journals are helpful in this regard because they are collective activities: they typically begin when a group of academics seeks to challenge the perceived shortcomings or lacunae of an established area of knowledge.

Journals provide a cross-section through a discourse over a given period of time. They constitute an archive of communication, and when read as whole, allow us to examine how collective voices emerge, and become prominent or fade into obscurity and disappear. In doing so they construct distinctive temporalities, or representations of time. In some cases, such as the *JSAH*, the shift in theoretical and epistemological foundations has been glacial for most of its history. By contrast, the editors of *Society and Space* have sought to attune the journal to ongoing developments in "theory" outside geography and, as a result, the journal has become a barometer of major theoretical developments in the Anglo-American academy over the last two decades.

Thus the value of journals as resources for understanding the shifting terms and conditions of discourse are clear. Until now, however, their potential as such has been largely ignored. For the most part, writing about scholarly journals has been produced by library science specialists, and has focused on the rapid growth in the number of serials over the last three decades, and its consequence for information management in libraries.[29] Perhaps the closest example to this study in methodological terms is Jane Gallop's book *Around 1981*. Her study of the history of US-based feminist discourse examines a series of anthologies published on the subject over a ten-year period. The anthology proved to be a useful vehicle for analyzing feminist discourse, for many of the same reasons I have chosen to analyze the scholarly journals. She writes that anthologies provide

> a method for getting at "symptoms" which recur across various authors. Rather than pointing to some individual's blind spots, these might indicate conflicts operating in a collective situation. I am interested in the marks produced in the discourse of knowledge by a subject, not an individual but a collective subject, the academic feminist critic . . . since anthologies not only have many voices, but are organized choruses, they are good places to witness the dynamics of collectivity. In contrast to idealized or romanticized portraits of collectivity, the hard work of collective action includes individual's attempts to speak for the whole, conflicts between centralizing and marginal discourses within the group, and the opposed pressures of solidarity and responsiveness to minority opinions.[30]

While journals provide a way for us to follow influential debates within or between disciplines, they are not simply conduits or containers for discourse. Anyone who has submitted an article to a peer reviewed journal will know that the idea of the journal as a neutral, uninvolved "frame" around an existing piece of writing is inaccurate. Each journal follows a specific set of protocols when bringing articles to publication. These often involve extended interaction between the editors, "blind" readers and contributors. The reputation of a journal acts as a powerful force in shaping what is printed in its pages: journals are, to a larger degree, "self-selecting." As they become established, their reputations can be both an advantage and a burden. Journals can, in fact, be "captured" and "held back" by their readers and contributors.

The format and organization of journals as classification devices also has a decisive impact on what is written. The table of contents organizes ideas into groups, separating certain themes from others, and orchestrating how we encounter arguments and their (non-)relationship to other arguments. Indeed, the subheadings that define the table of contents can be thought of as metaphorical thresholds between different spaces of knowledge. In the table of contents, thresholds are implied through categories that distinguish research from critical commentary (articles versus book reviews and letters). In this way, journals help constitute hierarchies that may serve to trivialize or marginalize some forms of knowledge while giving greater visibility and importance to others. Here, "lead" or "concluding" reviews are particularly important. The table of contents may also articulate a "master taxonomy" that is central to a discourse. For example, the *TDSR* itemizes the primary objects of analysis the journal studies in its title (traditional dwellings and settlements): the table of contents then subdivides this knowledge into a smaller classificatory grid, through keywords that designate location ("On America"), or methodology ("Field Notes").

Another threshold constituted by all the journals considered here is situated between what is constituted as "scholarly" writing and other types of writing. Footnotes are the primary distinguishing feature of scholarly writing: they not only define a social division of labor that all the journals have implicitly accepted: they also provide valuable insight into what are considered to be the "foundations" of interpretive activity. Footnotes describe who the contributors cite to support or verify their statements, whose voice they "speak" through in order to strengthen their own.[31]

Through their repetition and the links they make between authors, footnotes form discernible patterns in journals: they map the geographic and disciplinary location of a discourse. They also describe its temporality: in the case of the *JSAH*, for example, the foundational texts cited in the journal did not change significantly in the thirty years between 1960 and 1990. In the *International Journal of Urban and Regional Research*, the global diffusion of theories can be tracked through citations. The analysis of footnotes in *IJURR* reveals how critical paradigms travel from one part of the world to another as perceived conditions and "levels of development" change in different national contexts. Citations can also reveal the degree to which a discourse is moving to annex the terrain of another discipline, or to reinforce its position within a discipline.

THE PROLIFERATION OF JOURNALS

The explosive growth of book and journal publishing began in earnest in the 1960s when not only the academic system in the United States but those of most "advanced" industrial countries underwent a process of expansion and reorganization.[32] Over the last forty years there has been a generalization of the "scientific model" of research, in which the university no longer operates as an integrated unit commanded by a particular concept of education, so much as an administrative apparatus for managing a series of loosely integrated activities, each of which follows a particular logic determined by developments in the field, priorities set by funding agencies, pressing social and political issues, and increasingly, partnership with concerns outside the university. This growing emphasis on research over teaching has occurred together with an unprecedented expansion of the tertiary academic systems more generally in "advanced" economies of the "first world." The number of journals has therefore expanded, together with the increasingly specialist audience needed to read, edit and contribute to them.

Libraries of the 119 leading research universities in North America devote up to 60 percent of their acquisition budgets to journal subscriptions. Indeed, the growth and proliferation of journals over the time period covered by this study has been described by technical literature on library management as the "serials crisis."[33] Two processes – growth in numbers and the increasing specialization of journals – have occurred simultaneously. From the 1960s onwards, we see not only a dramatic increase in the number of periodicals, but also, a fundamental change in the type of journal being published.

Changes to the holdings at the Fine Arts Library at Cornell University over this period, for example, provide an indication of how these changes have affected the disciplines studied in this dissertation. Cornell not only offers some of the oldest graduate programs in the USA in the disciplines connected to this study, its library is also internationally known for its exhaustive historical archive of periodicals. Of the 122 scholarly journals currently held by the Fine Arts library on the subject areas covered here, fewer than 10 percent were in existence before 1960; another 14 percent were published prior to 1970. The remaining 76 percent of titles began publishing in the 1970s or 1980s.[34]

Prior to the 1960s the primary journals in architecture, urban planning, and geography were "field" journals – generalist publications that sought (and in some cases, continue to seek) to represent the totality of research and opinion in a particular field; they are typically published by national academic or professional associations. All predate the Second World War: *The Annals of the Association of American Geographers* (1911); the *Journal of the American Institute of Planners* (1935); *Town Planning Review* (1910); the *Journal of the Society of Architectural Historians*, the most recent of this group, began publishing in 1940. From 1960 onwards, while these older field journals remain, they are surrounded by an increasingly crowded array of "specialist" journals that do not attempt to include research over a wide range of competing positions or specializations across a discipline, but rather focus on a specific position or subtopic within a field.[35]

SITES OF DISCOURSE

All the journals in this study are part of the extraordinary transformation of theory in the built environment disciplines that emerged on the cusp of social change and unrest in the 1960s. Though the reorientation explored here is often associated with the notion of "postmodernism," it is a term I avoid, not only because it constructs a historical periodization that suggests modernity is "past," but because it also obscures the very real differences between intellectual currents under a single homogenizing term, thereby rendering important differences and contradictions in approach invisible. If there is a linkage between the journals that are examined here, it is in the commitment to find a way to understand space as a social and cultural process, as theorized in relation to different conceptions of authority and power.

While I explore the emergence and institutionalization of "counter-hegemonic" or oppositional discourses across the built environment disciplines more generally, my study is clearly weighted towards architectural history and theory. I have included two journals that, in different ways, have played a significant role in challenging the norms of Euro-American architectural history and theory. These are considered together with the *JSAH*, a "field" journal that, until very recently (i.e. since the early 1990s), has largely excluded the sort of critical theory and self-reflexivity that characterizes the more recent journals. The *JSAH* provides an important historical dimension to this study, not only because it deals explicitly with the historical analysis of space (especially represented in built form and urban design), but also because it helps to place the other four journals and the academic practices they embody in a larger historical context.

I have also included this journal because it makes the oppositional discourse of the other two architectural journals more fully comprehensible. *Assemblage* began by opposing what its founders regard as the conventions of architectural scholarship, many of which (in particular, the opposition between history and theory) are central to the *JSAH*. The *Traditional Dwellings and Settlements Review* questions not only the Eurocentric selection of objects of analysis, but also the attention to professional culture present in both *Assemblage* and the *JSAH*. It is only possible to understand the full dimension of the debates that shape these journals by considering them together, as part of an interrelated field of knowledge.

The remaining two journals in this study were selected because they both have made significant efforts to link social (as opposed to cultural) theory to the analysis of space. Both the *International Journal of Urban and Regional Research* (1977–) and *Society and Space* (1983–) are concerned with large-scale spatial units of analysis such as the national territory, the urban region or the locality. Indeed, in its entire publication history up to the mid-1990s, and in striking contrast to the architectural journals, the *International Journal* has never published an article about a building.

When considered in relation to the bounded, and often entropic forms of critical analysis that predominate in architectural writing, the discourses of these two journals constitute (at least hypothetically) a kind of breaking out: their capacity for generalization and abstraction, combined with a conception of agency that is defined through conflict between social groups, offers a starkly different image of the city, its spaces, and their meaning.

THE "JOURNAL OF THE SOCIETY OF ARCHITECTURAL HISTORIANS"

Founded in 1941 and published by its parent organization, the Society of Architectural Historians, the *JSAH* is the oldest of the journals studied here and the one I examine first. The *JSAH* is included in this study in order to examine dominant paradigms of architectural history. One of the central goals of the chapter has been to understand how the two central terms of the discourse, the "past" and "architecture," are defined and represented. How is the past constituted, and what does it include and exclude? Whose past is represented and for what purpose? What is the relation between the past and the institutions and agents that produce it in the "present?"

In the *JSAH* narratives of architectural history are typically treated as accurate reproductions of unmediated historical fact, "naturally" suited to representing historical events directly, and employing "ordinary" or natural, rather than technical, languages to do so. Indeed, the journal's editors have frequently reasserted the importance of "ordinary educated English." Until very recently, the *JSAH* has remained more or less untouched by the theoretical influences that have shaped the other journals in this study, particularly the practices of critical self-reflexivity and "located" writing, identity politics and deconstruction that predominate in *Assemblage* and *Society and Space* and, to a lesser extent, the *Traditional Dwellings and Settlement Review*. Indeed, the foundational literature on which much of the journal's research is built remained largely unchanged for the thirty years between 1960 and 1990.

The *JSAH* has played an important role in securing the social legitimacy of the discipline of architectural history. Although I initially regarded the *JSAH* as "apolitical" because of the impersonal, objectivist style of writing that predominates within it, as my research developed I came to see it less as an attempt to transcend politics through objectivity and reason, than as an attempt to enter into politics by the same means.

The journal, and the Society that supports it, was founded in response to the increasing marginalization of architectural history in the university curriculum, particularly in schools of architecture immediately prior to, during and following the Second World War. In the first decade of publication, the editor convened roundtable discussions on the status of architectural education, sought to link the SAH with more established scholarly societies, played a key role in defining the goals of the preservation movement, and established links with government agencies and officials responsible for the designation of historic monuments.

At the same time, the Society established links with the "interested layperson" through field trips to previously undocumented examples of "American architecture" thus playing a role in establishing an emerging canon of American architectural history, while persuading a broader public of its importance and, by extension, of the need for the profession to preserve and maintain it.

The *JSAH*, therefore provides a case study in the strategic use of publishing as part of a broader construction of academic and professional authority. It offers insights, not only into how the past is constituted in historical narratives, but how it is transformed into an arena of professional expertise and practice through the practices and institutions of architectural discourse.

"ASSEMBLAGE"

Founded in 1986, *Assemblage* was published by MIT Press until it ceased publication in 2000. Its contributors were largely based in a small number of Ivy League schools of architecture in the northeast United States. *Assemblage* sought to promote "the vigorous self-awareness of the history, methods and intentions of theory and criticism with practice."[36]

The journal began as an effort to deconstruct the relationship between theory and what are often represented as the opposed realms of history, practice, and criticism in "modernist" architectural scholarship and practice. Contributors to *Assemblage* examine the constitutive role of theory and its institutions in shaping the meaning of the architectural object and challenging modernist presuppositions of immanence and the a priori exteriority of the critic from the object observed. As editor K. Michael Hays noted in the first editorial, architecture is "enmeshed in circumstance, historical contingency, and particular currents of thought; connected in complex ways to the dissemination of values and world pictures, but also to power, to institutional authorities, and to canons handed down through disciplinary traditions."[37]

Drawing upon French literary theory, particularly deconstruction, as well as post-structuralist philosophy, contributors rejected the status of theory as an "appurtenance" to the architectural object,[38] and sought to develop the architectural text as an aesthetic object in itself. This form of writing may lead the reader from the description of the pyramid on the back of the US dollar bill to a speculation on the meaning of pyramids in Heidegger's philosophical writing. It is not narrowly "functional" in relation to the discipline of architecture but draws critical attention to the "rules of the game" by treating the written text as an object in itself; indeed, the editor described this genre of writing as constitutive of an "object-text" in which the reader's attention is directed towards the play of signification across the surface of the page, rather than towards some "extra-discursive provenance" that is revealed through the transparency of writing to the "facts."

Over its fourteen-year history, *Assemblage* raised important questions about the relations between "theory and practice" in professional disciplines. Writers for *Assemblage* sought, according to architectural theorist Mark Wigley, to cultivate an "ambiguous relation with professional practice."[39] One of the primary contributions of *Assemblage* was to draw attention to the historical subservience of theory to professional practice, and to create a space where alternative forms of analysis might emerge. Indeed, the journal's support for theory that did not simply hold an "ambiguous relation" with practice, but at times seemed to turn away from it altogether, sparked controversy within the profession.

In the case study, I focus my attention on the limits and contributions of the models of (counter) practice proposed by *Assemblage* both at the level of the design process and through writing. If theory is no longer written to legitimate the professionalized practices of architecture, then for whom, and for what purpose, is it written? Is it possible to write within a discipline and at the same time write with no purpose at all, other than to produce the pleasurable "dissemination" of codes? Does this constitute a form of resistance to the hegemonic practices of architecture? How is the location of these writers in some of the wealthiest universities in the world theorized in relation to the practice of writing theory?

I have also examined *Assemblage* in relation to those forms of writing and design that attempt to adapt the Foucaultian mode of the specific intellectual to architecture. This model offers the possibility of foregrounding a disciplinary apparatus that is largely tacit and, for the most part, taken as given, thereby raising many important issues about how and why subjects and objects of architecture have been constituted historically.

Foucault's theorization argues not only for an understanding of disciplinary practice *per se* but also for an understanding of how those practices have been linked to, and transformed by, their relation with historical forces such as the state, the economy, and indeed, other disciplines. Has the translation of "borrowed material" resulted in its subservience to the historically ingrained construction of architecture as an autonomous social force in and of itself? Or did such operations move towards the deconstruction of the very existence of the discipline as such? Was the deconstruction of fixed categories and ironic revelations of contingencies limited to some areas of practice and not others? For these writers, where did the "discipline" and its critique begin and end?

"TRADITIONAL DWELLINGS AND SETTLEMENTS REVIEW"

Traditional Dwellings and Settlements Review was launched in 1989 by Jean-Paul Bourdier and Nezar AlSayyad, both professors in the Department of Architecture at the College of Environmental Design at the University of California at Berkeley. The *TDSR* challenges the assumptions underlying the contemporary emphasis of "modern" architectural education and practice in most countries upon isolated monuments designed by architects and located in Europe or North America. For much of its existence, the journal has focused on communities defined according to "shared cultural values" as they are represented in "traditional environments" located primarily, though not exclusively, in the rapidly industrializing nations of the "third world."

While the journal has not developed the same analysis of the practices of architectural representation that occurs, for example, in *Assemblage*, both share a critical relation to what are defined as the norms of the discipline. However, instead of examining relations of power internal to the discipline (as constituted in the opposition between function and ornament, or theory and practice) the *TDSR* draws to how the "inside" of the discipline is constituted by focusing on spaces, histories, and forms of practice that have typically been excluded from it.

The *TDSR* is unique, not only among the architectural journals studied here, but within Euro-American architectural publishing more generally. While other journals occasionally publish articles on practices of building outside the geography of North America and Europe, the *TDSR* is the only journal that devotes extensive coverage to the built environments of the "third world." It takes the globe, rather than a small cluster of nations that have been historically defined as the "West," as its geographical unit of analysis. Although almost all of its articles have dealt with spaces that are located in "third world" countries such as Indonesia, China, and within Africa and South America, the definition of tradition pursued in the journal is not limited to a specific geography: tradition can be found wherever "ordinary people" construct "dwellings and settlements" according to shared cultural values.

The *TDSR* places importance on developing an international, rather than a national, or narrowly Euro-American, frame of analysis. One of my central concerns in this chapter has been to understand how writers for the journal constitute the world and their place within it. Attempting to develop a global frame of reference raises several vital questions, all of which are brought to the fore by the writing in the *TDSR*. Does the decision to take the world as the unit of analysis necessarily demand that only "universal" systems of explanation be used in order to write about that world?

A related question is whether tradition – though initially constituted in the journal as a basic human characteristic – is, in fact, something that is understood in the same way around the world. In order to explore this question, I have begun my analysis from the position that tradition is not something that simply exists in material form, awaiting discovery by a "scholar of tradition" (typically an anthropologist), but is constituted by the practices that the scholar brings to those objects. I therefore trace the debates that surround the meaning of tradition in the journal over its history.

When the *TDSR* began publishing it was primarily concerned with environments that are the expressions of shared cultural values of ordinary people. Here, tradition is largely constructed through opposition to historically, geographically, and socio-politically specific definitions of the modern, and hence is determined by it. Indeed, traditional dwellings and settlements are initially represented as unique and autonomous entities, separated from the "modern world" by geographic conditions and the internal resilience of tradition itself. These narratives of the "ethnographic pastoral" are as common in writing about isolated social groups in South East Asia as they are in writing about the "traditional house" in Turkey. Accounts of "traditional life" describe richly crafted buildings in painstaking architectural detail in an effort to preserve the vanishing material evidence of "traditional communities" and their "values."

These narratives constitute tradition as something that is about to be lost to the advancing forces of capitalist modernization. Although they continue to be an important part of the journal's research, a range of parallel debates has emerged that constitute tradition as something within, rather than outside, the space of capitalist modernity. This writing is less concerned with describing the global loss of tradition, than with its many different forms of production. As a result the journal has been opened to debates about traditions of hybridity and corrupted modernity in a global context. I consider how and why this shift in thinking about tradition has come about. Since its inception the *TDSR* has followed the unusual practice of inviting academics to comment on the *TDSR*'s research agenda. These commentaries, some presented first as keynote addresses at IASTE conferences, have often been deeply critical of the journal, particularly its theorizations of tradition and modernity. I discuss these critical dialogues as a distinct genre of writing, and explore their impact on the journal and wider debates on tradition.

THE "INTERNATIONAL JOURNAL OF URBAN AND REGIONAL RESEARCH"

The *International Journal of Urban and Regional Research* was founded in 1977 as a publishing project of Research Committee 21 of the International Sociological Association (established in 1970). *IJURR* defines the "urban and the regional" as "a problem area, rather than a locus for special disciplines and theory, or even a sub-branch of an established discipline or theory."[40] Drawing initially upon Marxist political economy, Weberian theories of social stratification and later, dependency theory and theories of the world economic system, the journal has played a leading role in theorizing urban processes under capitalism.

One of the strongest areas of investigation in the journal concerns the role of state policy in the unequal distribution of housing and other forms of "collective consumption" in the city. Especially in its earlier issues, the journal was a leading forum for adapting Marxist theories of the state, particularly those of Louis Althusser and Nicos Poulantzas, to the study of "urban change and conflict."[41] The journal became an important outlet for research of the so-called French school of urban research, and related studies into the role of urban social movements as political forces in challenging the penetration of an increasingly technocratic "state apparatus" into everyday life.

As the "advanced" capitalist societies studied in the journal began to undergo the privatization of government services and the general withdrawal of the state from many aspects of collective consumption, the initial emphasis on urban social movements came to an end and the journal shifted its emphasis from government policy and protest movements to the analysis of labor regulation, industrial location theory, and the rise of what might be called the "post-Fordist city," characterized by increasing class division, social polarization and new forms of labor exploitation.

The post-Fordist city is overwhelmingly a city of labor: the main acknowledgement of the private realm and gendered divisions of urban space appear in the journal's discussion of housing. However, housing is considered primarily as a public policy issue and examined as a "material resource" that is dispensed, rather than a social space that is constitutive of relations of power. I draw attention to the journal's somewhat cursory attention to, not only gender, but also race, ethnicity, and sexuality. I hope to problematize the functionalist paradigms of social inequality presented in the journal, and hence, open up this mode of analysis for debate and revision.

The journal has also played an important role in constituting the "world city" as an object of analysis. Based on narratives organized around an image of the world economy as a series of "nodes" in a larger network of capitalist forces, the world city's most privileged corporate inhabitants operate within glossy towers that form part of the "command and control centers" for the management and expansion of global capital. The world city is a "spatialized" duality, composed of both barrio and the citadel, the two polarized but also interdependent social spaces that are represented as existing together.

In the space of the barrio two versions of the "international" converge: like the traditional settlement, the barrio is viewed in the *International Journal* as a site of possible escape from the ravages of capitalism. It is represented as a nascent form of social democracy, where residents exploit their marginalization within global capitalism as a means to establish autonomous forms of self-government. Here, cultural narratives of loss, common in the *TDSR*, are replaced by their "social" reverse: they become narratives of emancipation and redemption, though in both cases the observer occupies a position of exteriority to the political subjects he or she shapes in representation.

Although the journal began by publishing articles that were limited, both in topic and contributors, to cities in Western Europe and the United States, in 1987 it began a concerted effort to develop a more global network of contributors and article topics. The *International Journal* has broadened its range of contributors – not least through the four yearly meetings in different cities of the world, of the International Sociological Association – to include substantial representation from North, South, East and West Africa, South America, the Middle East, South East Asia, Central America and the nations of the former

Eastern Bloc. How are such "international" networks of contributors formed? Do they follow existing lines of knowledge and power, or do they seek to challenge them? Upon what basis and according to whose terms has the journal's geography of knowledge extended to global levels of inclusion and exclusion? Is the inclusion of disparate national voices there to confirm the resilience and applicability of systems of knowledge developed through experiences of "Western" city planning and urbanism, or does the journal attempt to expand through the acknowledgement of difference and conflict, within common determinations such as colonialism and global imperialism?

The *International Journal* has made "capitalism" its object of analysis, using realist discourse to persuade its audience (planners, sociologists, and other urbanists, as well as policy makers and government officials) of the underlying cause of urban change and development. The signifying procedures used here suggest that the "real" is located in the processes of the city. In this formulation, Marxism is not regarded as a discipline, but as a set of tools somewhere outside a discipline, that by their very exteriority, enable the "real" to become visible. Yet in claiming to reveal the truth beneath the surface of urban patterns and processes, the *International Journal* has the potential to make the academic demystifier more powerful. Who benefits from these narratives of demystification? To whom are they addressed and for what purpose does this journal speak the "truth to power?" Is this another recoding of the social, appropriated by those already skilled in modeling it for academic study and manipulation?

"SOCIETY AND SPACE"

Environment and Planning D. Society and Space is the fourth in the series of journals published by Pion, an academic press based in the United Kingdom. The editors and contributors of *Society and Space* describe the journal's purpose to be the molding "of a social theory that will help directly unravel some of the key problems in contemporary society."[42] Indeed, many of the writers, though almost exclusively geographers, consider their primary contribution to be an expanded form of social theory that considers space as a constitutive force in social relations of power. *Society and Space* was formed by scholars working in the realms of human and social geography who sought to bring these areas of discourse together.

Launched in 1983, the journal began as an attempt to respond to growing criticism in the field that Marxist social geography has become "aspatial," assigning geographic space an epiphenominal position in relation to capitalist processes. It also sought to address criticism that the emphasis on human agency and imagination fetishized space by making it continuous with a voluntarist human consciousness free of the social processes of capitalism. This impetus for launching the journal can be understood as a contribution to a much larger debate over the role of structure and agency in social determination that became central to "Western" Marxist discourse in the 1970s and 1980s.

The journal's initial focus on various larger epistemological debates about structure and agency has led it to investigate "social theory" that has developed independently of the discipline of geography. The journal's contributors have engaged with many of the major theoretical debates that have predominated in the Anglo-American academy over the last two decades. The cumulative impact of these encounters has been to move the journal further away from its original goal of developing a unified, interdisciplinary model of investigation, and towards a "plural" theoretical position defined by an array of competing interpretations that link various scales of space to social relations of power grounded in feminism, queer theory, literary deconstruction, and most recently, post-colonial, and actor network theory.

The editors and contributors to *Society and Space* have referred to the journal not as one of geography or urban planning, but rather of "social theory." Indeed, Edward Soja, a contributor to the journal who has played a pivotal role in developing the "socio-spatial dialectic" that has featured prominently in its pages, titled his 1990 book *Postmodern Geographies: The Reassertion of Space in Critical Social Theory*, underlining the fact that his concerns were then, and continue to be, as much (if not more so) with "critical social theory" as with geography.[43]

To what extent has the emergence of a common category of analysis called "space" led to new theorizations of the simultaneity and interaction of different levels of urban experience? Professional disciplines have historically established their claims to expertise by monopolizing and setting up institutional measures to maintain exclusive control over specific forms of expertise and knowledge. As a result, attempts to understand the social production of the built environment within professional disciplines are impeded by forms of knowledge which assert the autonomy of a profession and its technical expertise. Do discourses such as those in *Society and Space* and the *International Journal* suggest the possible emergence of some new "common ground" that might act as a baseline for investigations into the spaces of the city that have until now been fragmented into highly specialized, non-communicating compartments of technical "expertise?"

Comparing *Assemblage* to *Society and Space* reveals different genres of "anti-objectivism" that raise different questions and critical issues. *Society and Space*, though now increasingly relying on the same realm of deconstructive theory as *Assemblage*, has employed it for different purposes. While *Assemblage* is largely concerned with revealing and then deconstructing the binary oppositions that structure relations internal to architecture's field of knowledge, contributors to *Society and Space* use deconstruction to express the partiality and socially situated quality of geographic interpretation, not only by revealing how those interpretations previously canonized as "neutral" tend to privilege the experiences and positions of white men, but also by developing other forms of interpretation keyed to specific experiences of race, gender, sexuality, and class, amongst others.

The journal has, for example, been particularly strong in developing feminist interpretations of space. Yet, in deconstructing the voice of white male patriarchal authority, and making room for feminist voices and objects of analysis, does *Society and Space* question the larger category of geographic expertise, and its own institutional and social geography? How far does the challenge to institutional structures of authority extend? Is the framework for geographic expertise being retooled to incorporate the voices of "women" who are already in the profession, and seek greater visibility, or does the discourse question the relation between those who are inside and those who are outside the journal's space of knowledge?

In the conclusion, I draw comparative insights from the case studies and return to a discussion of the relationship between journals, discourse and the formation (and transformation) of fields of academic knowledge. Although all the journals begin with criticisms of existing fields as internally determined, self-enclosed, and with bounded conditions, some have turned into versions of what they criticized: they have become "worlds unto themselves," with secure walls around the spaces they have constructed. Others have been subject to continual change in their assumptions, languages, methodologies, objects of analysis, and participants. They are "leaky habitats" where new ideas seep in, and where disruptions are welcome. These are shaped as much by the connections they foster with "outside" worlds, as by their own debates. Understanding how or why discourses change or remain fixed is a crucial step towards developing a model of interdisciplinarity that takes account of the spatial relations between disciplines, and with other spheres outside the academy, including professional practice. I summarize some of the reasons why these different "spatial" conditions of discourse have emerged, and in doing so hope to identify possible alternative practices.

NOTES

1 Eric Hobsbawm, *The Age of Extremes* (New York: Vintage Books, 1996), 403–432.
2 See, for example, Louis Althusser, *Essays on Ideology* (London: Verso, 1971); a more recent attempt to examine the organization of disciplines in the academy and the political consequences include Cary Nelson (ed.), *Disciplinarity and Dissent in Cultural Studies* (London and New York: Routledge, 1996). Within architectural studies, see Andrezej Piotrowski and Julia Williams Robinson (eds), *The Discipline of Architecture* (Minneapolis: University of Minnesota Press, 2001).

3   See John Frow, "Knowledge and Class," *Cultural Studies* 7, no. 2 (May 1983): 240–281; Barbara and John Ehrenreich, "The Professional Managerial Class" in Pat Walker (ed.), *Between Labour and Capital* (Boston, MA: South End Press, 1979); Pierre Bourdieu, *Homo Academicus* (Stanford: Stanford University Press, 1984); Alvin Gouldner, *The Future of Intellectuals and the Rise of the New Class: A Frame of Reference, Theses, Conjectures, Arguments, and an Historical Perspective on the Role of Intellectuals and Intelligentsia in the International Class Contest of the Modern Era* (New York: Oxford University Press, 1979); Daniel Bell, *The Coming of the Postindustrial Society: A Venture in Social Forecasting* (New York: Basic Books, 1973).

4   Cary Nelson, Paula Treichler and Lawrence Grossberg, "Cultural Studies: An Introduction," in Grossberg *et al.*, *Cultural Studies* (London and New York: Routledge, 1992), 1.

5   Rosalyn Deutsche, *Evictions. Art and Spatial Politics* (Cambridge, MA: MIT Press, 1996), 208.

6   See Cornel West's discussion of interdisciplinarity in architectural theory and criticism in "A Note on Race and Architecture," in *Keeping Faith. Philosophy and Race in America* (London and New York: Routledge, 1993). Writing about architectural criticism, he states that "the challenge is to try and understand architectural practices as power-laden cultural practices that are deeply affected by larger historical forces . . . but also as practices that have their own specificity and social effects . . . ," 47.

7   For an interesting application of these ideas to seminal discourses in urban theory, see James Duncan, "Me(trope)olis." In A. D. King (ed.), *Re-Presenting the City. Ethnicity, Culture and Capital in the 21st Century Metropolis* (London: Macmillan, 1996), 253–268.

8   Jonathan Culler, *On Deconstruction. Theory and Criticism after Structuralism* (London and New York: Routledge, 1983), 20.

9   Allan Bloom, *The Closing of the American Mind: How Higher Education has Failed Democracy and Impoverished the Souls of Today's Students* (New York: Simon & Schuster, 1988).

10 Hayden White, *Tropics of Discourse. Essays in Cultural Criticism* (Baltimore: Johns Hopkins University Press, 1978).

11 Ibid., 40.

12 Ibid., 5.

13 See, for example, the arguments presented in relation to Hayden White's research by Perry Anderson "On Emplotment: Two Kinds of Ruin," Amos Funkenstein, "History, Counterhistory and Narrative," in Saul Friedlander (ed.), *Probing the Limits of Representation* (Cambridge, MA: Harvard University Press, 1992), 54–81.

14 Michel Foucault, "The Order of Discourse," in Robert Young (ed.), *Untying the Text: a Postructuralist Reader* (London: Routledge Kegan Paul, 1981), 67.

15 Sara Mills, *Discourse* (London and New York: Routledge, 1997), 52.

16 Ibid., 47–76.
17 Paul Rabinow, "Representations are Social Facts," in James Clifford and George Marcus (eds), *Writing Culture. The Poetics and Politics of Ethnography* (Berkeley, Los Angeles and London: University of California Press, 1986), 258.
18 Dreyfus and Rabinow, *Michel Foucault. Beyond Structuralism and Hermeneutics* (Chicago: University of Chicago Press, 1983), 124.
19 Michel Foucault, "The Political Function of the Intellectual," *Radical Philosophy*, No. 17 (1977), 12–14.
20 Dreyfus and Rabinow, 124.
21 Adrian Forty, *Words and Buildings. A Vocabulary of Modern Architecture* (London: Thames and Hudson, 2000).
22 Tom Markus and Deborah Cameron, *The Words Between the Spaces* (New York and London: Routledge, 2001), 15.
23 Paul Rabinow, *French Modern. Norms and Forms of the Social Environment* (Cambridge, MA: The MIT Press, 1989).
24 Rabinow has described this form of analysis as "critical cosmopolitanism." He states that "The ethical is the guiding value. This is an oppositional position, one suspicious of sovereign powers, universal truths, overly relativized preciousness ... understanding is its second value, but an understanding suspicious of imperial tendencies. It attempts to be highly attentive to (and respectful of) difference. What we share as a condition of existence ... is a specificity of historical experience and place, however complex and contestable they might be, and a world-wide macro-interdependency encompassing any local particularity." See Rabinow, "Representations are Social Facts," 258.
25 Magali S. Larson, *The Rise and Fall of Professionalism* (Berkeley: University of California Press, 1977), 208–244.
26 Generally only larger and mainly private schools of architecture with significant financial resources have published journals that include scholarly articles, together with students' work and built projects by practitioners associated with the schools. The oldest of these journals is *Perspecta. The Yale Architectural Review*, which began in 1952. A flood of these journals began publishing in the late 1970s and 1980s, and reads like a roll call of the elite private universities in the United States, with the Pratt Institute, Columbia, Harvard University, Princeton, and the Cooper Union all launching glossy, high production annual or semi-annual journals within the space of several years. The practice has, in the 1990s, been extended to Britain with such recently formed journals as *Urban Design International* (Oxford Brookes University) and *Environments by Design* (Kingston University) stimulated by the demands of the UK's University Funding Council's Research Assessment Exercise, to produce evidence of research.

27 Pierre Bourdieu, *Outline of a Theory of Practice* (Cambridge: Cambridge University Press, 1991), 187.
28 Mills, op. cit.
29 See Clara D. Brown and Lynn S. Smith, *Serials: Past, Present and Future* (Birmingham, Alabama: Ebsco Industries Ltd, 1980); David Carson Taylor, *Managing the Serials Explosion* (New York: Knowledge Industry Publications Inc., 1982); Charles E. Osburn, "The Place of Journals in the Scholarly Communications System," *Library Resources and Technical Services* (October/December 1984): 315–325; Robin Denniston, "An Intellectual Explosion Without Precedent," *Scholarly Publishing* (October 1987): 3–17; Dennis P. Carrigan, "Publish or Perish: The Troubled State of Scholarly Communication," *Scholarly Publishing* (April 1991): 131–142; Dennis P. Carrigan, "Research Libraries Evolving Response to the Serials Crisis," *Scholarly Publishing* (April 1992): 138–151.
30 Jane Gallop, *Around 1981. Academic Feminist Literary Theory* (New York: Chapman Hall Inc., 1992), 7.
31 For interesting insights into this, see Anthony Grafton, *The Footnote. A Curious History* (Cambridge, MA Harvard University Press: 1997).
32 In his study of the US academic system, Alain Touraine notes, for example, that in the years between 1955 and 1964 alone, the percentage of those in eligible age groups attending higher education increased from 29 percent of the population to 41 percent of the total, where it has hovered since. See Alain Touraine, *The Academic System in American Society* (New York: McGraw Hill, 1997). In the UK it has increased from 14 percent in 1952 to some 30 percent in 2000.
33 Since 1960, the cost and volume of academic journals has been increasing more rapidly than related figures for books. In 1971, when the "serials crisis" began, the cost of serial subscriptions rose 20 percent in a single year. Between 1970 and 1976, spending at the 119 leading research libraries in Canada and the US increased by 39 percent. Within this figure, spending for journals increased by 100 percent and spending on books increased by 4.3 percent. By 1987, spending on journals had stabilized at 57 percent of acquisition costs. Dennis P. Carrigan, "Research Libraries' Evolving Response to the Serials Crisis," *Scholarly Publishing* (April 1992): 138–151.
34 Based on my August 1992 analysis of the serials holdings at the Architecture and Fine Arts Library at Cornell University.
35 The transition is documented in an article in *Lingua Franca*, describing attempts to reposition the field journal, *Cultural Anthropology*. Daniel Zalewski, "Inside Publishing. Can this Journal be Saved?" *Lingua Franca* (July/August 1995): 14–15.
36 K. Michael Hays, "On Turning Thirty," *Assemblage* 30 (August 1996): 8.
37 K. Michael Hays, "About Assemblage," *Assemblage* 1 (Spring 1987): 4.
38 K. Michael Hays, "Editorial," *Assemblage* 3 (Spring 1988): 4.

39 Mark Wigley, "Storytime," *Assemblage* 27 (Fall 1995). Wigley states that "one of the major reasons contemporary research is being condemned is that much of the writing being done today has a profoundly ambiguous relationship to architectural practice. This ambiguity is highly irritating to those who work so hard to preserve the big stories that I referred to before which organize the topography of the discourse, defining the position we take in the discourse and what a position is in the first place . . . ," 86.
40 Michael Harloe, "Editorial," *IJURR* 1, no. 1 (Fall 1977): 3.
41 This phrase was adopted by Michael Harloe for the title of a series of conferences he organized in the 1970s and 1980s that ran parallel to the founding and early years of operation of the *IJURR*. See Elizabeth Lebas, "Trend Report. Urban and Regional Sociology in Advanced Industrial Societies: A Decade of Marxist and Critical Perspectives," *Current Sociology* 30, no. 1 (Spring 1982).
42 Michael Dear, "Editorial," *Society and Space* 1, no. 1 (Spring 1983): 3.
43 Edward W. Soja, *Postmodern Geographies: The Reassertion of Space in Critical Social Theory* (London and New York: Verso, 1990).

Chapter 2: Silent Itineraries: Making Places in Architectural History

The "Journal of the Society of Architectural Historians"

This chapter examines the *Journal of the Society of Architectural Historians* (*JSAH*), the oldest and most widely read journal of architectural history in the United States. As with all the journals in this study, a complex history is compressed into a comparatively small space. This is particularly the case with the *JSAH*, which has been in existence for at least three decades longer than any of the other journals examined here. The *JSAH* is also (in the technical terms of library scientists) a "field journal" that strives for comprehensive representation of the activities of an entire discipline, rather than to represent the specialized research of one part of a field. It is therefore quite different from the other journals in this study because of its length and breadth of publication. But it is also the only journal that is administered by a nationally based learned society, with its own headquarters and staff. The *JSAH* is published by the Society of Architectural Historians (SAH), an organization founded in 1940 to advance the cause of architectural history in the United States. Beginning as a small, regionally based organization, the Society has evolved into a well-established institution with a staff of seven, whose national headquarters are located in a house designed by Frank Lloyd Wright in Chicago's elite "Gold Coast" district.[1] In addition to publishing the *JSAH*, the Society organizes study tours, holds an annual national conference, and adjudicates awards for books on architectural history, among other activities. Its base in a house designed by Frank Lloyd Wright is, as I will suggest below, emblematic of the leading role both the Society and journal have played in identifying, promoting and preserving significant works of American modern architecture of the nineteenth and early twentieth centuries.

Though it is difficult not to be distracted by the breadth of ideas contained in over sixty years of writing, in this chapter and those that follow, I will try to step back from the particulars of the writing to consider how individual articles are part of a changing set of shared assumptions, languages, and institutional processes. I suggest that there are powerful, if largely unstated, theoretical assumptions at work that have shaped the *JSAH*'s approach to history over time. These constitute a (tacit) theory of architectural history, and help to define the

Cover of the "Journal of the Society of Architectural Historians," vol. 59, no. 1 (March 2000), courtesy of the Society of Architectural Historians.

boundaries between what is considered architecture and "not architecture," the "West" and the "non-West," the past and the present, the professional and the non-professional, and indeed, history and theory. It is precisely the formalization of these boundaries in Anglo-American architectural culture that the two journals I discuss after the *JSAH* seek to contest. As a journal that struggled to put these boundaries in place and, with some alterations, continues to maintain them up to the present, the *JSAH* is a valuable place to start my discussion.

My focus is less on the content of individual articles than with what might be called their allegorical register. I argue here (as elsewhere in this book) that the discourses and debates in the *JSAH* tell at least two stories simultaneously: the first revolves around complex debates on authorship, style, periodization, the chronology of historical development; the second, at least as significant as the first, is about the shared methods, priorities and values such writing represents. My analysis is broken into three major sections. In the first part I situate the founding of the journal in relation to wider changes in the status of architectural history in higher education at mid-century in the United States. I consider the marginalization of history in architectural education by modernist agendas and explore how historians redefined the boundaries of the discipline. In the second part of the chapter, I examine the long period of stasis in which the journal's editorial voice becomes increasingly "univocal" and concerned with a relatively fixed collection of buildings and urban spaces. I consider how and why this closed space of knowledge developed and discuss its interdependent relationship to architectural education and professional practice. I conclude with an analysis of the journal's more recent history when, after a long silence, contributors have once again begun to examine the underlying assumptions that inform much of the journal's writing.

DEFINING THE FIELD

The Society of Architectural Historians (the parent organization of the *JSAH*) was founded in 1940[2] when the relevance of history to architectural education was being questioned in the United States.[3] When responsibility for architectural training passed from the apprentice system to the universities in the late nineteenth century, the teaching of architectural history played a crucial role in differentiating architecture from other more technical disciplines, like engineering.[4] Architectural history, once only a subject among others within university art history programs, assumed a new role, and a seemingly secure institutional future, narrating the origins and history of the profession. Under the Beaux Arts regime that acted as the model for the first American schools, architectural history was also closely tied to the studio, acting as a source for historical types in design projects.[5] However, by the 1940s, the privileged position of history in architectural education was well on the way to being overturned by a wave of modernist educators.[6]

Many of the founders of the SAH taught architectural history in schools of architecture.[7] The changing status of the discipline had a direct bearing on their careers. For example, the appointment of Walter Gropius as head of the Harvard Design School in 1937 led to a reorganization of the curriculum which made the study of architectural history optional. Kenneth J. Conant, a well-known architectural historian at Harvard and the first president of the SAH, was transferred, along with the entire subject of architectural history, out of the school of architecture and into the Fine Art Department. As early as 1932, the amount of time devoted to architectural history in some architectural programs had been reduced to as little as 4 percent of total curriculum hours.[8]

The Society played a crucial role in helping to redefine and secure the professional identity of the architectural historian. A small network of regional chapters that slowly grew to a national scale after the war extended the legitimacy of architectural history beyond the university. Using American architecture as the common object of discussion, the Society built bridges between the "interested lay person" and the professional architectural historian.[9] Members gave presentations on their architectural research, and illustrated talks about local monuments. Local chapters also organized weekend tours to those nearby buildings which were considered significant to American history.

The journal also drew attention to "historic" American architecture and the need to preserve it. A roundtable discussion on the importance of architectural preservation, held between prominent members of the architectural history establishment of the day, appears in the first volume;[10] in 1942 an entire issue was devoted to the subject. A special issue was also published in the first volume which examined how history could develop a new relevance within the emerging modernist curriculum.[11] This marked the beginning of a series of articles published throughout the 1940s which, in an effort to bolster the role of the historian in architectural education, re-examined the relationship between history and the design studio.

PRESERVATION AND EXCISION

It is hard not to be struck by the emotional tone of articles on preservation published in the journal in the 1940s and 1950s. Modernization, when it intruded on the newly emerging canon of American architecture, was considered tantamount to treason. The salvation of national heritage was linked to the knowledge of architectural historians in a manner that was at once both dramatic and juridical.[12] Soon afterwards, several of the founding members of the *JSAH* were asked to serve on Federal advisory boards charged with drawing up lists of nationally "important" buildings whose existence as monuments would be protected by law.[13]

Unlike the discourses of architectural history, those of preservation value not only monumental architecture, but also the spaces of everyday life, including streets, urban landscapes, and buildings not designed by architects. And just as preservation includes vernacular or everyday spaces among its objects of study, it also includes ordinary, non-academic forms of speech as part of its mode of representation. It is a discourse frequently written without footnotes, performed by "amateur" and professional historians alike, who speak passionately at public meetings, participate in local "watchdog" networks, and keep each other informed about possible threats to the preservation of important buildings. It is also an argument that the more scientific discourses of traditional architectural history cannot undertake without diluting and undermining its claims to objectivity.

In the journal's first two decades, discussions of architecture, education, preservation, and town planning fall together in an undifferentiated manner. A surprising number of articles, regardless of their subject matter, are not footnoted. However, in 1957, shorter and less "scholarly" articles about American architecture were transferred to a new section called "American Notes." This remained in place until 1967, when it was removed altogether. After the elimination of "American Notes," articles that would previously have been published there appeared in the *SAH Newsletter*, or migrated to other publications devoted exclusively to preservation. Studies on "high" architecture completed by American masters remained in the section for articles as examples of the American contribution to a traditional canon of architectural history.

The disappearance of "American Notes" and the channeling of what has come to be known as "vernacular" architecture into separate publications, sometimes with the less scholarly status of "newsletter," illustrates the workings of a group of oppositional relations central to the construction and practice of architectural history: between what are seen on the one hand as architectural monuments and on the other as "interesting buildings"; between "scholarly" and "popular knowledge"; and finally between a discourse which seeks to transcend its national context to achieve a "universal" character, and one which is plainly national in outlook, and justifies its arguments through appeals to the imagined or constructed cultural criteria of national significance.

The separation of the professional practices of preservation and history reflected not only irreconcilable differences between their modes of representation and objects of analysis, but also the growing institutional power base of each, and the varying resources each was able to command from both public and private sources. Architectural history no longer needed close proximity to preservation to underline the national relevance of the discipline as a whole. The great postwar expansion of university education was underway in the early 1950s. This, combined with a building boom that lasted nearly twenty years, resulted in the rapid growth of architectural education and with it programs in architectural history.[14]

The same forces that fueled the expansion of architectural education – the recycling and rebuilding of American cities to accommodate a new phase of capitalist investment and expansion – eventually brought preservation to new levels of prominence. As Osmund Overby has noted, the institutional tension that had developed in the journal between "traditional academic interests and some of the newer needs" of preservation was resolved by the latter's increasing "maturity" as a discourse. As the preservation movement developed its own institutions and specializations, new publications emerged (often with SAH members in key roles) which catered to its interests.[15]

UNIVOCITY

As the journal's outlook narrowed, the balance between its taxonomic categories was refined. The knowledge categories of the *JSAH* are organized within the same boundaries of temporal periodization that have traditionally classified forms of historical knowledge in the American university. The Eurocentric "eras" of ancient–medieval–modern are further subdivided into a sequence that begins with ancient Greece, passes through medieval, renaissance and baroque periods and culminates with nineteenth and twentieth century modernism.

Although based on morphological change and development,[16] and therefore putatively grounded in objective laws of measurement and observation,[17] the armature of neo-classical periodization[18] has been continually rebuilt in ways which expand some periods and diminish others, depending on who is mobilizing it, and for what purposes.

It is the way the regional is incorporated into the universal that typically defines differing versions of the system.[19] From its inception, the Society's members have been divided almost equally between those conducting research into European or American topics. The journal has gradually institutionalized this balance, and continues to maintain it as part of its "international" outlook. Only a small percentage of the articles published in the journal since its inception deal with research outside this axis. Though there is some discussion of seventeenth and eighteenth century buildings, architecture of the United States is represented in the journal mainly through a select set of buildings from the nineteenth and early twentieth century. Europe is represented through buildings dating primarily from the sixteenth to eighteenth centuries, though other European periods (particularly the medieval) have also risen and then faded in prominence over the years.

The balance between American and European subjects has been present in the research activities of the Society's members at least since 1944.[20] An article entitled "Where Architectural Historians Fear to Tread,"[21] published in 1967 by John Maass, underscored the predominantly Euro-American emphasis of the journal. Maass analyzed the articles published in the journal between 1958 and 1967, and discovered that of the 450 articles and book reviews published, only eleven dealt with "non-Western" architecture, and that American architecture outnumbered all other subjects in the *JSAH*. My own research confirms a similar pattern. I examined a total of 350 articles published in the journal between 1941 and 1993 inclusive, and found that 94 percent were on topics located in either Western Europe or the United States. This emphasis has remained relativley constant over virtually the whole life of the journal, with a minor, if important shift towards including "non-Western" research between 1998 and 2002.[22]

The *JSAH*'s bifurcation of periods along the geographical lines of the nation-state has the effect of making the United States the domain of "modern" architectural history, and Europe the repository of the past. Although separated geographically, these two periods are nevertheless linked by the underlying foundationalism of the entire system. American architecture, situated at the end of the morphological chain, is the "uniquely American" conclusion to the development of Civilization.

The assertion of the United States as the apex of history occurred when postwar nationalism was at a peak and the American economy was in a confident period of international expansion. At the same time, the identity of architects and architectural historians was undergoing a change as profound as the "great transformation"[23] which brought their professions into existence in the nineteenth century. In both cases, sectors of the middle class were seeking to improve their position in changing social stratifications of capitalist society. Legally enforced monopolies of practice depend on the parallel construction of a "monopoly of credibility"[24] with the larger public. In the socially unstable period of the late nineteenth century, professional groups obtained public confidence through association with the norms and practices of an aristocratic European culture. The same groups conquered their markets in the post-Second World War period by making themselves explorers, collectors, and guardians of the spaces of national identity.

A chain was formed linking the traditional canon of architectural history to American architecture, American architecture to preservation, and preservation to the law of the land. At one end of the chain were the local chapters of the Society, raising the alarm, and rallying fellow historians to fight the good fight;[25] at the other end were the academic architectural historians busy linking American architecture to historical developments extending back to ancient Greece. The chain served as a lifeline for the profession of architectural history, connecting it with a particular construction of American identity at one end, and an equally particular construction of Civilization at the other. In the process new roles for the historian were created in museums, local historical societies, civic trusts, and the emerging heritage industry.

The gradual departure of discourses of preservation, along with other, more informal, voices, is matched by a growing "statistical intoxication"[26] in the journal. By the mid-1960s, an article's footnote text often came close to the length of the article itself.[27] Sibyl Moholy Nagy, in one of the several critiques she wrote about the journal in the late 1960s and early 1970s, complains bitterly in a letter to the editor of the "footnote test," by then well established as a routine at the journal:

> The footnote test demands that at least half of an article be printed out of context, and that at least half the footnotes prove that what the author has to say has already been said by someone else. The article by Carl F. Barnes Jr., on "The Twelfth Century Transept of Soissons" . . . goes the foregoing assumption one better. To 431 lines of text he has 341 lines of footnotes![28]

An increased emphasis on empirical data was matched by the singular use of realist narrative genres to interpret and convey it. There is a decline in the number of articles dealing with preservation, city planning, architectural education and architectural history, and an increase in those concerned with biographies of architectural careers, cathedrals, monasteries, villas, palaces, country houses, castles, museums, and universities. With the settling of the balance between regional and universal, vernacular and scholarly, also came the delineation of a stable field of architectural objects.[29] Thus articles that examine differing institutional and epistemological characteristics of the field (architectural history, architectural education), or that tend to view architectural history from within other discourses (town planning, preservation), gradually assume less importance. Attention turns almost exclusively to single buildings and their architects. If we consider the periods extending from 1941 to 1963 and 1970 to 1993 separately, the number of articles about churches and palatial housing doubles between the first grouping and the second. Despite these changes, one factor has remained consistent throughout: in the 228 articles I examined which establish architectural authorship, all are about white males.[30]

After two decades of lateral shifts and excisions, a univocal editorial voice emerged that, until very recently, has remained largely unchanged.[31] It is a voice based on the predominance of an absent third person narrator, firmly located in what Hayden White calls "traditional history."[32] Our way of reading images and texts in the journal is disciplined through the promotion of realism as a basic mode of understanding. We read for "a content that is modeled on reality at the expense of awareness of the signifying system of which the work is constructed."[33] The narrative is therefore treated as a neutral container of historical fact, "naturally" suited to representing historical events directly, employing ordinary or natural, rather than technical languages to do so. The opinionated voice of the first person is confined to book reviews and letters to the editor, arenas where the historian evaluates other narratives according to what White calls the correspondence/coherence criteria.[34] Narration of the third person favors a "scientific" voice that allows the "I" to return as an arbitrating expert, simultaneously judge and jury, whose knowledge permits qualifying judgments about other narratives based on abstract criteria of truth and logic, sanctioned by the standards of the profession.

GENRES

Two narrative genres are prevalent in the journal: the "life-and-work" and "the work." The life-and-work is concerned with constituting professional subjectivities in relation to architectural space(s) through the trope of synecdoche; that is, the building stands for the life of the architect (or vice versa): "Richardson's American Express Building," "Palladio's Theory of Proportions," "Louis Sullivan's Building for John D. Van Allen and Son," "Vignola's Character and Achievement" – these apostrophized titles underline the ownership that is established between architect and building. The architect's consciousness is situated as the point of mediation between what the historian constitutes as influences (everything the architect experiences), and the presumed final product of that consciousness, the building. A typical example of this approach is the repeated attention given in the journal to determining the effects of Frank Lloyd Wright's kindergarten education on his later work.[35]

Because the synecdochial model requires that economic, social, political, and building forces are somehow assembled in the consciousness of the architect, character-types frequently assume heroic proportions.[36] The architect may be an inventor "of new spatial concepts," an infuser: "history offers sources and prototypes, but it took the genius of Wright and Le Corbusier to infuse mass architecture . . . with twentieth century meaning," a synthesizer, "his ability (lay) not in the development of new ideas, but in a synthesis of a very high order," a personality, "strong-willed and determined," a political ideologist, "creator of fascist architecture," or a visionary, "a prophet of modernism."

The genre of "the work" is constructed out of a chain of elements which suppresses the centralizing function of the architect-as-author. Instead, the metonymic trope dominates, and a series of contiguities represents the whole. This genre is inherently less singular than that of the life-and-work because, in terms of explanation, it privileges a chain of dispersed elements. It therefore takes in a range of research methods, extending from the abstraction of typological studies of building forms, to the contextual studies of social history. However, it is often the case in the *JSAH* that this genre is resorted to when the available data does not permit the use of the life-and-work model. Thus many of the objects that are narrated in the category of "the work" are what might be described as "mute" objects. They exist in the category of "the work" as a stage in (re)searching for "lives," or parts of lives, to pair them with.

Ambiguous authorship or date of origin assigns these objects to a historical purgatory. Here they must wait until sufficient evidence is compiled to establish "attribution." Journal articles pondering mute objects often present a range of documentary evidence in an effort to finalize the authorship or date of a building, as in this note appearing in italics at the beginning of an article about Amiens cathedral: "the combination of a new measured plan, detailed investigation of building fabric and spaces, and a reinvestigation of textual sources . . . leads to a revised chronology and new interpretation."[37]

Buildings that have the status of mute objects are often ones that were "previously unknown," or at the very least, unstudied, and therefore unwritten. They are "discovered" in the rubble of history, and in many cases do not actually exist in built form. They are historicized solely in two-dimensional representations and written texts; the discovery of a building is coincident with the discovery of representations of it. Thus the metonymic model of narration is informed by a metonymic model of investigation: a chain of events is pieced together that ultimately converges in a definitive statement. The starting point of the process is often research by other historians. A building may be treated as something which exists only as a proposition expressed through images; a second historian may decide to see if any such structures were actually built. Thus something as ephemeral as a shadow on an engraving provides "evidence" of the existence of a building, a crucial first step in the metonymic process of reconstruction.[38]

The narrator must intervene to both inaugurate and close off the metonymic chain, which is no longer "naturally" circumscribed by the life-and-death brackets of the architect-as-author. In effect, the contiguities of "the work" are represented as a collective author, which the narrator must bring to life and later silence. This genre therefore changes the way in which facts are dispersed, without challenging the epistemological status of the "facts" themselves, or the author's role in arranging them.

SPATIAL PRACTICES

The creation of a clearly demarcated past is essential to establishing it as a "real" object of scientific research which appears to exist outside consciousness, observed and interpreted, rather than constructed by the historian. The text "substitutes a representation of the past for an elucidation of the present institutional operations that manufacture the historian's text. It puts an appearance of the real (past) in place of the praxis (present) that produces it, thus developing an actual case of quid pro quo."[39] The effacement or disappearance of the historian's presence as narrator is necessary for history to appear as though it is a mirror of the past. The facts are presented as though they speak for themselves; that is, they are presented as a mimesis of the historical event. The disappearance of the narrator into the position of an absent third person thus describes a transition into the protocols of mimesis, where "the quantity of information and the presence of the informant are in inverse ratio, mimesis being defined by a maximum of information and a minimum of the informant."[40]

White argues that the differing ways in which mimesis is constituted in historical narration defines differing forms of historical consciousness.[41] The text constructs a perceptual regime that allows us to "see" history in a particular way, by directing us to take ensembles of representations as icons of events. In the *JSAH*, these ensembles are produced through a combination of narrative and descriptive modes of discourse.[42] Narrative discourse is employed for the "diachronic and discursive manifestation of events, things and beings"[43] and is successive in nature. Description, on the other hand, marks a resting point (and frequently the destination) of the narrative, where an object is viewed in a timeless present, as if it were "always already visually present, fully ordered to full and potential speech."[44] W. J. T. Mitchell states that although literary theory has traditionally categorized narrative discourse as temporal and descriptive discourse as spatial in character, both forms produce different spatialities: narrative discourse constitutes linear forms of space, while description constitutes those which Mitchell describes as tectonic.[45]

There is an assimilation in the *JSAH* between language and space, between route and site, and their enunciated expression in linear and tectonic forms of discourse. The genres of the work and the life-and-work can also be described as itineraries and stories of pilgrimage. Narratives lead us on a journey to a place or places; descriptions wander over the surface of these places once we arrive. We travel along the path of a life, or part of a life, passing through spaces in which parts of the biography unfold temporally (the kindergarten playroom, the home, the university, the architectural office); we examine spaces which putatively influence the architect's design of a building. In the case of the work, multiple but contiguous routes lead to the final destination, a building.

Thus the pilgrimage narrative "makes the complexity of the city readable, and immobilizes its opaque mobility in a transparent text."[46] Fragments of the city are isolated and read as objective signs of the real/past. The historian/narrator becomes a guide who directs perception towards particular objects and events, at the same time demanding "blindness" to other conditions – perhaps social, economic, or political – in order to maintain continuity. Each point on the itinerary is a step in the direction of a journey, "by which is accomplished a desire triggered by a discursive process or narrative chain whose mapped text traces out its realization."[47]

Many of the places of pilgrimage are in the past in the most tangible sense: they no longer exist. The architectural historian is therefore called upon to reconstruct them, assembling visual and textual data in a manner that will produce a convincing account of a "real" place. A physical topography is formed through reference to other accounts and documents, affecting a "domestication of textuality into a self-contained exercise of arranging and cataloguing."[48] A building described in the *JSAH*'s architectural history is often, as with Edward Said's Orient, "a topos: a set of references, a congerie of characteristics, that seems to have its origin in quotation."[49]

In such cases, there is nowhere to travel to, only archives to write from. The result is a closed circle of representational practice, where one form of disciplinary truth statement (the orthogonal projection, for example) is used to supply evidence to support the truth claims of another (the historical narrative). Reception is predicated upon the disciplinary knowledge that allows the receiver to "read" architectural drawings as direct transcriptions of physical objects. In this respect, the *JSAH* does not simply transmit historical narratives; it inscribes and reinforces the methodological techniques of the discipline in both its readers and writers.

STASIS AND CHANGE

From its founding until the late 1960s, the *JSAH* gradually demarcated a coherent field of knowledge drawing on the protocols of realist history. The extended period of stability connecting the late 1960s to the present emerges as one of the most remarkable features of the journal's history. Eugene E. Matysek's analysis of citations for articles published in the journal between 1986 and 1990 confirms that work published more recently in the journal shares many characteristics with the research of previous decades.[50] Much of the scholarship examined in Matysek's study is based on reasearch that dates from before 1970. Of the ninety-eight articles published between 1986 and 1990, 66 percent of the monographs cited were published before 1970, and 13.2 percent were published before 1900. Similarly, 56 percent of the periodicals cited were published before 1950, strengthening the journal's bond with the past, and separating its research from current developments in the field.

The list of most-cited monographs in Matysek's research is also revealing. The nine titles on the list include three from the Pelican History of Art surveys, two dealing with Great Britain and the third with Italy. The most cited authors include Nicholas Pevsner in the top position, followed by Frank Lloyd Wright, Frederick Law Olmsted, and Richard Krautheimer. As Maytsek has noted, the subject characteristics of these works correspond closely with the observations made by John Maass in his study of the *JSAH* between 1958 and 1967. Reflecting on the findings of his research, Maytsek states that "the *JSAH* has apparently changed very little over the past 30 years."[51]

The tendency towards atavism noted by Matysek has occurred at a time when the institutional and discursive fields around the *JSAH* have altered dramatically. Architectural history is now characterized by a wide range of specializations, some of which fundamentally challenge the assumptions and practices of the *JSAH*. Indeed, it is changes to the field outside the journal that the three editors since 1993 (Nicholas Addams, Eve Blau, and Zeynep Çelik) have pointed to, in an effort to transform its agenda from within. In the sections that follow I attempt to summarize the more recent history of the journal. I will suggest that, after a long period of minimal change, the *JSAH* is once again concerned with redefining the boundaries between what is considered "inside" and "outside" its discourse, and with it, the professional identity of the historian.

FOREIGN AFFAIRS

Recent debates at the *JSAH* are marked by (anxious) attention to the "international," not only in terms of the geography of the buildings and spaces analyzed, but in terms of the national origins of the contributors who publish in the journal. Concerns about "foreignness" have become a growing source of debate since 1990. These discussions illustrate how the practices, spaces, and people considered to be outside the concerns of the journal, continue to influence what goes on within it.

In 1993, Nicholas Addams became editor, and in his inaugural editorial wrote of the need to balance "tradition with change." He argued that the journal should "engage the breadth of scholars' interests . . . To seek the margins as well as the center, the new-fashioned as well as the traditional."[52] Addams listed some of the many sub-fields that have emerged in architectural history over the last two decades, including construction history, vernacular architecture, garden history, industrial archeology, urban history, military architecture, and "new methodologies" which "blend architectural history with philosophy, literature, and literary criticism." His remarks suggested that these new approaches would appear as pluralist additions to a set of "traditions" at the core of the journal.

This strategy is further outlined in a subsequent editorial entitled "International Conversations." Addams argues against including "non-Western" scholars in the journal in order to prevent confusion and non-communication. On the one hand, he suggests that the lack of familiarity with "foreign" languages in the United States demands publishing only those articles that are submitted in English; on the other, he states that an "American" lack of knowledge of interpretive techniques common to institutions outside the United States justifies the exclusion of "foreign" articles.[53] This suggests that "international dialogue" can only occur in the *JSAH* between scholars who share similar training, conceptual apparatuses, professional standards, and indeed, the same language. Most significantly, the basis of these similarities must be derived from the protocols of a US-based academic culture. In this formulation, the *JSAH*'s discourse can expand to include a potentially infinite array of buildings, geographies and cultures, but can only represent them through an a priori analytical system that has no necessary relationship to the context studied. The journal thus becomes international by expanding "naturally" from an epistemological and geographical core, in much the same way that branches on Bannister Fletcher's tree of architectural history grew outward from a Euro-American trunk.

Indeed the term "foreign" is used here to refer to everything that is "not American" (where America is immediately equated with the United States, but not, for example, the countries of South America). The question re-emerges several issues later. In a short commentary, one of the book review editors suggests that the continuing emphasis on European texts in the book review section is due to a combination of institutional forces, ranging from the priorities of the academic presses, to the status of European architecture as the dominant area of graduate research in the United States. The category of "foreign topics" (which is broadened here to include not only books on different geographical locations, but methodological perspectives provided by "readings outside architectural history"[54]) is represented as a potentially positive influence on the "interior" of the discipline: books on "foreign topics" can "help to clarify the boundaries of architectural history and interrogate its aims and hemeneutic value."[55]

In both cases, the term "foreign" assumes a curiously anachronistic meaning when considered in relation to the immense cultural and social changes that have occurred within the "America" to which it is implicitly opposed, not least in relation to the "foreign" origins of the overwhelming majority of the US population. The use of the foreign is based on the presumed existence of a culturally homogeneous and familiar "home" where traces of "outside" influences have either been assimilated or do not exist.

In 2000, Zeynep Çelik followed Eve Blau to become editor of the *JSAH*. Çelik is well known for her pioneering work on cultural self-representation at world's fairs in the late nineteenth and early twentieth centuries.[56] Her research has played an important role in redefining the geographic boundaries of Euro-American architectural history, to include both the colonial periphery and imperial metropole in a single space of global modernity. Her appointment would seem to mark a shift in the editorial direction of the *JSAH*. At the time of writing (2002), it is too early to evaluate the precise impact of her editorship. There has been an increase in the number of articles published in the journal that deal with buildings and urban spaces outside Europe and North America. Yet as Çelik notes in her first editorial, it is not the number of articles that matters.[57] As I have also suggested above, the canonical organization of architectural history is infinitely expandable, and capable of assimilating difference into its structure; indeed the incorporation of "new" topics broadens the scope of the existing canonical machinery, by showing its capacity to "adapt." A much more difficult undertaking involves simultaneously questioning how the "foreign" or "non-West" is represented, for whom and for what purpose. These questions extend past historical methodology to a reconsideration of the role of institutions such as the *JSAH* in producing and reproducing the discourses of architectural history.

It is therefore appropriate to conclude this discussion of the *JSAH* by turning to the journal's millennium issue, which undertakes precisely this task.

AT THE MILLENNIUM

The millennium issue was commissioned when the journal was being edited by Eve Blau to mark the arrival of the year 2000. It was an unusual departure for the *JSAH*. It sought to shift attention from the discussion of buildings to the historical methodologies, institutional practices and discourses that constitute them as such. The special issue is divided according to three meta-critical themes: "Institutional Frameworks," "Sites of Research," and "Perspectives and Parameters." These themes simultaneously seek to define the field of architectural history as it stands, and critically intervene within it. Though these themes each raise many important questions, here I focus specifically on "Sites of Research," and the status of the so-called "non-West" within it.

As Blau states, the intention of this section is to consider the way in which "traditional" categories of research "have been rethought under the influence of post-structuralist theories, and the historiographic methods of social, cultural and intellectual histories."[58] The categories, which include "The City," "The Dwelling," "Sacred Sites," "Cultivated and Vernacular Landscapes," are striking because monumental building types and a limited pantheon of Euro-American architects have, for many decades, been the primary "site of research" in the *JSAH*. The Christian church, perhaps the pre-eminent building studied in the *JSAH*, is subsumed here under the heading of "Sacred Sites," and considered alongside an article about methodological approaches to "non-Western Sacred Sites." Two of the research categories, the "dwelling" and the "vernacular landscape," were largely invisible in the *JSAH* for many years. Given this symbolic reorganization, it is interesting that the so-called "non-West" is represented as a taxonomical distinction within the categories of "The City" and "Sacred Sites." It is not clear why the "non-Western" distinction applies only to these two categories, or why the changing methodological relationship between the "West" and the "non-West" is not a category of research in itself.

The two articles that explicitly address the "non-West" signal different degrees of critical distance from the term. In the first of these, Zeynep Çelik indicates her partial discomfort with the term by placing it within quotation marks in the title ("New Approaches to the 'Non-Western City'"), while the second, by Labelle Prussin, accepts it as an unproblematic category ("Non-Western Sacred Sites: African Models").

Çelik begins her article by framing the problems associated with employing "non-West" as research category for everything that is "outside" the geographic boundaries of the "West": "while introducing a category that hitherto was generally omitted from the discourse it comes with an attendant train of charged meanings, collapsing most of the world into homogeneity, signifying binary oppositions, and defining by negation. It thus perpetuates a hierarchical order with its origins in 19th century European scholarship . . ."[59] She illustrates her argument by discussing reductive constructions of the "Islamic City" as a projection of a singular, timeless and unchanging set of religious beliefs. Drawing in part on the sociologist Janet Abu-Lughod's important research on the same topic, she suggests that the Islamic city as such does not exist, and it needs to be methodologically and conceptually reconsidered as a pluralized and impure condition whose distinctions are produced through interactions with other cultures and built environments.[60]

The contrast between Çelik's position and the other "non-Western" article in this section is striking. While Çelik cautions against unitary categories such as the "Islamic city," Labelle Prussin argues such categories are necessary for the "non-West" to free itself from "Western" assumptions, and become visible on its own terms.[61] Yet, in focusing on "African Models" of sacred sites, she ironically chooses the Western (post-imperial) category of "Africa" as her alternative. As a bracketing term, "Africa" also serves to homogenize rather than specify the distinctiveness of the diverse (and sometimes violently opposed) indigenous cultures contained within it. Thus the overlapping spaces of post-colonial, national, regional, local, and stateless tribal cultures are replaced with "African sacred space," "African sacred thought," "African nomadic tribes," and "African religious systems," all of which are studied by "scholars of African architecture." The continent represented here is also the site of rapid urbanization, and increasingly brutal encounters with the inequities of global capitalist modernity. As such, Prussin's Africa necessarily becomes the spiritualized, preindustrial, non-urban other to the Western modernity it is presumed to oppose. The reduction of entire cultures to a premodern Eden is not specific to "scholars of African architecture" and the issues that surround it will be re-examined in Chapter 4, on the *Traditional Dwellings and Settlements Review*, which initially shared many similarities with the approach outlined here.

DISCIPLINARY DISLOCATIONS

The "non-West" is not mentioned in the other thematic categories of the millennium issue. It is simply one of many "sites of research." The other two sections, on "Institutional Frameworks" and "Perspectives and Parameters," would seem to be appropriate points to consider how the ethnocentrism of architectural history is produced and sustained, both by the larger administration of knowledge in the academy, and by the methods of architectural history. Yet the "non-Western" remains disconnected from these concerns. Indeed, while claiming the breadth of a meta-critical analysis of architectural history *per se*, the entire issue is unapologetically framed at the outset in terms of the Euro-American context.[62]

Before concluding, I examine this criticism in more detail through two articles, each of which turns critical attention towards the practices and institutions of architectural historyand series. In the first of these texts, the historian and theorist Mark Jarzombek sets out to examine the consequences of increasing interdisciplinarity in architectural history. In an article entitled "The Disciplinary Dislocations of (Architectural) History," he argues that interdisciplinary "borrowings" and collaborations have created new contexts in which to consider the history of architectural production.[63] They have also brought architectural history closer to other humanities-based disciplines, while simultaneously moving it further away from professional education and practice. Jarzombek suggests that the priorities of architectural history are becoming increasingly responsive to debates within the academy, while losing sight of critical developments in design culture and the profession.

A similar argument is presented by critic Mitchell Schwarzer, but in relation to the discourses of architectural theory.[64] He argues that beginning in the 1960s, architectural theory began to draw more consciously on theoretical systems from other disciplines, and in doing so became increasingly specialized and directed towards other academics. At the same time, the possibilities for critical discourse outside academic networks gradually declined, as major trade journals and other extra-academic sites of criticism disappeared. Schwarzer argues that the current situation, with few (if any) contexts for publication and debate outside the academy, obligates academics to assume the role of public intellectuals, and write not only for specialized academic audiences, but also for those outside the academy, both within and beyond the profession.

Though it is described in both articles as a general condition, the image of the academy that is represented here is one that is specific to the United States. If Schwarzer's important arguments about theory had expanded to take account of conditions even within the limited "Euro-American space" that the editors initially cite as the context for the special issue, he would likely have reached somewhat different conclusions. In the UK, for example, a large and differentiated field of critical journals exists that spans between the academy and the commercial marketplace.[65] A comparative analysis of these two contexts may have explained the reasons for their divergence. But it is also possible to argue that, given the global reach of both the publishing industry and the architectural profession, it is necessary to think of architectural journals as transnational, and global, rather than national projects.

Jarzombek and Schwarzer draw similar conclusions about the inward turn of academic research. Yet Jarzombek's article is perhaps more pointed in linking new specializations to a sense of loss in relation to the history of the discipline. The "dislocations" of his title suggest the prior existence of a location that has disappeared, where architectural history had a direct relationship (critical or otherwise) to professional practice. In this scenario, architectural history has not only lost its traditional relationship with practice, but also its capacity to represent its own history as a discipline. According to Jarzombek, the postmodern distrust of historical meta-narratives has made the possibility of critical historiographies of architectural history almost impossible.

The argument is an interesting one, but it hardly applies when considered in light of the history of the very journal it is published in. It is difficult to think of a discourse of architectural history that is less interdisciplinary, less "open" to the relativism of "postmodernism" than the *JSAH*. Indeed, the disconnection between what Jarzombek argues and what the *JSAH* has stood for (and continues to stand for) permeates the entire issue. The larger intent – to examine the institutional structures that support and enable the discourses of architectural history – is both rare and innovative. Yet, the *JSAH*, an influential site in the production of architectural history, remains completely unanalyzed in this issue. The journal becomes present through its absence, viewing the field of architectural history it helps to define as if from the outside.

CONCLUSION

This chapter represents a brief and partial analysis of writing published in the *JSAH* over its sixty-year history. Though the range and volume of research is immense, I have suggested that it forms a remarkably consistent body of work, marked by incremental change, over a long period of time. While I have been quite critical of some of the approaches to history manifested in the journal, at different points (particularly when it began), the *JSAH* has also revealed a capacity to historicize its own operations in a way that is not present in any of the other journals in this study. Indeed, as I suggested in the first part of the chapter, it was the Society's understanding of the "history of architectural history" that led to the roundtables and later institutional alliances formed between historians and other organizations in the 1940s.

The millennium issue extends the analysis of the institutions and practices of history into the present. It constitutes a valuable departure from prior approaches that have stressed the agency of the architect, or the biography of the work as the primary frameworks through which to understand history. It is significant, however, that the millennium issue does not discuss the *JSAH* or the *SAH*, but focuses instead on the rapidly changing field around both. The *JSAH* emerges, by implication, as an observer exterior to changes in the discipline, watching from afar, but largely unaffected by the very debates it notes and comments upon. And while the discussion of media and institutions is a methodological departure, the millennium issue is unapologetically concerned with architectural history as it is produced and understood within a select group of largely US-based contexts.

The journal's Eurocentrism persists in the use of both the "foreign" and "non-Western" as categories of research and publication. The fact that these terms continue to circulate in, and even organize the representation of ideas in the *JSAH* is an indication of the journal's distinctive construction of scholarly time and cultural and geographic space.[66] The non-West first emerged in the *JSAH* in the mid-1960s, and then disappeared for three decades, only to reappear in the 1990s as part of a debate about how the journal's "international conversations" should be conducted. At this point it acquired quotation marks and became for editor Zeynep Çelik, the "non-West" – a gesture of critical distance from the term's problematical meanings.

Yet, as Çelik has suggested, the question is not so much whether buildings and urban spaces located outside Europe and North American are included in the journal, but how, and according to what terms, this inclusion takes places. For much of its history, the *JSAH* has expanded outside its Euro-American axis of influence only if monumental, architect-designed buildings exist that correspond to its system of classification. The boundaries constituted by the journal have therefore depended upon the presence of subjects and objects of knowledge that fit into pre-established theoretical and historical discourses and taxonomies, recognizable modes of representation, protocols of scholarly research and "proper" language usage. As a result, the "non-West," when considered as such, is typically an expansion of "Western" boundaries, rather than an attempt to examine buildings and urban environments in relation to the specific histories and cultures of the distinct social, economic, and political contexts in which they exist.

If recent developments at the *JSAH* are any indication, this may be about to change, or perhaps has already done so. In her inaugural editorial in 2000, Çelik announced that she planned to undertake a survey of how architectural history is taught in different places around the world. The very conception of this project overturns many of the assumptions that divide the world into the separate and opposed zones of "American" and "Foreign" topics. It suggests a theory of history where connections between multiple locations are studied and their institutional effects compared. When read together, the articles convey an approach to architectural history that reflexively acknowledges the social, institutional and not least, national and post-colonial contexts in which it is produced and taught, and how it is situated in relation to world historical forces. The first part of the survey appeared in the September 2002 issue.[67] Though outside the time frame examined in this book, its methodology and results are of such major significance to my criticisms of the journal and the field of architectural history as a whole, it is important to mention it here, if only briefly.

Five articles examine how architectural history is taught in Belgium and the Netherlands, the United Kingdom and Australia, South Asia, Germany, Austria and Switzerland, and Ethiopia, Ghana, Nigeria, and South Africa. The articles reveal how "universal" notions of architectural history and theory undergo local transformations as they are appropriated and redefined in specific contexts.

Among many other issues, Jyoti Hosagrahar describes, for example, the continuing influence in India of canonical British texts that were first published in the early twentieth century. Her analysis addresses many of the critical themes of this chapter in relation to the South Asian context. The significance of colonialism, both in setting the agenda of architecture as well as influencing how historical knowledge is produced and taught, is a key theme in four of the five articles (ironically, the relationship between imperialism and the normative construction of architectural history and theory is not discussed in the survey of the field in the United Kingdom, nor in relation to Germany or Austria).

When taken together, the essays in this "global inquiry" address some of the criticisms I have made in relation to the millennium issue. Each contributes to an understanding of architectural history, its institutions and their relation to various interconnected national histories, and in some cases, transnational ones.

If there is a question to be raised about this project, it is this: what will happen next? Will the insights that emerge from this ambitious undertaking be reflected in the future agenda of the journal? Some of the most stringent criticisms made by the journal's own contributors in the past (for example, the articles by John Maass in 1969, and the concurrent arguments of Sibyl Moholy Nagy) have either not been acted upon, or have been addressed in ways that have left the underlying Eurocentrism of the journal's taxonomical system in place. While certainly valuable as a teaching tool and starting point for discussion of how architectural history and theory might change, the inquiry is perhaps more diagnostic than strategic. Will the critical insights it presents develop into alternative approaches, and will the *JSAH* reflect these changes? These questions are of particular importance as the innovative editorship of Çelik comes to an end.

The next two journals I will discuss examine the spaces "outside" what might be called the *JSAH*'s normative space of history. Both *Assemblage* and the *Traditional Dwellings and Settlements Review* reflect an impatience with the perceived status quo of architectural history and theory. Both differ from the *JSAH* in terms of their organizational structure and relationship to a larger disciplinary field. Neither are field journals. Nor are they concerned with representing the production of an entire discipline. Both have comparatively small audiences. Despite these differences, they share conceptual ground with the recent history of the *JSAH*, particularly in relation to the millennium issue, and the subsequent "Global Inquiry." Over its history *Assemblage* (1986–2000) devoted considerable attention to examining how architectural institutions shape, and are shaped by, critical thought. Since its inception, the *TDSR* has explored built environments constructed by "non-professionals" outside the imaginary space of Euro-American modernity, primarily in the newly industrializing nations of the "third world." It is to these debates that I now turn.

NOTES

1. Osmund Overby, "From 1947: The Society of Architectural Historians," *JSAH* 49 (March 1990): 12.
2. When the Society of Architectural Historians was founded, it was called the Society of American Architectural Historians. The word American was dropped from the name when the Society was incorporated in 1947.
3. See J. A. Chewing, "The Teaching of Architectural History during the Advent of Modernism, 1920s–1950s" in Elizabeth Blair MacDougall (ed.), *The Architectural Historian in America, Studies in the History of Art 35* (Washington, DC: The Smithsonian Institution, 1990), 101. See also Gwendolyn Wright, "History for Architects" in Gwendolyn Wright and Janet Parks (eds), *The History of History in American Schools of Architecture 1865–1975* (New York: The Temple Hoyne Buell Center and Princeton Architectural Press, 1990); and Kenneth Frampton and Alessandra Latour, "Notes on American Architectural Education," *Lotus* 27, no. 2 (1980): 5–39.
4. Frampton and Latour, op. cit., 7.
5. Wright, op. cit., 13.
6. Ibid., 14.
7. Based on my analysis of the journal. For the years 1941–1944 inclusive, 74 percent of the articles published in it were by writers teaching in schools of architecture; a small percentage of these were practicing architects. In the 1941 and 1942 volumes of the journal, scholars teaching in schools of architecture outnumber all other writers by a margin of two to one.

    See also Chewing, 101; Overby, 11; and, on the academicization of the journal, John Maass, "Where Architectural Historians Fear to Tread," *JSAH* 28, no. 1 (March 1969): 3–8 and Sibyl Moholy-Nagy, "Mass for Measure," *JSAH* 29 no. 1 (March 1970): 60–61.
8. Wright, ibid. Chewing disagrees with the claim that the amount of time devoted to history declined substantially in the 1940s; instead, he rightly emphasizes that the real change was in the content of courses and their role in the curriculum. See Chewing, 101.
9. Turpin Bannister, the first editor of the journal, described its audience in this way: "Membership should be drawn from the staffs of professional schools of architecture and collegiate art departments, from practicing architects, from the governmental agencies dealing with the preservation of historic monuments, and from interested laymen . . ." as quoted in "Summary of Round Table Discussion on the Preservation of Historic Architectural Monuments," *JSAH* 1, no. 2 (April 1941): 22.
10. See "Summary of the Round Table Discussion on the Preservation of Historic Architectural Monuments," *JSAH* 1, no. 2 (April 1941): 21–24.

    Among those present were noted historians Henry Russell Hitchcock, Richard Krautheimer, Paul Zucker, and officials from the National Parks

Service, then responsible for administering the Historic Sites Act, including Thomas Vint and Frederick D. Nichols.

11 *JSAH* 2, no. 2 (April 1942).

    The issue published papers from a symposium held jointly with the Association of Collegiate Schools of Architecture entitled "The Function of Architectural History in the Modern Professional Curriculum." The editor, Turpin Bannister, stated in his contribution that he wished "to survey the contributions that the study of the history of architecture can make to the students in our schools today, to help them master more completely the creative solution of contemporary problems . . .", 5.

12 Hans Huth, writing in the July–October issue of the journal in 1941, states that the American preservation movement began in 1864 when Congress declared Yosemite Valley a State Park, and "war was declared against the vandals who threatened to destroy our cultural and national heritage," 5.

13 Fiske Kimball, a regular contributor to the *JSAH* in the 1940s, acted as architect for the restoration of, among other "national" monuments, Monticello. He was also on the advisory boards of Colonial Williamsburg and the National Park Service, which was initially responsible for administering the Historic Sites Act.

14 See Clausen Weatherhead, *The History of Collegiate Architecture in the United States* (New York: The ACSA, 1942); *The Architect at Mid-Century* (Washington, DC: The AIA, 1952); Robert Gutman, *Architectural Practice: A Critical View* (New York: Princeton Architectural Press, 1988), and the SAH's *Graduate Degree Programs in Architectural History* (Philadelphia: The Society of Architectural Historians, 1992) for an indication of how architectural education has expanded since 1945. By 1955, the number of schools had increased by one third from the time of the last survey in 1935. Enrollment in first professional degree programs continued its upward climb until the 1970s, when it stabilized at approximately 15,000 students, an increase of two-thirds over the 1940 level.

15 Overby, 15.

16 See William A. Green, "Periodization and World History," *Journal of World History*, (Spring 1992): 15–53. Green stresses that the "morphological exercise emphasizing disciplined concepts of change and continuity" is derived from the practices of eighteenth century botany. It is a mode of classification that relies on the comparative assessment of visible characteristics, and hence, though it is putatively concerned with placing things in a chronological sequence, its method for establishing characteristics is based on observations of structure and form conducted "outside time." Universal, as opposed to particular manifestations in the object must be scrutinized, 14.

17 See Stephen G. Nichols, "Periodization and the Politics of Perception: A Romanesque Example," *Poetics Today* 10, no. 1 (Spring 1989): 131–154.

Nichols describes how the eighteenth century naturalist Gerville developed his classification of Romanesque by referring to Jussieu's principles for studying and classifying plants. He determined the characteristics of Romanesque through the observation of relations in space, as though one were "comparing plants in vegetal chains, or to a geographic map on which each being occupies a fixed point whose relationship to the whole may be determined . . . [by] . . . a universal yardstick against which to measure and plot phenomena," 131.

18 E. H. Gombrich has emphasized that although we accept the normative categories informing both art and architectural history, like "Romanesque" as neutral and value-free, they are derived from discourses that favored or opposed classicism. The terms of contemporary historical periodization evolved as terms of abuse related to one of these two positions. See E. H. Gombrich, *Norm and Form. Studies in the Art of the Renaissance* (London and New York: Phaidon, 1971), 81–98.

As Paul Rabinow has noted, although the opponents of anti-classicism were successful, the categories remained and were recuperated into a "scientific" system of classification: "much scholarly energy was . . . expended in seeking a scientific classification of form. Some historians sought universal morphological principles as the means to unify and ground the burgeoning historicist catalogue of difference. Others emphasized a plural unity within each of a multiplicity of cultural or historical periods; each era had its own internally coherent norm(s) and form(s)." See Paul Rabinow, *French Modern. Norms and Forms of the Built Environment* (Cambridge, MA, and London: MIT Press, 1989), 7–8.

19 Yasemin Aysan and Necdet Teymur, "'Vernacularism' in Mete Turan (ed.), Architectural Education" in *Vernacular Architecture* (Aldershot: Avebury Press, 1990). Aysan and Teymur state that a "parallel regionalism presenting itself within universalism exists within each Western discourse and education which consists of a selection of a very small proportion of the local production of artifacts and buildings assumed to qualify for the privileged title of Art or Architecture. It is this internalized universalism that provides the framework on which the art and architecture of different parts of the world are equally selectively judged in the name of 'universal values'," 308.

20 Successive surveys of the members in 1944, 1949, 1956, and 1963 revealed that at least 50 percent of research was based on American topics, primarily in the nineteenth century. In 1967 a slightly higher proportion dealt with European subjects. In 1990 the editor claimed that the typical balance between European and American subjects was still in place.

See Tod Marder, "Note From the Editor," *JSAH* 59, no. 5 (March 1990): 5.

21 John Maass, "Where Architectural Historians Fear to Tread," *JSAH* 28, no. 1 (March 1969): 3–8.

22 My sample includes volumes from the following years: 1941–1943; 1950–1952; 1960–1963; 1970–1973; 1980–1983; 1990–1993. I also examined the period between 1995 and 2002, and in particular 1998–2002, the dates of the editorial policy of Zeynep Çelik, which called for more attention to "non-Western" topics.

   In my survey, I also found that since the 1980s the balance between Europe and America has shifted, with articles on European topics outnumbering those based in America. In 1990–1993, 67 percent of the articles were on European subjects, while 29 percent dealt with American topics.

23 Magali Sarfatti Larson, *The Rise of Professionalism. A Sociological Analysis* (Los Angeles: University of California Press, 1977), 4.

24 Ibid., 17.

25 In the "Round Table on Architectural Preservation," H. R. Hitchcock suggests that a "nationwide group of watchful historians could perform a valuable service in warning of danger weight [sic] with those responsible for an endangered building," 23.

26 Michel de Certeau, *Heterologies. Discourses on the Other* (Minneapolis: University of Minnesota Press, 1989), 208.

27 Sibyl Moholy Nagy, "Maass for Measure," *JSAH* 29, no. 1 (March 1970): 61.

28 Ibid., 61.

29 When the history of the journal is considered as a whole, my research suggests that Christian religious monuments are the most common object of analysis in the journal (18 percent of all the articles in my survey were dedicated to this topic); this is followed by architectural biographies (14 percent); and articles on villas, palaces, castles, country houses, and modernist mansions (12 percent). Articles on city planning took up 5 percent of the total, while museums, government buildings, and architectural style each comprised 5 percent of the total; corporate office buildings, domestic architecture (row housing and mass housing) and architectural theory each registered at 4 percent.

30 While discussion of European architects shows a diffuse selection with very little repetition, the work of several American architects has attracted continuous attention in the journal. Of the 228 articles which establish or discuss architectural authorship in my survey, all the architects discussed are white men; the four most frequently analyzed are Frank Lloyd Wright (25), H. H. Richardson (12), Thomas Jefferson (8), and Louis Sullivan (7).

31 In his history of the journal, Osmund Overby suggests that its current form was established as early as 1951. He remarks that in response to a questionnaire issued in the back of the 1951 bills respondents stated that 50 percent of the journal's articles should be on American topics: "In this, and most other ways as well, many of the salient and familiar features of the Society were in place by the 1950s."

32 Hayden White, "Historical Emplotment and the Problem of Truth," in Saul Friedlander (ed.), *Probing the Limits of Representation. Nazism and the Final Solution* (Cambridge, MA: Harvard University Press, 1992), 37.
33 Mieke Bal, "De-disciplining the Eye," *Critical Inquiry* 16 (Spring 1990): 506.
34 White, 90–91.
35 See, for example, Stuart Wilson, "The 'Gifts' of Frederich Froebel," *JSAH* 26, no. 4 (December 1967): 238.
36 For an interesting study of the changing professional identities of the architect since the nineteenth century, see Andrew Saint's *The Image of the Architect* (New Haven, CT and London: Yale University Press, 1983).
37 Steven Murray and James Addiss, "Plan and Space at Amiens Cathedral: With a New Plan Drawn by James Addiss," *JSAH* 49, no. 1 (March 1990): 44–66.
38 Clay Lancaster, "The Philadelphia Centennial Towers," *JSAH* 19 (March 1960): 11.
39 Michel de Certeau, *Heterologies. Discourse on the Other* (Minneapolis: University of Minnesota Press, 1989), 205.
40 Gerard Genette, *Narrative Discourse. An Essay in Method*, trans. Jane E. Lewin (Ithaca, NY: Cornell University Press, 1980), 166–167.
41 See Hayden White, *The Tropics of Discourse. Essays in Cultural Criticism* (Baltimore: The Johns Hopkins University Press, 1978).

White claims that discourse is characterized by movement through archetypal modalities of figuration, which attempt to liken events to already known modes of comprehension or consciousness. Discourse, according to White, "is intended to constitute the ground whereon to decide what shall count as fact in the matters under consideration, and what mode of comprehension is best suited to the understanding of the facts thus constituted," 3.

Because differing modes of comprehension are articulated through differing modalities of figuration, themselves forms of mimesis, mimetic text can be understood as representing a form of consciousness. "Consciousness in its active, creative aspects, as against its passive, reflective aspects . . . is most directly apprehensible through discourse, and, moreover, in discourse guided by formulable goals, or aims of understanding," 20.
42 I take this distinction from Louis Marin in *Utopics: The Semiological Play of Textual Spaces* (Atlantic Highlands, NJ: Humanities Press, 1984): 201–202.
43 Ibid., 210.
44 Ibid., 202.
45 W. J. T. Mitchell, "Spatial Form in Literature: Towards a General Theory," in W. J. T. Mitchell (ed.), *The Language of Images* (Chicago: University of Chicago Press: 1980), 271–299.
46 Michel de Certeau, *The Practice of Everyday Life* (Berkeley: University of California Press, 1984), 92.

47 Marin, 206.
48 Paul Rabinow, "Representations Are Social Facts: Modernity and Post-Modernity in Anthropology," in J. Clifford and G. E. Marcus (eds), *Writing Culture* (Berkeley and Los Angeles: University of California Press, 1986), 243.
49 Edward Said, *Orientalism* (New York: Phaidon, 1977), 177.
50 Eugene E. Maytsek Jr, "Three Recent Literatures in Architectural Research: A Citation Analysis, 1986–1990," Unpublished student research paper, University of Maryland.
51 According to Maytsek, in the ninety-eight articles published between 1986 and 1990, 66 percent of the monographs cited were published before 1970, and 13.2 percent were published before 1900. Similarly, 56 percent of the periodicals cited were published before 1950. Maytsek, 18.
52 Nicholas Addams, "International Conversations," *JSAH* 55, no. 2 (June 1996): 137.
53 Ibid., 124–125.
54 "The Changing Scope of Foreign Topics," *JSAH* 57, no. 1 (March 1998): 5.
55 Ibid.
56 Zeynep Çelik, *Displaying the Orient* (Berkeley: University of California Press, 1992).
57 Zeynep Çelik, "Expanding Frameworks," *JSAH* 59, no. 2 (June, 2000): 152–153.
58 Eve Blau, "Architectural History 1999/2000. A Special Issue of the *JSAH*," *JSAH* 58, no. 3 (September 1999): 278.
59 Zeynep Çelik, "New Approaches to the 'Non-Western City'," *JSAH* 58, no. 3 (September 1999): 374.
60 Janet Abu-Lughod, *Cairo: 1001 Years of City Victorious* (Princeton, NJ: Princeton University Press, 1971).
61 Labelle Prussin, "Non-Western Sacred Sites: African Models," *JSAH* 58, no. 3 (September 1999): 424.
62 Blau, op cit., 280.
63 Mark Jarzombek, " The Disciplinary Dislocations of (Architectural) History," *JSAH* 58, no. 3 (September 1999): 488–493.
64 Mitchell Schwarzer, "History and Theory in Architectural Periodicals: Assembling Oppositions," *JSAH* 58, no. 3 (September 1999): 342–349.
65 See, for example, *Building Design*, *Blueprint*, *Architecture Today*, *Architectural Review*, *Journal of Architecture*, *ARQ* (*Architectural Research Quarterly*).
66 At the time of writing (2002), even the book reviews continue to be divided according to "American" and "Foreign" topics, with an editor assigned to each.
67 The first part of the survey is entitled "Teaching the History of Architecture: A Global Inquiry I," *JSAH* 61, no. 3 (September 2002): 333–396. It includes the following articles: Zeynep Çelik, "Introduction": 333–334; Hilde Heynen

and Krista de Jonge, "The Teaching of Architectural History and Theory in Belgium and the Netherlands": 335–345; Deborah Howard, "Teaching Architectural History in Great Britain and Australia: Local Conditions and Global Perspectives": 346–354; Jyoti Hosagrahar, "South Asia: Looking Back, Moving Ahead – History and Modernization": 355–369; Dietrich Neuman, "Teaching the History of Architecture in Germany, Austria and Switzerland": 370–380; Ikem Stanley Okoye, "Architecture, History, and the Debate on Identity in Ethiopia, Ghana, Nigeria, and South Africa": 381–396.

Cover of "Assemblage. A Critical Journal of Architecture and Design Culture," no. 41 (April 2000) courtesy of the MIT Press.

Chapter 3: Strategies of Disturbance and the "Generation of Theory"

"Assemblage. A Critical Journal of Architecture and Design Culture"

The history of the *JSAH* examined in the last chapter ended with a discussion of the millennium issue, which in many ways marked a departure for the journal. By choosing to investigate how social and political institutions and media shape architectural history, the issue pointed towards a very different conception of historical inquiry from what has predominated in the journal for most of its history. The *JSAH*'s contributors argued that museums, conferences, journals, books, and academic institutions (to name a few) play a significant role in shaping what counts as history. In doing so these institutions were transformed from being regarded as backdrops or frames, and instead have become legitimate sites of historical research. As my analysis of the journal suggested, the *JSAH* itself has been shaped by the changing status of architectural history within the institutions of architectural education. I also argued that *what counts* as architectural history depends on *who counts* as an architectural historian, as the issues surrounding "foreign" scholarship in the journal suggested. The focus on institutions is therefore not just a matter of showing that history is socially constructed: it is also about how it is constructed, for whom, and for what purpose. The importance of this latter point has been underscored by the journal's "global inquiry" into the teaching of architectural history, which attempts to examine national institutions in relation to world historical forces.

While these questions have received attention in more recent issues of the *JSAH*, the institutional and disciplinary critique of architectural theory and criticism was central to the agenda of *Assemblage*, the journal examined in this chapter. From its inception in 1986, to its demise in 2000, *Assemblage*, a "critical journal of architecture and design culture,"[1] sought to question the boundaries between specialized areas of architectural scholarship that typically isolate architectural theory from history and professional practice. In the journal's inaugural editorial in 1986, K. Michael Hays, the founding editor, described *Assemblage* as the only English language journal devoted to supporting architectural theory and criticism that had "a vigorous self-awareness of its own history and methods, and of the potential for interaction with practice."

Assemblage, he writes, will "assess and sustain the development of this critical enterprise . . . *Assemblage* is a format for oppositional knowledge that continually questions received ideas, challenges entrenched institutions and values, that strays from permissible terrains."[2] Conventional architectural criticism, Hays argued, isolates the architectural object in a purely "abstract and idealized realm" where it is freed from the "molestation" of history and "distanced" from material contingencies; the critic enters into a self-referential process that maintains rigidly defined disciplinary boundaries, dominant institutions, and "disengaged" modes of practice.

The origins of this "cycle of affirmation" is traced to the conventions of high modernism in architectural thought, where, according to Hays, critical writing operates as an "attachment" to the object. A dividing line is constructed that separates the meanings presumed to be inherent in the object from the critics and historians who write about it. As a result, that object assumes a transcendent status, because its meanings are presumed to be embedded in the object, unchanging and always available to the perceptive critic. *Assemblage* argued that although the modernist discourses of autonomy represented the meaning of architectural objects as being outside history and culture, they were intimately connected to the interests of the writer: modernist critics constructed the very meanings they claimed to discover. Thus the premise of autonomy mystified the connections between critics and architects:

> One thinks, for example, of the classic texts of Giedion, Banham, or Hitchcock and Johnson, where critical writing about selected objects constructs criteria against which all works of architecture are judged, and form canons by which the mediation between the various practices of architecture and design and the various institutions of culture is accomplished. In this way, criticism has provided the ideological apparatus for architectural practice, setting not only the terms for theoretical discussions, but also the practical parameters of cultural legitimacy.[3]

Assemblage attempted to open up new horizons for architectural scholarship, where, for example, "theorized" history might be possible; where the tacit assumptions of professional practice might be recognized as an unspoken form of theory, and where the often undisclosed relationship between critics and practitioners might be exposed. As a result, theory became a crucial part of the attempt to overcome the perceived introversion of architectural thought. *Assemblage* sought to transform the modernist "apparatus of autonomy" into "discourses of context and exteriority recalibrated according to what [was] sayable or thinkable in the idiolects of deconstruction, psychoanalysis, critical theory and other interpretive systems."[4] Hays argued that these systems were not "merely yoked together with architecture." Instead, contributors to the journal "transcoded" borrowed materials, as they adapted them to the analysis of architectural practices. The intended result was a historic shift of level as well as perspective, in which

> . . . architecture's specific forms, operations, and practices [can] now be more clearly seen as producing concepts whose ultimate horizon of effect lay outside of architecture "proper" in a more general socio-cultural field.[5]

Yet the writing in *Assemblage* sought to use "borrowed theory" not only to inform critical interpretations of architectural production. It also sought to make such theory the basis of the design process. The best-known and most controversial examples of this operation were design experiments with deconstructive literary theory – such as the architecture of Peter Eisenman – and later the philosophical writings of Gilles Deleuze. The issues raised by such procedures are complex, because deconstructive theory originally developed in relation to written texts. In translating literary theory into the basis of architectural production, the work published in *Assemblage* raised important questions about the limits of architectural theory and the knowledge that might inform architectural design. Is it possible to inform the architectural design process with literary theory? And if so, what changes do our conception of both buildings and literary theory undergo in order for such an operation to take place?

As with the other chapters in this book, I do not attempt to provide a comprehensive summary of everything that was published in the journal. Rather, I focus on several interrelated debates that help illuminate some of the key issues the writers attempted to confront. In this case, my focus is on writing that helps to foreground the issues surrounding the "translation" of theory from other disciplines for use in the critical interpretation and design of built form. In particular, my emphasis is on writing that is organized around two interrelated metaphors: the text as architecture, and architecture as text.

The first of these themes, "the text as architecture," is concerned with writing that reflects critically on the conventions and practices of architectural writing. Here the written text assumes a status that is equivalent to buildings and urban spaces: the text is regarded as an "architecture" built out of mental concepts and their interrelationship. The space between disciplines, the problems of moving from one disciplinary location to another, implicit hierarchies of ideas, the way in which critical concepts are preserved and built upon over time – all comprise facets of this imaginary architecture, which, it is argued, shapes the outcome of physical space. The goal is to make a tacit and hence invisible architecture of assumptions and disciplinary conventions a visible site of critical operation, and having done so, to disrupt, subvert or transform its order.

The second theme, which deals with "architecture as text," examines attempts to make various forms of text-based theory from the humanities the basis of the architectural design process. In some cases buildings assume the status of constructed texts, whose messages are to be "read" by their inhabitants; in others, critical concepts, sometimes expressed in spatial metaphors from philosophy or literary theory (such as Gilles Deleuze's concepts of the "fold" and the "rhizome"), are translated into built form. In both cases, the critic/designer attempts to dismantle the modernist opposition between text and building, critical subject and architectural object, theory and practice, and re-situate architecture in its "worldly" condition. By destabilizing the epistemological foundations that constitute the discourse of architecture, the journal aimed to reveal architecture as contingent rather than autonomous and self-fulfilling, as "enmeshed in circumstance" rather than transcendent from it, thereby showing how architecture is "connected to power, to institutional authorities, and to canons handed down through disciplinary traditions."[6]

FROM ZERO POSITIONS TO "ASSEMBLAGE"

It is difficult to fully understand *Assemblage* without first discussing what many regard as its predecessor. *Oppositions* was founded in 1973 by architect and theorist Peter Eisenman as the house journal of the Institute for Architecture and Urban Studies in New York. It ceased publication in 1984, two years before *Assemblage* was launched. *Assemblage* operated within the same network of East Coast US academic and professional networks as *Oppositions*. Two of the founding editors of *Oppositions*, Peter Eisenman and Mario Gandelsonas, were also connected with *Assemblage*: Gandelsonas, a Professor of Architecture at Princeton University, was a member of the *Assemblage* Advisory Board until the journal's demise; Peter Eisenman was an "individual sponsor" of the journal in 1989 and 1990. His professorial work is examined in *Assemblage* 5 (1988).[7]

Oppositions and *Assemblage* represent two overlapping stages in the transformation of US-based architectural theory. At the time of *Opposition*'s founding, Eisenman (who completed a PhD at Cambridge University in the United Kingdom) was influenced by linguists on both sides of the Atlantic, particularly Noam Chomsky in the United States, as well as French structuralists Lévi-Strauss and Roland Barthes.[8] The title of the journal (conceived by Eisenman) was a play on the term "zero positions," and eliptically referred to Barthes' influential text *Writing Degree Zero*.[9] At the time, Eisenman was attempting to develop an "architecture degree zero" through formalist design procedures that sought to return architecture to its presumed syntactical essence. The purifying operations were intended to free the design process from entrenched functionalist ideologies. Eisenman and others involved in *Oppositions*, such as the critic and historian Colin Rowe, argued that the functionalist paradigms of modernist design had been largely co-opted to serve the means-end logic of postwar corporate capital.[10] Experiments in formalism attempted to restore the possibility of architectural autonomy through design strategies that were not determined in advance by functionalism.[11]

The breadth of ideas published in *Oppositions* was by no means limited to Eisenman's interests, and during the life of the journal he also moved beyond the constraints of these experiments in autonomy. *Oppositions* also explored architectural debates in Marxism, phenomenology, and the "return of history" via precedent and typological studies. It fostered debates on the influence of popular culture in architecture through the work of Venturi and Rauch, and featured English translations of texts by Italian Marxist historians Manfredo Tafuri and Francesco Dal Co, as well as architects such as Aldo Rossi, all of whom were part of the "Venice School" of historians, architects, and critics. But perhaps the lasting significance of *Oppositions* is located less in any particular theoretical position, than the fact that it put architectural theory on the agenda of US-based architectural education and practice. It was one of the first scholarly journals in North America to historicize theory, and to explore the different theoretical underpinnings of history.

Assemblage continued *Opposition*'s transatlantic emphasis, bringing a second wave of continental (French) theorists to the attention of US architectural audiences. It was closely aligned with post-structuralist approaches from its inception, and while continuing the debates around theory initiated by *Oppositions*, it attempted to move beyond structuralist positions. The first wave of continental theorists that became influential in *Oppositions* attempted to treat human activities scientifically, by finding basic elements (concepts, actions, classes of words) and the rules by which they were combined.[12] At the level of architectural theory, structuralism was manifested in critical writing that argued that architecture was determined by a larger social totality that could be objectively represented and understood.

Social totality, and the idea that there is an underlying order to the world that can be discovered through scientific research, is replaced in *Assemblage* by the idea of "the social" as a text. In this post-structuralist interpretation, the world is accessible only through representations, to which there is no "outside." The acknowledgement of the irreducible role of representations meant that buildings themselves, along with other social forms, had to be rethought as representations, rather than as the built projections of representations. In an editorial reflecting upon the achievements of the journal at the time of its thirtieth issue, Hays wrote that:

> . . . if the theory of the "Assemblage" generation has taught us anything, it is that what used to be called the sociohistorical context of architectural production . . . as well as the objects produced are both themselves texts (call them constructions if

you don't like texts), in the sense that we cannot approach them separately and directly, as distinct unrelated things in themselves, but only through their prior differentiation and transmutation.[13]

If architecture and the socio-historical context of production are both defined as representations, then it is no longer possible to think of "the social" as a given or objective condition to which architecture responds, adapts to, or simply "reflects." Both are now cultural artifacts whose meanings change depending on how they are constructed and related, not only to each other, but to other "texts."

There is not space here to present a detailed overview of deconstruction and its position within the history of philosophy. Jacques Derrida, the French philosopher who is most closely associated with the term, has argued that language does not have a point of origin or ending: its meanings are defined through differences, deferrals, and supplements in a potentially endless play of signification.[14] Flows of meaning are constrained and ordered by devices such as binary oppositions.[15] To deconstruct a text therefore involves "dismantling" the authority of these oppositions, and disrupting their effects. Thus, the opposition between text and architecture is predicated as defining architecture as part of a "real" world that exists outside culture, whose condition the text is presumed to simply mirror. As I will suggest below, it is this dichotomous representation of a "real/architecture" that is independent from texts (and hence culture), that *Assemblage* set out to challenge.

ARCHITECTURES OF DECONSTRUCTION

Contributors to *Assemblage* argued that architectural theory should "transcode" theories of deconstruction in ways that do not "dissimulate" the architectural object into a written text. For example, in a 1988 article, Mark Wigley states that deconstruction offers a model of "internal subversion" of "traditional ways of thinking." The architect/critic adopts "conventional codes and meanings" in order to "enter into the very heart of architecture" to do "internal violence" against its "logic." These maneuvers are aimed at deconstructing the institutions of architecture from within. Architecturally specific deconstruction evolved as a way of preventing architecture's "dissimulation" into the forms of expression (i.e. the text) and techniques of analysis common to other disciplines:

> We would understand the importance of architecture, and reject the tradition in architecture that says that architecture is really not so important, that the object is

not so important, and that what counts is the derivation of our theory from other disciplines, that if one really wants to talk about what's important in architecture, one must use philosophy, literary theory, and so on, while we ourselves, from our humbled discipline, just manage to scrape into universities and do so in a very undignified way . . . it is necessary for me to . . . reject this undignified servility. Because the theoretical tradition is already an architectural tradition. To tamper with architecture is already to tamper with the basis of theory.[16]

Thus it is possible for critics to move beyond the architectural discipline, finding architecture where it "should not properly exist" in literature and philosophy. If philosophical writing has an architectural structure, how could the procedures employed to analyze and deconstruct the architecture of philosophy become relevant to architectural thought? Wigley explores this process further in "The Translation of Architecture, The Production of Babel"[17] (1989), where he asks "How then to translate deconstruction in architectural discourse?" In his answer, architectural knowledge assumes the metaphorical status of a material form. Discourse becomes a surface that is "knotted," and marked by conceptual crevices and epistemological fault-lines.[18] At the same time, the constructed architectural object is understood as "text" that signifies and transmits socio-cultural meanings, but in a manner that is specific to architecture.

Material reality and conceptual apparatus are thus tied together into one "textual" weave. The representation of architecture as a surface of interwoven texts is accompanied by a renunciation of the search for conceptual or theoretical depth. "We are" writes John Whiteman, "looking for an architecture that does not shun the look and feel of things, an architecture that works, as it were, on the surface."[19] Mark Taylor argues in *Assemblage* 5 that "if architecture is textual and the textual is architectural, then the relation between text and building is transformed. Or more precisely . . . text can no more explain architecture than architecture can exemplify text."[20] He claims that when the search for deep meaning is abandoned "writing and construction become the same (without being identical) textual practices. Text and building intersect in writing which, though it is never about the architectural, might be archetextural . . . the true world we have abolished."[21] In the same issue, Mark Wigley states that dismantling the text/object relationship would enable the production of the theoretical object:

> The critical work has been loaded into the object. The object takes over. Its formal moves call the theoretical moves into question. The theoretical test of the object is the critical work of the object itself, what we would have previously denigrated as merely its aesthetic . . . All that matters is the condition of the object. This is a theoretical object to be understood as a piece of criticism.[22]

The question of how to "translate" deconstruction into architecture is also addressed by Peter Eisenman, the New York-based architect, former editor of *Oppositions* and occasional collaborator with Jacques Derrida, in a letter Eisenman wrote to Derrida and subsequently published in *Assemblage* in 1990. Like Wigley, Eisenman argues that deconstruction must take account of the "specificity" of architecture. He referred to the work of Valerio Adami, a painter Derrida admires, in order to illustrate the "critical relationship" that must be developed between architectural practices and deconstruction:

> I am fascinated by your discourse, yet when I look at the painting, I find it lacking: it lacks the aura possible in marking a surface with lines, paint, color, texture etc., I feel the same way about psychoanalysts who put symbolic and ritualistic drawings and paintings in frames on the walls of their offices and think of them (because they are framed) as art. While these works may have psychological content and intent, they are for me, illustrated psychology, not art, because they do not establish a critical relationship to traditional art. They are not analytical or critical in terms of their own medium of either painting or drawing. They do not take into account the history and specificity of painting.[23]

Deconstruction must therefore be used to address the conventions of representational practice "specific to architecture." One of Eisenman's largest and most complex projects at the time, a group of science laboratories in Frankfurt, attempts to carry out this critical program by "subverting" the conventional relation between structure and ornament. The building is discussed at length in two articles published in *Assemblage* in 1988, the first by Eisenman, and the second an interview with Mark Wigley by K. Michael Hays entitled "The Frankfurt Projects. The Displacement of Structure and Ornament."[24] Wigley explains that the spaces in Eisenman's science laboratories, which are designed to look functional, are not where the functional work of the laboratories is undertaken; similarly, the areas that are reserved for laboratory space adopt an "ornamental" or decorative use of geometry. The result, according to Wigley, is that it is impossible to determine the use of the interior spaces of the building through its exterior coding. This inversion, though conducted at the level of architectural aesthetics, is presumed by Eisenman to have a "domino effect," ultimately undermining the "traditional relationship between aesthetics and practice because that relationship is thoroughly dependent upon the tradition in which ornament is added to structure."[25]

TEXTS AS ARCHITECTURE

The argument outlined above – that the text is architectural and that architecture is textual – defines what was perhaps the central theoretical proposition of *Assemblage*. In this section I examine the production of "object-texts," or the "text as architecture," more closely. Here, critical writing, "formerly an appurtenance or attachment,"[26] ceases to be merely an interpretive description of an object exterior to perception. It takes on the status of a parallel and equally important combination of codes that are open to interpretation, plays of meaning and rewriting. The writer "is now involved in registering and repeating (though not duplicating) systems of signification, whose provenance lies beyond the individual writer or designer."[27] The reader's attention is drawn to the "surface" of the text, and the way ideas are organized, expressed and developed, resulting in an opaque form of writing that is deliberately "unclear." These articles are encountered first as aesthetic objects: the "excess" of the text calls attention to itself and the techniques used to compose it, in an effort to undermine the traditional codes and stability of meaning associated with the scholarly discourse.

Paradigmatic examples can be found in the work of Mark Taylor and Jennifer Bloomer. Both write in a playful manner that constantly changes voice and does not follow a linear path of development. The suggestion of a single position of knowledge is questioned, and the partiality of the text is stressed. In Jennifer Bloomer's 1990 "Abodes of Theory and Flesh: Tabbles of Bower" she "produces a design that is for and about Chicago, and is an effect of the fire of 1871."[28] She explores "theory as a potentiality, a possible pattern; it is dynamic, tracing a fragmentary process of object-making. This essay and the project it attends are about such a tracing; they are as well, objects resulting from the process."[29]

Like much of the writing in *Assemblage*, Bloomer's goal is the production of "heterogeneity" or the release of "difference" from a previously unified field of knowledge. She seeks to reveal the alterity of ornament to the dominant discourse of structure. She claims that ornament is typically construed as feminine in architectural discourse, and as such it is placed in a subordinate position: "the duplicity and degeneracy of the feminine is a metaphor for many forms of alterity to the dominant. Throughout our project this convention is mimed and exploited."[30]

Bloomer conceives of theory as the record of process, which in this case is grounded in her own personal history. Thus it is not the structure/ornament relation that she discusses and deconstructs as such, but rather the specific way it is constituted in relation to her own experiences. The article connects an apparently arbitrary chain of associations, beginning with a description of a foot-stool in her bedroom, a photograph of her great aunt's husband who worked in Chicago until the fire; reference to Louis Sullivan and his use of ornament; a description of a feminist theory of ornament; and finally, the design of a pavilion that attempts to suspend the structure/ornament pair by literally suspending a cowhide from an elaborate system of decorative pulleys over a gallery space.

A similar strategy is employed in *Assemblage* 11 by Mark Taylor in his article "The Archetexture of Pyramids." Like Bloomer, Taylor links together a cluster of seemingly unrelated elements. The notion of a thread pulled through a labyrinth of meanings, which ultimately does not lead to a conclusion but to more labyrinths, is omnipresent:

> If the object is archetexture – the arche of texture as well as the texture of the arche – if the subject is in one way or the other, the arche or the beginning, then where are we to begin? I will try to begin by exploring something near and dear to us all . . . a pocket. What is a pocket?[31]

The initial reference to a pocket leads to a complex chain of loose associations that connect the pocket to the pocketbook, to the image on the US dollar bill, to capital, and finally to the capital of Paris, and a discussion of the way in which Merleau Ponty, Derrida, and Bataille represent the axis of Rue d'Etoile in their work. A significant characteristic of this writing is its tendency to call attention to itself. The reader is drawn back to the surface of the text, away from deep meanings, through the sudden shifts and cancellations in lexical development the text produces. Each time a new association is introduced as the signifier of an apparently stable concept, its stability as such is immediately undermined by altering its meaning and the expectations that have been set up around it.

Part of the "pleasure of the text" resides in its "undecidability" – its ambiguity demands that the reader suspend the desire to have the text lead to a fixed set of conclusions, and the voice in the text changes as it proceeds. In the case of Taylor's article, for example, the narrator shifts from etymologist ("The exerge is a small place, usually on the reverse of a coin"[32]) to philosopher ("Ontotheology is Heidegger's term for the dominant philosophical tradition in the west"[33]) to detective addressing the audience as fellow sleuths ("might this past have something to do with the strange arche for which we are searching?"[34]). Thus the text becomes less a revelation of meaning than a search for its multiple forms.[35] Indeed, both Bloomer's and Taylor's goal appears to reside in the paradigmatic "postmodern" activity of provoking fragmentation – itself conceived as a transformative act when cast against an apparently unified architectural culture.

This writing also seeks to construct an ambiguous relationship between "theory" and "practice." The idea is that by creating texts whose meanings are "undecidable" and contradictory, the practice of writing will be rescued from the means-end logic of conventional architectural criticism and its post-facto legitimations of built form. This version of "deconstructive" writing has therefore been seen as opening up a space of critical agency for architectural theory, in and through the strategies of representation.

A second goal is to dismantle the opposition between the text and the architectural object, in which architecture is constituted as something "real," and exterior to perception, and writing as a transparent representation of that reality. In the discourse of "textuality," writing and architecture are treated as a fluid and interdependent system of codes.

There is no question that these strategies have made a singular and important contribution to architectural debates by revealing the way in which representational practices construct the objects we write about. What I want to question here is the wider claim that is made together with this form of writing: that its production will somehow transform the institutional relationship between architectural writing and professional practice, and that its subversion of codes will create a space of critical activity that is free from the means-end logic of professional practice.

Indeed, there is a suggestion of triumphalism in Mark Taylor's abolition of the "true world," just as there is a note of romantic heroism in John Whiteman's declaration that "we must forget the lure of the abstract, with its accompanying notions that we are dealing with something deep or structural or profound. Such notions are bogus . . ."[36] I want to suggest that these statements can be read not only as programmatic guidelines for deconstuctive criticism, but also, following the literary theorist Bruce Robbins, as allegories of professional vocation.[37] Doing so allows us to raise uncomfortable questions about the larger system of knowledge and power in which a supposedly authentic (i.e. not bogus) deconstructive critic is situated. On the one hand, casting architecture as a rigid, inflexible, and normative system positions the critic as a liberator engaged in a struggle with a regressive textual form. On the other, this heroic and "difficult" work is located exclusively in the realm of signifying practice, a move which isolates writing from its material conditions of production and reception. This means that the critic who wants to challenge the subservience of criticism to practice does not need to analyze the interrelation between institutions, economies and agents that structure their relationship: instead (s)he is released into a field of signification which is now presumed to be coterminous with the field of the social itself.

ARCHITECTURE AS TEXT

The strategies of disturbance outlined above attempted to destabilize the architecture of critical texts. In this section I explore a series of interventions that extend these ideas to the design of constructed buildings, theoretical designs and unbuilt works. These projects attempt, as Wigley has written, to "load theory into the object."[38] Just as deconstructive writing sought to release the text's suppressed heterogeneity from the counterweight of convention, so too does "architecture as text" attempt to unleash what was constituted as the subversive potential of architectural form by challenging its subordination to normative design conventions. I begin by discussing several small-scale projects that were funded by cultural or educational institutions, built for a short time and then dismantled. I then discuss the production of "textual architecture" at an urban scale, through design commissions concerned with large sections of cities. In tracing the evolving debate on architecture as text through projects of increasing scale and complexity, I hope to identify where the deconstructive procedures begin and end, and point to fundamental contradictions in their method.

Many of the contributors to *Assemblage* were trained as architects, and are employed as academics in schools of architecture, where they teach design or architectural history and theory. For some, the academy or other cultural institutions have provided both physical context and financial support for the production of "textual architecture" in the form of prototypes and interventions in existing buildings. Writing that describes the designs and temporary installation of these projects constituted a small but specific genre of writing in *Assemblage*. These articles are unique within the writing examined in this study, since they document attempts by their authors to literally construct theory, sometimes through their own labor, in built form. Yet the primary experiential context is within essays published in *Assemblage* and similar books and journals.

An example is the installation entitled "Divisible by Two," a polemical public toilet designed by John Whiteman as part of an outdoor art exhibition in Vienna in 1987.[39] According to Whiteman, the goal of the project is to question the "banality of architecture." He writes that the "political considerations in architecture could be awakened through an attack on banality created by the attitude of naive functionality that is so predominant in most discussions of buildings."[40] The lavatory is considered to have a repressed "power" in it that is buried or hidden by the demands attached to it by functionalist discourse.

By Whiteman's definition, the "political" in this project centers on an encounter with the difficulties created by a disturbance of the ordinary, made by setting up, and then denying, the desire for architecture to support the disposal of human waste. Claiming that the public lavatory is "architecture at its most abused," Whiteman's pavilion design employs the semiotic codes typical to the public lavatory – notably two doors, each labeled male and female. However, the interior space was not a functioning toilet, but an empty space in which attention was focused on the experiential qualities created by reflective stainless steel surfaces. Pursuing a similar strategy in 1993, Mark Rakatansky describes his attempts to intervene in the realm of the "banal" or the "everyday" in "Transformational Constructions (For Example: Adult Day)." In this case, the author does not appropriate a generic space like Whiteman's public lavatory, but an element within a space. The handrail of an old person's home is modified to hold attachments that construct an architectural counter-narrative. Following Bertolt Brecht, Rakatansky states that

> Whatever progressive aspects the institution allows or engages, all its practices, all its architectural forms, all its apparatuses – all its narratives, all its theater – encourage the stupefication of convention, precisely in order to give the institution t he appearance of seamlessness and fixity . . . Architecture . . . following the institution, encourages thus stupefication and enacts it by "means of hypnosis."[41]

Like Whiteman, Rakatansky argues that architecture plays a hypnotic role by making "everyday practice a matter of functional or decorative problem-solving,"[42] and in doing so constitutes ideological demands as objective problems. Here "functionalism" is considered to be equivalent with a form of passivity on the part of the architect, where the creative imprint of the architect is denied and replaced with the technical function of satisfying needs that are stipulated or given in advance, either by institutions or clients themselves.

The possibility that architectural form might, in and of itself, transform the conditions of social life is central to the discourse of this "textual architecture" and is pursued at an urban scale by Greg Lynn in a 1993 project entitled "Multiplicitous and Inorganic Bodies." Lynn argues that "in architecture, the present static alliance between rigid geometry and whole organisms cannot be entirely overcome, but it can be made flexible and fluid through the use of suppler deformable geometries."[43] Thus he undertakes a project called "The Stranded Sears Tower" in which he proposes that the nine-square grid of the office tower is bent over, laid out horizontally, and the squares of the grid separated into strands that "interrupt or empower local circumstances around the base."[44] Yet precisely who inhabits these local circumstances, how they might be "empowered" by this "stranded form" and why, remains unexamined. In the end, the object of emancipation is not only the repressed power of a fluid architecture, but its double, the architect, whose capacity for critical knowledge is supposedly constrained by the formal strategies associated with "functionalism" and "tradition." Local circumstance remains the silent target of these operations.

Although the journal identified overcoming the arbitrary separation between critical theory and building practice as a central concern, it is difficult to understand how these articles address this relationship: indeed it would appear that the normative theory/practice dyad is sidestepped by moving outside the realm of conventional building production. Rather than support writing that examines, for example, how architectural criticism helps to promote some architectural practitioners and demote others in the global competition for commissions, or the increasingly exploitative labor practices commonplace in firms that specialize in "high" or "critical" architecture, attention is shifted to theorists whose "clients" are cultural agencies and whose work is either produced by unpaid labor in the academy, or is small enough to be fabricated – from drawing to "crafted" installation object – by the theorist as autonomous producer.

TRANSGRESSIVE METAPHORS: BECOMING DELEUZIONAL

As the foregoing discussion suggests, the textual discourses of architecture in *Assemblage* attribute an instrumental rationality to conventional forms of geometry, representation and spatial organization. A corpus of historically determined formal practices are identified as "normative" and linked to the repression of difference and heterogeneity. The response to the perceived rigidity of "conventional" or "proper" architecture assumed the form of its reverse: a landscape of folded and "fluid" spaces. Writing about these formal operations reached a rhetorical apex in *Assemblage* in relation to design propositions inspired by the work of French post-structuralist philosopher Gilles Deleuze.

Deleuze's writing is notable for the many spatial and architectural metaphors it employs, and this is undoubtedly one of the reasons why it has become so influential in the upper reaches of Euro-American architectural culture: it contains a metaphorical language that is already fully architecturalized. As the cultural critic Grant Kester has argued, the key figures of Deleuze's philosophical language (the rhizome, the body without organs, the fold) were integral to his effort to develop a non-Cartesian model of political identity: each figure "takes on a life of its own and is endowed with an inherently liberatory capacity to transmit or express modes of being and social organization."[45] The rhizome is an ethereal and non-linear social condition that emerges spontaneously, and cannot be defined in advance. It describes the mutating space of a fluid and decentered ontology of being that has no origins or telos. As Kester notes, it is in this lack of overarching determination that its liberatory power is located: "unplanned, unadministered, unanticipated new collectivities or configurations of bodies are formed that elude the instrumentalizing grasp of political 'theory' and that may break up as easily as they have congealed . . ."[46]

Deleuze did not intend his writing to be interpreted as a political manifesto. To "organize" a Deleuzian political "movement" would be to contradict the anti-foundational logic of the system; in Deleuze's terms, a collectivity can only form as a random political "assemblage" through unplanned intersections of unconscious desire and spontaneous action. Given these anti-essentializing characteristics, the idea that particular arrangements of built form might act as political stimulants for rhizome-like social formations seems spurious. Whatever one may think about Deleuze's "agentless" political philosophy, it is clear enough that he was not arguing in favor of social determination by physical form: nowhere does he suggest that inhabiting worm-like or "folded" spaces will somehow engender a "rhizomatic" political condition. He would almost certainly be surprised at the way the figures he used to articulate a mutable and indeterminate ontology of being have been translated into physical forms that are presumed, by virtue of their formal qualities alone, to be capable of inducing liberatory political conditions.[47]

The tendency to appropriate the Deleuzian theoretical schema and transform it into an autonomous but emancipatory formal order is implicit in projects such as Lynn's folded Sears tower, and plays a formative role in his more recent "blob" architecture.[48] Here computer animation programs that "randomly" generate curvilinear forms supposedly translate the immanence of a Deleuzian political moment into the design process.[49] Indeed, *Assemblage*'s larger project of "loosening" the rationality of architecture through "subversive" formal operations restates these Deleuzian strategies at the level of the journal's broader editorial program (and even its title, which has been used by Deleuze and Guattari to describe the emergence of a rhizomatic condition).[50]

The contradictions inherent in transforming Deleuze's obtuse and difficult theory of political ontology into an increasingly global meta-theory of architectural form is encapsulated in the elliptical remarks of *Assemblage*'s projects editor Stan Allen, in a review of a building by the Dutch architect Wiel Arets. This review marks a turning point in the Deleuzian discourse in *Assemblage* because it acknowledges the international appropriations of Deleuzian theory (and their basis in the marketing of differentiated "theory" identities in architectural culture), while simultaneaously mobilizing it in relation to a specific project. Allen first describes Arets' career as a carefully constructed brand image:

> Arets' production of work and projects has been accompanied by a carefully choreographed strategy of publications . . . The projects and images participate in a complex system of exchange.[51]

Allen cites an article published by Arets in *AA Files* entitled "Grid and Rhizome," as part of this system of exchange.[52] He writes that the "paradoxical conjunction of grid and rhizome can, of course, be interpreted as simply opportunistic, deferring to predominant critical models in an effort at legitimization."[53] And indeed, the building in question (an Academy of Arts in Amsterdam organized around rectilinear grids), does not bear an immediate formal resemblance to any of Deleuze's figures. Yet Allen turns this apparent mismatch, or what he calls the "incommensurability of the project and its theoretical description" into a Deleuzian moment.

The fact that the building does not look like one of Deleuze's mutable figures makes it Deleuzian: "After all, a rhizome does not have to look like a worm."[54] Thus the streets of Amsterdam become a rhizomatic source of "root like circulation." Yet the building itself, whose visible portions suggest their "vertical dominance over the root like circulation at and below the level of the street," also turns out, on closer inspection, to be a Deleuzian form with unstable meanings.[55] The rectilinear form "may function less as a stable regulator of meaning than as an empty slot awaiting the unpredictable event."[56]

Allen carries this argument further through a discussion of Arets' dance theater in Delft. Here the entrance driveway to the theater is described as a "rhizome," while the theater space above is represented as the embodiment of the modernist "grid." Yet the theater space and the entry zone "interpenetrate." The floor plane is "twisted," allowing the visitor to experience both volumes at the same time. According to Allen, the project intensifies the "co-presence" of grid and rhizome hinted at in previous work:

> . . . no longer held apart in their distinct realms, the grid inhabits the rhizome and the rhizome inhabits the grid. The separatrix has begun to be twisted. . . . Its internal structure is heterogeneous; the grid begins to stammer . . . the pedestrian who arrives through the labyrinth of the streets and the automobile (relic of the machine world) introduced into the volume of the theater from below, infecting the stable geometries with another modality.[57]

Allen questions the formal reflexivity that equates Deleuze's political ontology with curving forms, and the oppressive mastery of Cartesian modernism with the grid. Yet the underlying assumption that architectural form – whether it is worm-like or grid-like – can somehow induce "rhizomatic" social conditions remains intact.

"Theory" operates here in a manner that *Assemblage* set out to challenge: as an attachment to the object – or a set of ideas that are represented as being immanent in the form, but in fact are "attached" to it by the critic. The process is doubly ironic here because Allen observes Arets attaching Deleuze to his work with some skepticism and then does the same thing himself. Yet perhaps the most telling indication of the modernist reversals within these supposedly postmodern narratives is the beleaguered figure of the "occupant": an invisible, culturally undifferentiated, disembodied subject who is the presumed beneficiary of the building's transgressive messages.

URBAN DELIRIUM

The Deleuzian narrative described above allows its proponents to have their rhizomatic cake and eat it. One can design a formalist object and claim it is politically transgressive to do so because the forms themselves are presumed to be coterminous with the unconscious desires of the fluid and mutating (if entirely invisible) social body that inhabits them. In this scenario, the otherwise routine decision to connect a building to an urban street system becomes a subversive political act, because within the Deleuzian architectural imaginary, it allows the unplanned spontaneity of everyday life to "infect" and subtly transform that "bad" rationality of the late capitalist state.

In this section I want to explore what happens when these ideas are extended to an urban scale. I will argue that a discourse of architectural design results in which the city is represented as a "disciplinary apparatus" that represses the inherent social and cultural differences of everyday life. Urban life becomes a set of "flows" and fragmentary incidents that large-scale buildings "latch onto," "channel," and "heighten." Fragmentation, randomness, and unpredictability are orchestrated in relationship to a rigid ordering system: buildings become "event stages" for the "proliferation of difference"; the building envelope becomes a "frame" which allows unpredictable events to take place within its boundaries.

The metaphor of architecture as a stage that supports the "proliferation of difference" and the "unpredictable" is most developed in a pair of related texts concerning the work of Dutch architect Rem Koolhaas. The first, an introduction to a selection of Koolhaas's architectural projects by Sandford Kwinter, is followed by an illustrated essay by Koolhaas. Kwinter claims that Koolhaas's architectural firm (known as the Office for Metropolitan Architecture, or OMA) attempts to "engage the contemporary forces that both carve up and produce our modern world" by intervening in "the space of the socio-technical formation of collective subjectivity; in other words the politics of metropolitan 'delirium.'"[58] Kwinter suggests that the work of OMA comprises "some of the most daring – and perhaps exhilaratingly dangerous – practical speculations to be found anywhere in late twentieth-century culture."[59] He begins his introduction to Koolhaas's work by describing the city as a "historico-material assemblage that has begun to multiply, mutate and atomize so quickly that it itself could no longer be conceived as anything other than a turbulent punctuated fluid."[60] With the city metaphorically reconstituted as ceaseless, unpredictable flows, Kwinter suggests that OMA's work recognizes these flows, and uses architecture to unleash, trigger, or capture them.[61] Thus architecture is concerned with the appropriation and juxtaposition of existing processes and forms of organization in ways that will heighten their intrinsic character. There is a

> refusal to repress either the material fact, the economic reality, or the technological brutality of rampant infrastructural systems . . . those vitalistic circulatory systems of all modern civilizations . . . these infrastructural systems . . . are generally approached as

capillaries, engravings, or developmental pathways or canalizations to be inflected, redirected, or simply followed like the surf or the mise-en-delire.[62]

According to Kwinter, the idea is to program space "like a dramaturge or film director . . . The envelope follows and fills in the wake of concrete yet unpredictable events."[63] The intention is to use programmatic elements to "set in motion artificial ecologies that in turn take on a genuine self-organizing life of their own."[64]

While Kwinter's arguments represent an attempt to read a Deleuzian conceptual landscape into a large-scale design proposition, the architectural orchestration of randomness, unexpected juxtapositions as a political strategy was already established as a subject of debate. In *Assemblage* 16 (1991), Jeffrey Kipnis argued that a "radical heterogeneity" should be pursued, that "supports the proliferation of differences without alignment, and without allowing difference to sediment into any reified hierarchy . . . this pursuit holds the most promise for providing architectural/urban design with an affirmative political direction."[65] In the next issue, the entire strategy is aligned with the grand-sounding politics of a "post-civil society" by the Marxist literary critic Frederic Jameson. In an interview with Michael Speaks entitled "Envelopes and Enclaves: The Spaces of Post-Civil Society,"[66] Jameson expands Stanley Allen's figural literalism (in which a floor slab is equated with a textual slash) to an urban scale. The wall dividing the inside of Koolhaas's urban megastructure from its surrounding context is now the "separatrix." According to Jameson, the radical political gesture undertaken by Koolhaas is to render the separatrix "impotent" by making the conditions on either side the same. In the visionary architecture of the post-civil society he attributes to Koolhaas, there is no longer an opposition between "inside" and "outside" or between "urban" and "rural." Instead, large-scale formal elements channel pre-existing urban "flows," in an effort to duplicate and indeed exaggerate the supposedly "random" juxtapositions of the surrounding metropolis. Jameson states that Koolhaas's work

> does not simply glorify differentiation in the conventional pluralist ideological way: rather he insists on the relationship between this randomness and freedom, and the presence of some rigid, inhuman, non-differential form that enables the differentiation of what goes on around it . . . Koolhaas offers the picture of imposition on the differential of a rigid . . . contingent or meaningless structural form, a form that, like the elevator, has no internal meanings of its own, but whose function is to allow this improvisation and differentiation to go on outside of itself and around itself. Thus the free spaces are enabled by the rigidity of the framework. It's almost a political paradigm in the sense that the combination of formal requirements of a certain order without content permits all kinds of forms of freedom or disorder within the interstices.[67]

Although Jameson attempts to invest the fragmentation of post-civil society with radical political meaning, it is worth noting that even here the designer is treated as an autonomous subject engaged in a heroic struggle with architectural form. Here, as elsewhere in the discourse of textual architecture, the hierarchical relations of power associated with the professional context of architectural production are exempt from criticism. Nor is any attempt made to examine the relationship between the architect and the (undifferentiated) occupants who actually inhabit or pass through these "delirious" or "rhizomatic" structures. Indeed, the occupants remain a "set of flows," differentiated but mute, reduced to almost protoplasmic status as mere organic materials in an "artificial ecology."

BEYOND STRATEGIES OF DISTURBANCE

In the arguments presented here, I have suggested that *Assemblage* reproduced many of the characteristics of the modernist writing it criticized. Both the critic and the designer become heroic figures who endow form with the capacity to capture and transform the social world. While the identity of the architect constructed by this writing is heroic, the architecture that results is an intensification of existing contexts, rather than the production of Utopian alternatives. In some cases, the goal is to construct a didactic experience about architecture as a discipline trapped within its own norms; in others, it is to "loosen" those norms in order to allow unspecified, unpredictable activities to take place. Both strategies result in "replications" of what already exists: the first turning attention towards the discipline and its normative assumptions, and the second exaggerating the "randomness" of metropolitan life.

The writing of contributors such as Mark Rakatansky, Catherine Ingraham and John Whiteman is valuable for its powerful capacity to evoke an image of "proper" or "conventional" architectural discourse of "sham somnolence." Their goal was to destabilize the normative opposition between accepted categories of architectural thought (such as ornament and structure or theory and practice), and in so doing, create moments of open-ended possibility in which the "proliferation" of difference might occur. Yet, despite their laudable intentions, it is difficult to see how their destabilizing practices led to anything but the reorganization of existing categories, a sort of epistemological interior renovation that left the boundaries around the discipline intact. The continual struggle between architecture and related disciplines to claim exclusive control over a segment of the built environment, how that terrain has shifted historically, and its consequences for the subjects of professional knowledge, remained unexamined.

Similar issues arise in relation to the examples of architectural production I have examined here. Just as critics attempted to unleash the play of difference across the surface of the text, so too did designers attempt to disrupt the conventions of design with fluid forms, random juxtapositions of functions, and dissolved boundaries between building and city.

The problem with these strategies, however, is that architecture remained both the subject and object of investigation. Though both discourses developed sophisticated techniques to represent the condition of architecture as a self-enclosed, and self-referential discipline, the alternatives were equally internalized, because disturbances occurred within the given boundaries of the discipline. The idea of architecture as disciplinary apparatus became both the villain and the hero of social change: if "architectural texts" repressed, classified, and homogenized, then they could also possess, in and of themselves, the power to liberate, declassify, and heterogenize. Missing here was a consideration of how, and why, such a disciplinary apparatus came into being, and how its capacities for classification, order, and hierarchy have been intertwined with wider historical forces such as the state, the economy, and education.

Another limitation I have identified concerns the way the "institutions of architecture" were defined. *Assemblage* was primarily concerned with representations as institutions of architectural knowledge. While certain forms of architectural representation (such as Cartesian geometry, or the metaphysics of space) constitute disciplinary traditions in architecture, they do not achieve their influence on their own. They require bureaucratic organizations, educational programs, professional bodies, journals, books, and conferences to do so. Yet the institutional supports that warrant their authority were rarely examined in *Assemblage*. Analysis of architectural representations as the primary "institutions" of architectural culture tended to displace consideration of other institutional sites. Strategies of disturbance thus became strategies of displacement.

This point is most clearly illustrated in the critical relationship formed between *Assemblage* and its contributors. Despite *Assemblage*'s goal of examining the institutions of architecture, the arguments were seldom extended to the journal itself. The contradiction is similar to the one I noted in relation to the *JSAH*, but it assumes more significance here, because the editorial program of the journal was organized around "criticism through representations." If the journal sought the strategic disruption of fixity, shouldn't the journal itself have been subject to continuous critique and disruption?

The latter point can be extended to an analysis of the self-enclosed social geography of the journal, which also remained unexamined. It is ironic that a publication endorsing interpretive strategies that stressed the multiplicity of meaning was unable to acknowledge the multiple but intertwined cultural meanings of "architecture." Reference to "architecture" and "architectural culture" were unqualified, when in fact the buildings, objects analyzed and techniques employed were common to a culturally specific group of academics located primarily in the northeast of the United States. This is particularly contradictory given current conditions, in which US-based architectural norms and forms are being globalized through practices of transnational property development, professional education, regulatory controls, architectural media and popular culture. In as much as *Assemblage* universalized a parochial position that was based in a small group of wealthy institutions, it participated in, rather than challenged, such processes.

Could the blindness towards *Assemblage* as an institution be connected to the fact that the writers saw themselves as part of Deleuzian moment, a momentary and random intellectual "swelling" which they were a part of, but did not control? This much is suggested by Mark Wigley's comments about *Assemblage* in a special issue entitled "The Politics of Architectural Discourse."[68] This issue of the journal contains papers presented by *Assemblage* board members and editors at Tulane University in 1995. Each paper is preceded by a large photograph of the presenter, and a group photograph is published at the beginning of the issue. Of this photo Wigley writes:

> All groups are to some extent fictional, but I think contemporary work is marked by, even shaped by, a profound ambivalence between the image of a group or even a generation . . . and a series of heterogeneous and only rarely intersecting, let alone overlapping or mutually reinforcing, research trajectories. To some extent, "Assemblage" has sustained the fiction of a group, a fiction sometimes useful, sometimes not, but always a fiction. This conference takes it a step further. The significance of the group photo at this event cannot be overestimated. It is a risk. The magazine could easily tip the balance toward the idea of a definable, compatible group, a club like all those architectural clubs that have gathered on steps all over the world throughout this century for highly charged snaps. The image will become a key piece of evidence in the trial of contemporary theory . . .[69]

Wigley's characterization of *Assemblage* contributors draws on the trope of the Deleuzian rhizome: they are a fluctuating field of rarely intersecting forces, a non-totalizable assortment of "heterogeneous and only rarely intersecting" research trajectories. These social particles were apparently joined together, if only temporarily, by the "grid"-like fiction of a group, which was produced and sustained by *Assemblage*. It is as if *Assemblage* were exterior to Wigley and the other presenters, an anonymous, authorless machine that held an equally decentered group together long enough to sustain the "fiction" of its existence.

The *Assemblage* group was indeed a fiction, or, better still, a representation. However, it was a representation that was constructed in and through the discourses and institutional practices of its contributors, editors, and readers. The decisions about what to include and what to leave out, what theories to "transcode," what theories to ignore, which writers to include and exclude from the *Assemblage* conferences, all played a part in constituting the *Assemblage* "group." Close analysis of these practices (and their role in defining particular arrangements of power and knowledge) becomes impossible when they are defined as random trajectories, and their cumulative effects as "fictions."

And although Wigley was worried by the capacity of the group photo to "fix" the image of a group, elsewhere in his article, *Assemblage* was a group after all, but an underappreciated one, formed through its collective struggle with a regressive discipline. Referring to professional perceptions of the journal outside academia, Wigley writes that *Assemblage* had been portrayed as "the work of the devil. And I am not exaggerating."[70] He adds that contributors to *Assemblage* "were "attacked, on the one hand, for detaching themselves from the world of architectural practice, and, on the other, for having completely contaminated the world of architectural practice."[71] His comments describe *Assemblage* as a disruptive, threatening, and even heretical force. Despite these attempts to place *Assemblage* on the "outside" of US-based architectural culture, it is evident that the journal and the mainstream it sought to disrupt were, in fact, intimately tied together: interdependent, rather than opposed, and therefore both on the "inside."

Assemblage had an ambitious agenda: to disrupt and transform the disciplinary machinery of architecture. It was also a "project" that was conceived, sustained, and ultimately terminated, by a relatively small group of contributors and editors. It was a collective representation of the shared interests and disputes of those who participated in its discourse. Their relationship to each other was closer, both from a geographical and institutional standpoint, than is possible in a large national organization such as the *JSAH*, with over 3,000 subscribers. The social, institutional, and written worlds that *Assemblage* helped to define are also very different from the "international associations" I will discuss in the second half of this book.

One small mark of this familiarity and closeness (and indeed the sense that the contributors are talking to each other, with us, as readers, listening in) is the frequent use of "first names only" in the last issue, as in Beatriz Colomina's "farewell" entry. She begins with a personal recollection: "I first met Michael through Lauren." Although we are never told the last names of Lauren or Michael, it quickly becomes clear that Michael is K. Michael Hays. The subsequent text describes, in fond terms, how their professional connection was formed: "Lauren would often end up saying at one point or another 'Michael says' . . . Michael it turned out had been Lauren's teacher."[72] Colomina bonded with Hays after an article she solicited from him met with controversy from her co-editors:

> Now it was not just Lauren who thought our work had something in common, but the entire Revisions group. Moreover this something was dangerous, worth fighting against, denouncing. Now I was really reassured.
>
> While all of this was going on and through completely different channels, Michael was hired to teach in the School of Architecture at Princeton, and I was

asked to replace Alan Colquhoun's seminar on Le Corbusier while Alan was on sabbatical.[73]

Indeed, as the nostalgic atmosphere of Colomina's writing suggests, the last issue is like a scrapbook of an institutional life, containing everything from recollections of the moment of conception in a conference hotel room ("I met many Assemblagers in Miami in the Spring of 1987 during an ACSA conference. There was a scene in a hotel room . . ."[74]), to reflections on the journal's premature death. George Baird argues this took place in issue 29, when a dispute between Beatriz Colomina and Greg Lynn revealed the journal's unacknowledged "generational" alignment with the elder figures of the East Coast theory establishment.[75] The intimate stories, familiar language, and knowing asides all suggest a closely bound world, but one whose ideas are now established in the upper reaches of the US academic system. This point is underscored in the editorial, when K. Michael Hays and Alicia Kennedy describe *Assemblage* as a "journal and a group project" that helped to constitute an "*Assemblage* generation" of theorists, thereby confirming Lynn's prior claim.[76]

In conclusion, the discourses in *Assemblage* found "the social" inside "architecture." While carefully deconstructing oppositions internal to Euro-American architectural discourse, the journal left the polarized relationship between the "inside" of the discipline and all those practices that remained outside it, at the level of theory and professional practice, unexamined. Rather than situate architecture in interpretive frames which would reveal the way it related to other social forms (such as the state, the economy, education) the writers of *Assemblage* went more deeply into the discipline itself, seeking to reveal its hidden structures and presuppositions. While this writing usefully foregrounded the protocols of Euro-American architectural theory and design practices, in doing so it tended to reproduce what it sought to disrupt: a self-reinforcing, socially abstracted architectural culture. With "architecture" defined as both the medium and outcome of "the social," the writer could once again focus exclusively on architecture, attributing both causal properties and critical agency to the manipulation of architectural representations – whether expressed through texts or the design of physical space.

NOTES

1. This was the official subtitle for *Assemblage*, as it appeared on the cover and within the journal.
2. K. Michael Hays, "About *Assemblage*," *Assemblage* 1 (October 1986): 5.
3. K. Michael Hays, "Editorial," *Assemblage* 5 (February 1988): 4.
4. K. Michael Hays, "On Turning Thirty," *Assemblage* 30 (August 1996): 8.

5 Ibid.
6 Hays, "About *Assemblage*": 4.
7 The majority of articles published in *Assemblage* are by students or faculty based at one of four institutions: Harvard, MIT, Princeton, and the University of Iowa at Ames. The founding editor of *Assemblage*, K. Michael Hays, began teaching at Harvard as an Assistant Professor in 1986, the year *Assemblage* was launched. Mark Wigley and Beatriz Colomina (both of whom acted as contributing editors), in addition to Mario Gandelsonas, were based in the Department of Architecture at Princeton University.
8 See, for example, Kate Nesbitt, *Theorizing a New Agenda for Architecture: An Anthology of Architectural Theory, 1965–1995* (New York: Princeton Architectural Press, 1996), 129–132.
9 Joan Ockman, "Resurrecting the Avant Garde. The History and Program of *Oppositions*," in Beatriz Colomina (ed.), *Architectureproduction* (New York: Princeton Architectural Press, 1988), 180–199.
10 Colin Rowe, "Introduction" in *Five Architects* (New York: Oxford University Press, 1975), 3–8.
11 Peter Eisenman, "Cardboard Architecture: House 1," in *Five Architects* (New York: Oxford University Press, 1975), pp. 15–17.
12 Paul Rabinow and Herbert Dreyfus, *Michel Foucault. Beyond Structuralism and Hermeneutics* (Chicago: University of Chicago Press, 1983), xvii–xcvii.
13 Hays, "On Turning Thirty": 8.
14 For an overview of post-structuralism and architecture see: Neil Leach, *Rethinking Architecture* (London and New York: Routledge, 1996), pp. 283–390.
15 For a concise introduction to Derrida's work, see Jacques Derrida (trans. by Alan Bass), *Positions* (Chicago: University of Chicago Press, 1981).
16 Mark Wigley, as quoted in K. Michael Hays,"The Frankfurt Projects: The Displacement of Structure and Ornament," *Assemblage* 5 (1988): 55.
17 Mark Wigley, "The Translation of Architecture, The Production of Babel," *Assemblage* 8 (February 1989): 6–21.
18 Wigley writes that deconstruction involves "locating that moment in each discourse where the other is made thematic, where the other comes to the surface. The line of argument that surfaces there can then be folded back on the rest of the discourse to locate other layers of relations. These hidden layers are not simply below the surface. They are within the surface, knotted together to form the surface. To locate them involves slippage along fault lines, rather than excavation."
   See Wigley, "The Translation of Architecture": 8.
19 John Whiteman, "On Hegel's Definition of Architecture," *Assemblage* 2 (February 1987): 16.
20 Mark Taylor, "The Archetexture of Pyramids," *Assemblage* 5 (April 1990): 16.

21 Ibid.
22 Mark Wigley as quoted in Hays, "The Displacement of Structure": 53.
23 Peter Eisenman, "Post/El Cards: A Reply to Jacques Derrida," *Assemblage* 12 (August 1990): 14.
24 See Hays, "The Displacement of Stucture": 51–57.
25 Wigley as quoted in Hays, 52.
26 Hays, "Editorial": 5.
27 Ibid., 4.
28 Jennifer Bloomer, "Abodes of Theory and Flesh: Tabbles of Bower," *Assemblage* 17 (April 1992): 6–30.
29 Ibid., 7.
30 Ibid., 9.
31 Taylor, "The Archetexture": 17.
32 Ibid., 18.
33 Ibid.
34 Ibid., 19.
35 Bloomer's article "In the Museyroom" also brings together fragments of existing historical texts related to Sir John Soane's Museum in London. The text displays a "multiplicity" of competing interpretations of the building. See Jennifer Bloomer, "In the Museyroom," *Assemblage* 5 (February, 1988): 59–65.
36 Whiteman, "On Hegel's Definition of Architecture": 16.
37 See Bruce Robbins, *Secular Vocations. Intellectuals, Professionals, Culture* (London and New York: Verso, 1993).
38 Mark Wigley, as quoted in Hays, "The Frankfurt Projects: The Displacement of Structure and Ornament," *Assemblage* 5 (1988): 52.
39 John Whiteman, "Divisible by Two," *Assemblage* 7 (1988): 43.
40 Ibid.
41 Mark Rakatansky, "Transformational Constructions (For Example: Adult Day)," *Assemblage* 19 (December 1992): 7.
42 Ibid.
43 Greg Lynn, "Multiplicitous and Inorganic Bodies," *Assemblage* 19 (1992): 37.
44 Ibid.
45 Grant Kester, "Not Going with the Flow: The Politics of Deleuzean Aesthetics" in Amitava Kumar (ed.), *Poetics/Politics: Radical Aesthetics for the Classroom* (New York: St Martin's Press, 1999), 29.
46 Ibid. 28.
47 Ibid., 31 See also Michael Hardt, *Gilles Deleuze, An Apprenticeship in Philosphy* (Minneapolis: University of Minnesota Press, 1993).
48 Greg Lynn, *Folds, Bodies & Blobs: Collected Essays* (Brussels: La Lettre volée, 1998).

49 See Alexander Stille's interesting analysis of this tendency in "Invisible Cities" in *Lingua Franca* (July/August 1998): 40–48.
50 Gilles Deleuze and Felix Guatarri, *A Thousand Plateaus*, trans. by Brian Massumi (Minneapolis: University of Minnesota Press, 1987), 23.
51 Stanley Allen, "Leveraging Theory," *Assemblage* 17 (April 1992): 41.
52 Wiel Arets, "Grid and Rhizome: Recent Work by Wiel Arets and Wim Van der Bergh," *AA Files* 21 (Spring 1991): 16–25.
53 Allen, op. cit., 41.
54 Ibid., 43.
55 Ibid., 42.
56 Ibid., 43.
57 Ibid., 45.
58 Sandford Kwinter, "Rem Koolhaas, OMA. Urbanism after Innocence: Four Projects. An Introduction," *Assemblage* 18 (August 1992): 84.
59 Ibid.
60 Ibid., 83.
61 Ibid., 85.
62 Ibid.
63 Ibid.
64 Ibid.
65 Jeffrey Kipnis, "Moonmark," *Assemblage* 16 (December 1991): 10.
66 Frederic Jameson and Michael Speaks, "Envelopes and Enclaves: The Spaces of Post-Civil Society," *Assemblage* 17 (April 1992): 30–37.
67 Ibid., 33
68 See the special issue entitled "The Politics of Architectural Discourse," *Assemblage* 27 (August 1995).
69 Mark Wigley, "Story-Time," *Assemblage* 27 (August 1995): 89.
70 Ibid., 89.
71 Ibid.
72 Beatriz Colomina, "Farewell to *Assemblage*," *Assemblage* 41 (April 2000): 19
73 Ibid.
74 Colomina writes: "I met many Assemblagers in Miami in the Spring of 1987 during an ACSA conference. There was a scene in a hotel room which Jeff likes to reminisce about, which seemed to me out of that Marx Brothers movie where an unbelievable number of people keep piling into an ocean liner cabin." Ibid.
75 For a critical review of the conference see Greg Lynn, "In the Wake of the Avant Garde," *Assemblage* 29 (April 1996): 116–125, and Beatriz Colomina's response entitled "At Home with his Parents," *Assemblage* 30 (August 1996): 108–111.

76 K. Michael Hays and Alicia Kennedy, "Editorial," *Assemblage* 41 (April 2000): 3. *Assemblage* had a circulation of 1650 "unspecified' readers when it ceased publication in 2000. Source: Ulrichsweb.com, 2002.

Cover of the "Traditional Dwellings and Settlements Review," vol. 12, no. 1 (Fall 2000) courtesy of the International Association for the Study of Traditional Environments.

Chapter 4: Unsettled Traditions and Global Modernities

The "Traditional Dwellings and Settlements Review"

The discourses of positivist architectural history and post-structuralist theory and criticism discussed in the previous two chapters operate within the same disciplinary space, but from positions that are almost diametrically opposed. For much of its history, writing in the *JSAH* has remained disengaged from debates in critical theory, not only in other disciplines, but also in related specializations in historical research. Until very recently, there has been little interest in considering the theoretical basis of historical interpretation, and how these have changed over time. By contrast, *Assemblage* was concerned with "criticism through representations." It examined how critical thought in architecture was shaped by assumptions, categories, and ways of representing specific to architecture, and argued that history was always theoretical. The question was not whether, but how history was "assembled" as a representation, and according to which interpretive systems.

Despite their methodological differences, these discourses share common ground. Both are written and read almost exclusively by US-based academics. Although they employ very different methods, both examine canonical histories and theories of professionally produced architecture within Europe and North America. The *JSAH* has typically been concerned with enlarging, or conserving this stock of accumulated knowledge. *Assemblage* attempted to disturb or dismantle it, and in the process defined a space for a specialized discourse on architectural theory. In as much as the very systems of classification, taxonomies, and modes of representation in the *JSAH* became the subject of the critical operations in *Assemblage*, the discourses of the two journals are interdependent and relational. Though *Assemblage* and the *JSAH* made limited forays into the spaces of the "non-Western" and have periodically considered buildings that are produced by non-professionals (which by one estimate accounts for more than 95 percent of all buildings), these considerations are peripheral to both journals.[1]

Since its founding in 1989, the *Traditional Dwellings and Settlement Review* (*TDSR*) has published research that attempts to move beyond the bounded domain of Euro-American architectural history and theory represented by *Assemblage* and the *JSAH*. The *TDSR* seeks to challenge the global hegemony of modern architecture and its professional and pedagogical fixation on single, often monumental buildings that have been produced through specialized aesthetic judgements, rather than shared cultural processes. This is connected to a broader conviction that the professionalization of building production is a form of cultural domination, in which humane and equitable values are rejected in favor of those which are exploitative and self-serving. The editors have argued that "tradition," like the "modernism" it seeks to counter, is also a global phenomenon, and occurs as much in the United States as, for example, in China: tradition exists wherever "ordinary people" produce buildings "with a strong connection to place."[2] Thus, while often drawing attention to spaces and modes of building production that have typically been overlooked by architectural education in the "West," the *TDSR* is also fundamentally concerned with a form of knowledge that takes the world, rather than a nation-state (or cluster of nation-states), as its geographic unit of analysis.

The research on traditional environments published in the *TDSR* has always been concerned with more than the form of buildings, whether it is carefully crafted, or commercially "manufactured." The interest in exploring the social dimensions of built form (not only in how it is used, but how it is constructed as a representation of "shared cultural values"), initially aligned the research in the *TDSR* with parallel debates in cultural anthropology. Influential ideas from that discipline are redefined in the *TDSR* to deal with buildings rather than people (or as I will discuss in more detail below, with buildings as the reflection of the consciousness of "traditional" people). As the conception of the "social" within the "traditional" has changed in the journal, so too has the interdisciplinary character of the writing: recent issues draw upon current developments not only in anthropology, but also geography, planning, heritage studies, post-colonial theory, and research on globalization, among others.

The *TDSR* is published biannually by the International Association for the Study of Traditional Environments (IASTE). Just as the journal looks beyond the conventional geographic and professional terrain of hegemonic forms of architectural education and practice, so too does it seek to transgress the epistemological boundaries common to architecture as an academic discipline. The IASTE mission statement calls for the establishment of a research community that is organized around the same "collective," "egalitarian," and "non-specialized" values the ideal traditional society is presumed to hold. IASTE is defined through opposition to "disciplinary associations," in much the same way that traditional environments are defined through opposition to those produced by industrialized professional practice.[3]

The Association convenes conferences for its membership, which take place every two years. With the exception of the first two, these have been staged in diverse locations outside the US, and have played an important role in expanding IASTE's international membership and recognition. The journal can be linked to the large-scale demographic changes that have occurred in the United States over the last three decades, as the primary axis of immigration has shifted from Europe to Asia, Latin America and the Caribbean. Indeed, the journal has benefited from the migration of students to one institution in particular – the College of Environmental Design at U.C. Berkeley and the subsequent return to their country of origin after graduation, or entry into other levels of the United States academic system.[4] To date, about a quarter of the contributors either work at, or have obtained their degrees from Berkeley, where the two founding editors, Nezar Alsayyad and Jean-Paul Bourdier both teach.[5]

With its emphasis on research conducted in parts of the world that are, in many cases, remote from the scholar's institutional base, and on conferences that bring together scholars of diverse national origins, the *TDSR* and IASTE are dependent on the relatively recent growth in international travel and communications possibilities. For IASTE participants who are situated in the comparatively affluent university systems of the "West," international travel as well as regular access to sophisticated communications systems such as the internet and fax are increasingly commonplace. However, the cost of international mobility often remains prohibitively expensive for scholars working in many of the newly industrializing nations that the journal studies, and may help to explain the imbalance of contributors to the journal from outside the United States. In this respect, the journal is both a product of, and dependent upon, processes of globalization and the global centers of knowledge and power they construct.

Debates about tradition have played an important role in the *TDSR* during its relatively short history. When it began, much of the writing in the journal constructed the meaning of tradition through an (unacknowledged) opposition to modernity. The two terms were opposed, not only through contrasting ideas of social organization and built form; they also were opposed geographically, with traditional dwellings and settlements examined in the premodern, pre-industrial nations of the so-called "third world," and modern environments in the post-industrial spaces of the first. Recent research represents tradition and modernity as interdependent and mutually constitutive terms. The journal is currently more concerned with analyzing the rapidly expanding production of tradition and "heritage" on a global scale, and increasingly situates tradition within, rather outside the global space of capitalist modernities. It is this change in emphasis, and how and it came about, that I explore in this chapter.

In the first part of the chapter I discuss the historical background to the *TDSR*'s debates on tradition. I examine the history of "tradition" in architectural research and, in particular, the emergence of positive or "recuperative" discourses on tradition in the 1960s. These set the stage for the *TDSR*'s initial debates about traditional settlements as idealized depictions of "premodern" environments. In the second part, I examine some of the criticisms that were made of these narratives of the "ethnographic pastoral." From its inception the *TDSR* has followed the unusual practice of inviting academics to comment on the journal's research agenda. These commentaries, some presented first as keynote addresses at IASTE conferences, have often been critical of the journal, particularly its theorizations of tradition and modernity. I discuss these critical dialogues here as a separate category of writing, and explore their impact on the journal.

In the final section of the chapter, I examine writing on tradition that moves beyond the narratives of the ethnographic pastoral by taking account of these criticisms. I focus on writing that is less concerned with describing the global loss of tradition, than with its many different forms of production. The transition I describe here does not occur as neatly or completely as this overview suggests. What happens is at once messier and more complex: over a relatively short period of time, new ways of envisioning tradition are built out of old narratives. In some cases, the sense of loss that shapes the ethnographic pastoral remains, but in a new, more globalized form. I hope what follows conveys not only the beginning of this more outwardly directed and global approach, but also the paradoxes of what one author has called the "traditions of tradition."

DEFINING TRADITION

As noted above, the question of how to define tradition has been a central preoccupation in the *TDSR* from its inception. In this section I want to briefly situate the *TDSR*'s initially positive, or recuperative debate on the subject in a wider historical context. The *TDSR* began by arguing that traditional environments should not only be preserved, but could serve as models of social organization in the West. In the larger history of the ethnographic and anthropological debates on tradition in "pre-industrial" or primitive societies, this constitutes a remarkable reversal of fortunes for the term. As the anthropologist Nelson Graburn has noted:

> . . . the concept of tradition was originally negative in the European world, referring to the irrational, pagan survivals, the burdens of superstition. But as changes sped up after the industrial revolution, tradition came to be seen in a different light, as a reservoir, a source of continuity and identity. Indeed, by the late 19th century, tradition was at the center of many European nationalisms, and traditions became selectively, things to be saved, preserved, or even invented.[6]

Graburn's comments link the emergence of a positive discourse on tradition within the West to the rise of the nation-state and industrial capitalism. These comprise the so-called "invented traditions" described by Eric Hobsbawm and Terrence Ranger in their 1990 collection.[7] Their definition stresses the role of invented traditions in creating a (national or imperial) past where one did not previously exist:

> Invented tradition is taken to mean a set of practices, normally governed by overtly or tacitly accepted rules of a ritual or symbolic nature, which seeks to inculcate certain values and norms of behavior by exception, which automatically implies continuity with the past.[8]

The examples in the Hobsbawm and Ranger book span from Highland Scotland to colonial territories in Africa. All are focused on the pivotal period in the late nineteenth and early twentieth centuries when the expansion of industrial capitalism and the proliferation of the nation-state coincided. But as Hobsbawm suggests, the "invention of tradition" was not limited to Western Europe. While European nation-states were busy inventing tradition to consolidate the idea of national identity, similar processes were underway in relation to colonial territories.

During the initial period of French and British colonization, indigenous buildings were often characterized as "primitive" or "uncivilized" and replaced by colonial adaptations of European buildings and infrastructure. The negative classification legitimated the operation of colonial power, which claimed a civilizing mission. In certain "late colonial" cases, colonizing nations redefined indigenous cultures in positive terms, and selectively preserved their "traditions." In colonial Morocco, for example, indigenous building practices were used to inform the architecture of new colonial cites. These were built alongside carefully preserved medinas, which served as built exhibitions of "traditional" indigenous culture. The colonizer was represented as a benevolent force that guaranteed the continued existence of the unique "traditions" of the colonized society, while simultaneously modernizing them to European norms.[9]

Tradition has always held very specific meanings in the architectural discourses of metropolitan, European modernism. Various national vernacular traditions developed in the nineteenth and early twentieth centuries in response to discontent with the effects of rapid industrialization, such as the arts and crafts movement, the English vernacular tradition and the Deutsche Werkbund movement.[10] In the early part of the twentieth century, avant garde movements in literature, art and architecture represented tradition as unwanted irrationalities, or manifestations of a decadent bourgeoisie to be swept aside by modernist design ideologies. In this context, tradition assumed largely negative meanings, and was associated with everything from reactionary political positions to a refusal of scientific rationality.

But the complex history of European architectural modernism also embraces tradition. Even Adolph Loos, who equated ornament with crime, argued that tradition was central to modern architecture: for Loos, tradition represented the process of rigorous critical thought that eventually brought everything to an equivalent plane of rationalized perfection.[11] As Hilde Heynen argues in her interesting book on architectural modernity, the contradictory embrace of tradition within modernity was central to some of the most complex visions of modernist architecture. She suggests, for example, that the modernist housing projects of interwar Vienna fused mass-produced materials and techniques of construction and machine age aesthetics with forms of planning that acknowledged local patterns of domestic organization.[12] Heynen reads across the history of modernism, locating its most interesting moments in propositions that created a dialectical synthesis between local traditions of social and spatial organization, and the universal techniques of mass-produced, industrial modernism.

While this reading finds tradition at the center of modernism, European architects in the colonies generally had little or no interest in the built environments and everyday landscapes outside the West, as sources for design within it. Though the later work of certain modernists in the post-colonial "third world," such as Le Corbusier's designs for Chandigarh, or Kahn's plans for the national assembly at Dhaka, have been interpreted as monumentalized references to indigenous built form, prior to the Second World War there were few attempts to draw upon "third world" sources to inform high modernism.[13] This began to change in the 1960s, when modernism entered a period of crisis and critical revision. Teymur and Aysan link this recuperative discourse on tradition "outside the West" to two geocultural events: the need for academic research to inform economic aid and development programs initiated following post-Second World War decolonization and a growing dissatisfaction with the aesthetic principles and design ideologies associated with "architectural modernism":

> These events converged into an ever-growing interest not only in so-called primitive societies, but also in the study of under-developed countries and cultures, rural settlements, and communities in local, regional, and national idioms of architecture. This growing interest coincided with the realization of the results of urbanization and the effects of international idioms in planning and architecture.[14]

It is significant that two of the foundational texts of vernacular or "traditional" architecture in this period were written by architects Paul Oliver and Amos Rapoport, who were both teaching at schools of architecture in London, not least connected to the immediate post-imperial role of developing programs in architectural education for "students from developing countries."[15] The third, written by American architect Bernard Rudofsky, preceded both Rapoport's and Oliver's books by several years, and was prepared as a catalogue for a 1964 exhibition at the Museum of Modern Art.

Both Rudofsky's book *Architecture without Architects* and the exhibition it was based on reached audiences that extended far beyond the many visitors to the Museum of Modern Art's New York galleries: the exhibition traveled internationally for eleven years after being launched at MOMA, and the book remained in print until 1980, and was translated into six languages.[16] Although its immense popularity was due in part to the way it tapped into rising popular and professional criticisms of architectural modernism, it cannot be understood as simply an anti-modernist tract. As Felicity Scott has argued, the environments documented in Rudofsky's striking black and white photographs are not represented as an alternative to modernity, but rather as its simple, uncorrupted essence.[17] The buildings and urban spaces he captured were intended as instances of "true functionalism, and timeless modernity."[18] They were meant to act as correctives to the excesses of modernism, a reminder of the simple truths that were obscured by the complexities of industrialized building production.

Rudofsky's photographs represent "traditional" societies maintaining a bond with "nature" that he believed industrialized societies had lost. The book begins by showing indigenous inhabitants of Africa, Asia, South America, Saudi Arabia, among others, living in natural forms (hollowed-out trees and troglodytic caves "that form multistoried apartments"[19]); other examples are photographed to suggest intricate geological formations. The underlying theme of naturalism, in which settlements located in so-called "under-developed" countries, are represented as symbiotic outgrowths of the landscape, was intended by Rudofsky to be

> Frankly polemical, comparing as it does, if only by implication, the serenity of the architecture in so-called under-developed countries with the architectural blight in industrial countries; here the accent is on communal enterprise. The untutored builders in time and space . . . demonstrate an admirable talent for fitting their buildings into the natural surroundings.[20]

Yet, the "natural" conjunction that the exhibition formed between modernist aesthetics and the environments it studied was due in large part to the fact that the images were themselves the product of compositional strategies that stressed formal abstraction.[21] As Scott notes, the photographs were

> a construction of [Rudofsky's] highly trained modernist eye, mediated through the lens of the camera . . . the retroactive construction of a universal modernism was also facilitated through Rudofsky's own blindness to historical questions, as well as to the specificities of the subjects who inhabited those structures, in favor of aesthetic and formal polemic.[22]

Paul Oliver's edited collection *Shelter and Society* (1969)[23] is also directed towards correcting a particular instance of "architectural blight": the climatic and cultural insensitivity of architectural and urban planning techniques exported by Western architects and planners to the third world, or produced by indigenous architects and planners according to "modernist" norms. Oliver hoped that the "documentation and preservation" of "primitive and vernacular communities" would inspire "culturally responsive" design:

> It is hoped that these new studies in vernacular shelter will be of benefit to architects and will provide not only a documentary record, but also material which may be of use in the future.[24]

Oliver's principal contribution at the time, however, was his insistence that "vernacular building" and "monumental architecture" be considered together as part of an interdependent totality, rather than a series of specialized and contained disciplinary categories. He has argued not only for a broader geographical horizon for architectural history and theory, but also a conception of building that would study the relation between so-called monumental and everyday architecture. As he states in *Shelter and Society*,

> It would seem appropriate to consider both the domestic prototype and the ceremonial edifice: to encompass the provision of shelter in man's history as well as the provision of focal centers in his symbolic, ritual and political life.[25]

The significance, and indeed, lasting influence of Amos Rapoport's 1969 book *House Form and Culture* is undoubtedly linked to the fact that he manages to take all the tacit characteristics of so-called "traditional society" produced by writers such as Oliver and Rudofsky (i.e. non-Western, non-professional, non-industrialized) and represent them positively, as descriptions of an idealized traditional society with its own apparently autonomous and distinct characteristics. While this model of tradition is still defined through opposition to dominant norms, the way in which the opposition is expressed – through a series of positive attributes, rather than negative statements – makes the book a pivotal document in the institutionalization of the discourses on tradition.

Rapoport describes a fully developed model of an ideal traditional society in the abstract, and then proceeds to show, through a series of case studies, how that theory can be operationalized in field research. The traditional society represented in Rapoport's book is based on an assumption of collective, rather than individualized or specialized values, through the notion of "collective assent." Rapoport states that tradition

> has the force of law honored by everyone through collective assent. It is thus accepted and obeyed, since respect for tradition gives collective control, which acts as discipline.[26]

In a 1992 article entitled "On Cultural Landscapes" published in the *TDSR*, Rapoport recapitulates the central arguments of *House Form and Culture* (which he advocates with little change today) and provides a concise summary of how he believes the transmission of tradition occurs. He suggests that the values of groups be formalized into "schemata" and translated into built form that "try to recreate, however imperfectly, the ideal landscape embodied in the schemata."[27] As such, the traditional landscape embodies a process of correspondence or matching up between the rules and values of the group and its environment, making "rule systems group-specific."[28] A homogeneous group, within a localized area, follows rules that lead to "systematic choices typically producing a distinctive cultural landscape."[29] It is the degree of correspondence between a schematic ideal and its materialized form that is, according to Rapoport, to be used in "evaluating" a landscape. This establishes a powerful system of classification and aesthetic judgement: "Real landscapes are evaluated in terms of ideal landscapes. If congruent with ideals, landscapes are evaluated positively; if non-congruent, they are evaluated negatively."[30]

In their different ways, Rudofsky, Oliver, and Rapoport have made significant contributions to developing the study of tradition or the vernacular, to use Teymur and Aysan's phrase, as a "conscious" field of activity. Together these texts describe not only a set of appropriate objects ("pre-industrial," "collectively produced," "crafted rather than manufactured," "sensitive to the landscape"), they also describe an ethical position to be taken towards those objects. They give tradition distinctive temporal and spatial boundaries: it is something that is located either in the socially constructed third world or in the past of a "pre-industrial West," but not, apparently, in the present. The study of tradition is motivated by a desire to find a way to combat the "mental oppression"[31] imposed by the imported "Western" architecture of everything from "new towns" and "resettlement projects," to "high rise flats," all of which fail to "give the deepest sense of belonging"[32] offered by vernacular communities. According to Oliver, these impart qualities "to which we all respond – human scale, to human dimension, human values, human society."[33]

Perhaps most significantly, these books also share a common conception of how the traditional society is organized and how collective "values" are preserved and passed on over time. They are represented as societies of assent, whose underlying principles form a "schemata" that is transmitted into built form according to "informal practices," handed down from generation to generation.

A direct link between "group-specific values" and their materialized form is presumed to occur through the actions of "disciplined" communities. A traditional environment is only "congruent"[34] with its ideal form (the shared values of the traditional society) if the process by which those values are transferred into built form is the result of common assent: the clarity of the transmission process is therefore predicated on the degree of unity within the collective traditional consciousness.[35] Because the results of the "transmission" process are inevitably evaluated in relation to an idealized norm, most traditional environments fall somewhere between two opposed categories: the ideal or the lapsed. Those environments that are closest to the "ideal" are often represented as paradisiacal societies that have managed to transmit traditional values into built form for centuries without interruption. Societies that embodied lapsed ideals are represented as having undergone a gradual transformation, largely due to their contact with an exterior capitalist world that is hostile and disruptive to the traditional environment. The transmission of ideas between generations is therefore mediated by the outside influences, which change the ideas transmitted.

Although Rapoport's definition posits a common structure for all traditional societies (as embodied in the assent to shared values), each society differs from the next because each is the projection of "group-specific values." Thus while connected by structural characteristics that situate such cultures in the larger category of "traditional environments," each is unique and "group specific" from the next. It is as if indigenous societies were gathered together in a box, and separated from each other by gridded divisions. Each traditional society is conveniently small (and hence manageable), socially bounded, and possesses its own point of origin.

There is something of this imaginary system of display in the organization and content of the *TDSR*, particularly when it began. The *TDSR* is primarily a journal of case studies, and even now for the most part they remain analytically removed from each other. The range of geographies presented in each issue may extend from Indonesia to New Orleans. However, the space between the case studies is often undefined. And while the approach to tradition changes in later issues, the journal is initially concerned with studying a single "community" or environment as a bounded and self-enclosed domain. At this point there are few attempts to explore the historical connections formed by trade networks and regional patterns of commerce and culture, and more recently, flows of labor, ideas and money may have constructed global lines of social and political influence.

As I will suggest below, the language used to represent the traditional environment is very different from the writing of *Assemblage* or the *JSAH*. If anything the *TDSR*, with its emphasis on the collective agency of ordinary people, presents almost the reverse of the "life and work" narrative of the solitary creator that is common in the *JSAH*. Shared beliefs and social practices, rather than the romantic version of a self-actualizing individual, form the basis of collective authorship in the *TDSR*. Yet it is not only the emphases on how "unique," even primordial, social groups collectively produce buildings that distinguishes this writing from the previous two journals: the *TDSR* also draws upon a different set of narrative conventions to "emplot" its traditional worlds. Here the premodern, pre-industrial spaces of collective identity are also spaces about to be lost to the encroaching threat of capitalist modernization. The underlying sense of urgency and even impending tragedy that accompanies much of the initial writing in the *TDSR* is also part of its persuasive force. I refer to these accounts, in which an almost Eden-like paradise is about to be lost to modernity, as narratives of the "ethnographic pastoral."

THE ETHNOGRAPHIC PASTORAL

I have borrowed the term from James Clifford, who uses it to describe the allegorical register of academic writing that describes (distant and "exotic") cultures from a specific temporal distance, and with a presumption of transience or mobility on the part of the writer. Often written from a "lovingly detailed but disengaged standpoint," these discourses attempt to salvage historical worlds as textual fabrications that are

> disconnected from ongoing lived milieu and suitable for moral allegorical appropriations by individual readers. In the properly ethnographic pastoral this textualizing structure is generalized . . . to a wider capitalist topography of Western/non-Western, city/country oppositions. "Primitive," non-literate, underdeveloped, tribal societies are constantly yielding to progress, "losing" their traditions . . . The most problematic and politically charged aspect of this encoding is its relentless placement of others in a present-becoming past.[36]

As Clifford notes, one of the central characteristics of the ethnographic pastoral is its tendency to isolate the society studied in time and space. The first step in the abstraction of the traditional settlement from "ongoing lived milieu" in the *TDSR* occurs through contextualizing descriptions that emphasize the traditional society's geographic isolation. The traditional settlement is initially portrayed as being surrounded by extensive and largely unbroken natural boundaries – usually either tropical jungle, ocean, or both – which separates the settlement from the rest of the world. These descriptions tend to combine physical separation with social, economic and political isolation, not only from a larger world economy, but also from national, regional and local forms of social organization that operate beyond the scale of the traditional setting. Settlements are described as "elaborate compounds nestled in the foothills"[37] of mountains, or located on plateaus "broken by valleys and entangled ravines."[38] They are far-away and "insular," separated from the rest of the world by deep bays and hidden in landscapes whose "configuration is . . . peculiar"[39] thus allowing them to evolve peacefully, untouched by outside intervention or influence. These geographical frames not only create "natural" boundaries around the settlements studied, they also reinforce the representation of these societies as organic outgrowths that "co-exist" with the spiritualized landscape that surrounds them.

The spaces of the ethnographic pastoral are also framed by their own, often "premodern" temporality, appearing as fragments of a remote and distant past that have survived into the present. Their very existence in a state that is largely untouched by the outside world, makes them "valuable" and adds urgency to the need to preserve them textually. They are isolated as "pure" or uncontaminated examples of tradition (and hence abstracted from large-scale social processes) thereby making the "clarity" of the transmission process one of the primary criterion for their selection as objects of analysis. Joseph Aranha offers a paradigmatic example of this rationale in his 1992 paper on traditional settlements in Nepal and Bali. He states that

> The processes of colonization and modernization have changed the forms of traditional settlements in much of South and Southeast Asia. Fortunately, a few places remain where patterns of living and physical forms remain largely untouched by the forces of change. Places like these provide an opportunity to study architectural environments that are determined by factors other than functionalism and profit . . . in the towns of Kathmandu Valley, a unique medieval urban culture that is more than 5000 years old still survives. This culture [has] changed little since classical times.[40]

The strength of a collective inner spirit also forms a powerful protective barrier around societies of the ethnographic pastoral. Because traditional settlements are represented as the projection or "transmission" of shared values, each traditional society assumes the status of a collective spiritual consciousness whose outer limit coincides with the physical boundaries of the settlement. A "strong" or "vigorous" traditional community is one that has not succumbed to "outside influence" linking the resilience of traditional architecture to the enduring presence of a common inner spirit, which may be spiritual, religious, or even poetic in nature. For example, Saif-Ul-Haq suggests that "the roots of traditional Bangladeshi architecture are dug deep into the psyche of the common people . . . Bangladesh is a land where poetry and philosophy are inherent in every person."[41]

At the same time, however, tradition can survive only if it becomes detached, not only from its larger "lived milieu," but also from the immediate exigencies of everyday life within the traditional settlement. Although traditional environments are represented as the projection of common values, the transmission of tradition is predicated on the assumption that those values become "tacit" and are passed down from generation to generation without question. As Maria-Christina Georgalli writes,

In order for tradition to survive, certain elements and rules of composition must acquire a certain typicality independent of their time and place of generation. Such forms may be thought to have acquired an a-spatial and a-historical nature."[42]

As suggested above, the journal's discourses of the ethnographic pastoral tends to associate each side of the modern/traditional dyad with two contrasting models of social organization. Modern societies are represented as dynamic, constantly changing, and invasive, while the traditional societies are represented as passive and sustained by collective assent to the "discipline" of tradition, changing only in relation to "external pressures" over which they apparently have little or no control. The traditional society is a unified society, free of internal conflict. The world is effectively divided into two geographical and conceptual zones, one isolated from the other.

Traditional societies are also abstracted from time and space by the way in which archival sources are used in the ethnographic pastoral. As noted above, the traditional settlement is frequently represented as a projection of "shared cultural values." The cultural values that form the basis of the traditional settlement are usually linked to religious or spiritual beliefs that are considered to be unique to particular groups rooted in a specific place and outside historical determination. Because the documentation of such beliefs is considered to be objective or transparent to these beliefs, it is also dehistoricized. Existing ethnographic "data" compiled decades (and in some cases almost a century) earlier are reassembled to form a composite description of the "cultural traditions" and "belief systems" of the traditional society. The juxtaposition of "evidence" also reveals how the processes of documentation and interpretation are often treated as two separate activities. Photography, sketching, field research, and notes compiled *in situ*, are presumed to be transparent to the "reality" they describe, rather than constitutive of it. The "logic" discovered in the analysis of the photographs and maps is presumed to pre-exist the process of representation when in fact the media chosen, and the position from which it is analyzed, has a determinate effect on how the traditional settlement is understood.

The "documentation" stage of the writing process thus reduces the traditional settlement to a series of morphological relationships that are mapped through putatively "objective" techniques. The traditional settlement is reconstituted according to the "protocols" of the researcher before analysis can begin. In this way, the traditional environment is made over into a research object that is "congruent" with the techniques that are used to analyze it.

The now-extensive critical literature on ethnography and anthropology that has emerged over the last two decades has devoted considerable attention to the relations of power masked by the apparent neutrality of the ethnographic observer.[43] The most significant aspect of this critique for the *TDSR* concerns the way in which the desires and values of that observer shape the conditions observed: the indigene and his or her inhabitation becomes ur-text of the observer's fantasies of the "other" as an inverted projection of his or her own "modern" subject position.[44]

THE ARCHITECTURAL TRANSLATION OF TRADITION

By stressing the opposition, rather than the co-implication between tradition and modernity, discourses of the ethnographic pastoral ironically constitute a "traditional" version of the high architectural history and theory the *TDSR* set out to challenge: a corpus of "exquisitely crafted" ritual buildings of indigenous cultures that are physically and theoretically removed from the social and spatial processes of urban development. In doing so, this writing not only overlooks the potential of traditional buildings and modes of social organization for coping with, and even contesting, the processes of rapid urbanization; it also defers a critical analysis of the global professionalization of tradition. The reduction of traditional environments to decontextualized formal and aesthetic properties permits them to be assimilated into professionalized architectural production. It is this process of translation that I want to explore in more detail here.

The architectural translation of tradition takes place in the *TDSR* through the graphic reconstruction of traditional environments in measured drawings, and narrative descriptions relayed in the technical language of the professional observer. For example, in his discussion of sacred housing in Indonesia, Joseph Aranha describes the "layout of the plan," through modernist categories of spatial organization, translating each of the spaces he describes into their professionalized, architectural equivalent: the "ground floor" contains "a small shop," the second floor, a "private sleeping room," the third floor, the "main room for public entertainment," while the "topmost serves as the kitchen." The façade, which contains "exquisitely carved windows," maintains "vertical as well as horizontal hierarchy."[45]

The translation process is marked by the continual slippage of the word "architecture" from the realm of professionalized industrial practice, into that of "traditional" building. In "Architecture as Social Expression in Western Samoa," Anne E. Guernsey Allen begins by stating that the Samoans build according to the "canons which govern their architecture." She describes the "basic structuring of architectural space"[46] which, like the façade in Aranha's paper, is informed by an abstract formal system composed of "linear hierarchies and complementary relationships."[47] The outer limit of the town's formal organization defines the outer limit of Allen's analysis: the "village boundary" operates as a "physical frame" for the activities which take place within it, and "reflects the conceptually unchanging aspects of society."[48] Having demarcated the village with distinctive formal and conceptual limits, the components of the village "social space" are translated into the language of Euro-American architectural discourse, moving from the analysis of "village internal structure," "public orientation," and "compound structure" to detailed analysis of "house internal structure" (including "interior decoration") in much the same way that Aranha moved from the "layout" of "floor plans" to "exquisitely carved window details."

These examples suggest that built forms are understood and represented in the language of Euro-American architecture. Yet it is not only the constructed landscapes of tradition that undergo a symbolic reorganization. The traditional society itself is discursively constructed as a "collective consciousness" that materializes its common beliefs as the "codes and maxims" or "traditional canons" of "Balinese"/"Samoan"/"West Cameroon"/"Chinese"/ "Turkish"/"Islamic"/architecture. The collective author of the traditional landscape is also redefined as an "architect," for whom questions of "identity" are central. Thus, for example, Dominique Malaquais writes that the indigenous population of a Bamileke enclave in western Cameroon constitutes a collective "architect" who designs according to "concepts" which, in this case, allow "architecture and social identity to go hand in hand":

> Architecture and architect for the Bamileke are linked in a symbiotic relationship . . . The link between man and structure hinges on one key concept: a vision of houses as embodiments of the people who construct them.[49]

Like Allen, Malaquais focuses her attention on a single ritual building as a metonym for the social organization of the Bamileke people as a whole. Although her concern is primarily with the façade design of a ritual "shang" or meeting building, her goal is also to analyze the building in modernist terms, as a dialogue between "form, meaning and function."[50] Yet it is perhaps in the general lesson that these articles draw from "traditional architecture" that their interrelationship to modern architectural production becomes clear. All three conclude by presenting the traditional settlement as a formal device that is ultimately capable of transforming "human" consciousness. Ironically the study of traditional environments is used as a means to reaffirm the modernist assumption of architecture's capacity to initiate and direct social change.

Malaquais suggests, for example, that "the architectural process comes to the fore as a powerful tool of social organization. It emerges as a forceful means of conditioning attitudes and behavior; or as a model or a heuristic device that actively shapes and directs patterns of thought and intercourse."[51] The case of the Bamileke reaffirms the power of "architecture" as determinant of social conditions, and hence its autonomy as a social force. Allen suggests that the Samoan model reveals how "architecture" can accommodate "both continuity and adaptation . . . buildings and the units they define are given a theoretically fixed external configuration and a flexible interior by the application of linear hierarchies, diametric and concentric dualism, and fixed focal points."[52] Aranha concludes by suggesting that the Balinese and Nepalese houses he has described provide powerful morality tales for modern architects. They are examples of

> design determined by more than function and profit. Studies such as these emphasize the societal and human aspects of architecture. They support suggestions like that of a prominent Balinese architect that architecture should be viewed as a dharma (spatial obligation) rather than an economic commission. If more architects followed this advice, they might realize that meaningful architecture is born, not made.[53]

These texts present the canons and concepts of "traditional architecture" as an alternative to what is implicitly defined as its spiritually exhausted, inhumane, profit-driven, and socially unresponsive modern opposite. However, they ultimately reaffirm rather than challenge one of the central assumptions of "high" architectural modernism: that the formal properties of architecture can produce social transformations independent of larger social, economic, and political contexts.

More broadly they suggest that traditional dwellings and settlements are studied primarily as a means to improve "modern" architecture. For example, James Steele writes in "The Translation of Tradition: A Comparative Dialectic" that

> the rapidity of environmental degradation and the recent popularity of the concept of sustainability have made clear how successful traditional societies have been in co-existing with nature. Architects, in responding to this rising awareness, are searching for modern forms of tradition, seeking examples and guidelines.[54]

Steele describes the work of three architects who have "re-examined vernacular principles when translating their cultural heritages into architectural form,"[55] which in two of the three cases housed large-scale urban institutions. The largest of these is the UAE embassy in Amman, by architect Rasem Badran. Like the other projects Steele discusses, this one draws upon the characteristics of local building types and street organization to inform the design. Steele describes Badran studying the city in much the same way that Aranha, Malaquais, and Allen examined the isolated traditional settlements: as an intricate set of formal and symbolic elements that are presumed to reflect the "originality and identity" of the inhabitants. Steele writes:

> Moving in hierarchical progression, Badran next studied the formal aspects of residential neighborhoods on Sana'a. At this level he noted fortress-like formations and the importance of water in locating buildings. Badran categorizes urban

typologies and their morphological patterns . . . in addition to gates, walls, streets, alleys and intersections. From these investigations he arrives at a set of general planning principles.[56]

The building that results is a walled compound whose interior resembles a condensed version of the larger city in which it is set. The wall (designed to recall the traditional gates and walls elsewhere in the city) is the only indication that the space inside is a high security compound housing the diplomatic functions of a modern nation-state, which the historical traditions of "old Yemen" are used to cloak. While "tradition" is used to help the building "relate" to its immediate formal and climactic "environment," it is unable, like the writing of the ethnographic pastoral, to acknowledge how the building is connected to its larger socio-cultural field.

These writings on "traditional architecture" fulfill Bernard Rudofsky's vision of twenty years earlier. While Rudofsky did not explicitly define the professional implications of his argument, his photographs also translated indigenous environments into the language of modernist abstraction, completing the first step in the translation process. And, as I have suggested above, the traditional environment was presented less in opposition to modernity than its uncorrupted source: the traditional "other" converted to the architectural "same." Here the process of translation is taken much further, and culminates with a discussion of how the collective practices of the "traditional architect" can inform those of the professional at work in the realm of industrialized building production. The process is not without irony, since one of the goals of the journal includes recognizing and preserving the "values" of the environments it documents. Those environments become projections of the goals, perceived inadequacies, and strategies for reform of the professional culture that observes them.

In some cases, the translation of tradition is not only a means to transform architectural practice but the compartmentalized structure of the Euro-American academic system. Keynote addresses at IASTE conferences have explored the possibilities of tradition as the basis of both an "interdisciplinary science" and a new form of building, "Ethno-architecture." Changes in education are proposed as the foundation for professional reform. For example, in a plenary paper presented at the 1996 IASTE conference, Amos Rapoport argues that IASTE conferences and the *TDSR* should conduct research on traditional environment as a means to "influence and improve design, planning and development."[57]

For Rapoport, the traditional environment is a laboratory in which the "environment-behavior studies" (EBS) scientist might observe the relation between humans and environments in their simplest, archetypal form. The EBS paradigm suggests that there are fundamental human responses to the built environment that transcend time and place and that can be effectively isolated and studied in "simple" traditional settings, and then abstracted and applied to all forms of building. The goal of the journal and the society should therefore be, according to Rapoport, the development of an "interdisciplinary science" of tradition that is concerned with "learning from the traditional domain":

> The five conferences and the journal have from the start emphasized one very important goal for the study of the domain – learning from it for the purpose of the design, planning and development, and also for the development of an explanatory theory of environment-behavior relations.[58]

The suggestion that the study of tradition should form the basis of a new interdisciplinary science is echoed in Gerard Toffin's paper presented at the 1992 IASTE conference. He argues that the *TDSR* and IASTE have played an important role in beginning to redefine Euro-American architectural history and theory by studying buildings for the way they represent "cultural identity."[59] For Toffin, the purpose of studying tradition is to "decenter" Eurocentric models of architectural history and theory: however, this decentering is undertaken in order to recenter existing structures of knowledge and power around the study of tradition. Toffin does not challenge the existence of professionalized knowledge and training located in powerful institutions in the West. Instead his goal is to reform the canons of knowledge that define such institutions from within, and in doing so, develop a new and improved form of architectural history and theory, which he calls "Ethno-architecture."[60] Toffin imagines the world represented by this new "composite science"[61] as a mosaic or patchwork of distinctive cultural identities materialized in built form, each separate and distinct from the next.

Like Rapoport, Toffin claims that the traditional environment offers a model that architects and the ethnologist alike might learn from when seeking to understand how the "social, the mental, and the material" are "blended" together. While this relationship can be studied in any building, it is "particularly clear" in the traditional environment:

> This interweaving is particularly clear in non-Western, "traditional" civilizations where all aspects of life are interconnected, and religion often controls all aspects of social life. Against all formalist temptations, Ethno-architecture grants man priority and gives privilege to the question of meaning.[62]

These arguments suggest that much of the research on traditional environments is ultimately directed towards professional ends in the first world academy and that its value is measured by its relevance or applicability to practice. I have suggested that the construction of the traditional environment as a socially abstract, and geographically isolated, primordialist milieu is the first step in its professional appropriation.

FROM TRADITION TO "TRADITION"

A range of other theoretical positions have developed in the *TDSR* that challenge the assumptions associated with the ethnographic pastoral. One of the reasons these alternative positions have emerged and flourished is undoubtedly because both the journal and the Association have made a point of inviting scholars to make pointed critiques of the central assumptions of ongoing debates. The practice is unusual when viewed in the context of the other journals in this study: it is difficult to imagine, for example, *Assemblage* asking an anthropologist or cultural geographer to comment on how the idea of "discipline" is constructed and then "disturbed" in that journal. The critical reflections published in the *TDSR* often refer directly to the journal and the Association, and make the representation of tradition and its consequences the object of study. The authors question the organization of writing around dichotomies such as first world/third world, East/West, modern/traditional, rational/intuitive, individual/collective, spiritual/capitalist; and the tendency to represent societies through the viewpoint of an objective, omnipotent subject. The latter concern has led to writing in which reflexivity defines a politics of intellectual identity, through the consideration of how one positions oneself in relation to an object of study.

Janet Abu-Lughod's 1992 article entitled "Disappearing Dichotomies" is one of the first articles to appear in the journal that is devoted to the defining opposition between the traditional and the modern that underpins much of the writing in the *TDSR*. Her article dismantles the opposition by arguing that the spatial dichotomy upon which it was based no longer exists. She states that the colonial origins of "tradition" and its related meanings (primitive, underdeveloped, uncivilized, preindustrial etc.) were reinforced by global relations of power in which a distant imperial metropole dominated the colonized periphery. According to Abu-Lughod, it is no longer possible to assume a correspondence between social formation and spatial location, due to the proliferation of "intermediate types" that have characteristics associated with both the West and the third world. In a comment that has a pointed relevance for the *TDSR*, she states that, in an increasingly "hybrid world," researchers are forced to take smaller and smaller units of analysis in order to continue to work within a homogeneous context:

> In desperation we break off from the present globalization process some small pieces of relatively insulated "local" culture or regional specificity . . . we can then put them into a residual category we call "traditional" or "vernacular."[63]

She argues in favor of replacing tradition with "traditioning," an "ever-changing social process," in which past practices and spaces are constantly "recycled and reused" to meet present needs. The example she selects to illustrate the idea concerns the creative adaptation of existing abandoned housing in New York to the needs of a feminist community. Here "traditional" plan forms are modified to meet the needs of the women who occupy them (and hence accommodate the "living traditions" of domesticity and social life). In a 1993 article entitled "The Tradition of Change," Dell Upton also questions the tendency to divide the world into neatly opposed categories. He compares the study of traditional architecture to a paralyzed body, and suggests that because researchers are "too interested in continuity and authenticity, we tend to ignore change and ambiguity."[64] He calls for an "impure" understanding of the world "in which the static is replaced with the evanescent, narratives of spatial and temporal fixity with those of migration."[65]

HYBRIDITY AND HERITAGE

As primordialist assumptions have come under increasing scrutiny, a different set of terms have entered the *TDSR* that describe tradition as an impure, even "corrupted," category. Tradition has become "tradition," just as the non-West has become the "non-West" in the *JSAH*. Both terms have been placed in relativizing quotation marks to suggest critical distance from them. The transformation in the meaning of tradition has been underscored by the use of hybridity as a keyword for the impure and processual qualities now associated with it. Once the dualities of first world and third, traditional and modern are unpacked, it becomes possible to revisit environments once unproblematically taken as self-contained sites of tradition, and to see them in the light of their global interdependence as "hybrid" conditions.

In some ways hybridity is as problematic as the unitary concept of tradition it is intended to replace. Its biological origins suggest a splitting of genetic influences, and thus point towards a combination of two or more "pure" sources. Yet as Duanfang Lu argues in her discussion of the term in the *TDSR*, a more radical conception of the term understands it as the relation between situated subjects and objects. Here perception itself is a hybrid condition, because it is linked to the historical experiences and modes of understanding of the viewer.[66] Thus one object can sustain numerous readings, each different from the next, but ultimately linked through their common participation in systems of power mediated by class, gender, race, ethnicity, religious belief, and national identity.

It is the understanding of modernity as an irrevocably hybrid condition that Ananya Roy points to her in her plenary address to the 2000 IASTE conference, published in revised form in the *TDSR* as "Traditions of the Modern: A Corrupt View."[67] Roy traces how the meaning of modernity has changed over the last century, beginning with its singular definition at the end of the nineteenth century when, as a Euro-American concept, it was constructed through opposition to "tradition" and "traditional" societies. She argues that, by the end of the twentieth century, this had been replaced by the idea of multiple modernities, "not simply in terms of a globalized modern, but as modernity that is inherently and inevitably tainted."[68] The term multiple modernities is intended to signal the "corrupting impact of history" on the claims of purity associated with "the new." Her argument suggests a research trajectory in which "traditions" are studied as figures of these impure, global modernities. In its "de-essentialized" and "hybrid" form, the term resists fixity, both historically and geographically, and is equally difficult to identify with a redemptive moral position.

Some of the ambiguities attached to this understanding of tradition are exemplified by Jyoti Hosagrahar's article on housing extensions in New Delhi under British colonial rule.[69] She explores how customary building practices challenged the normative cultural authority of colonial building codes, as building extensions planned between 1936 and 1941 were subsequently taken over by private real estate development, allowing customary building practices marginalized by colonial power to return. There is no clear divide here between capitalism and tradition; in this case, one actually serves to reinforce the other, while simultaneously challenging the authority of the colonial regime. Other recent articles have explored tradition as an ideological production of modernity, rather than an uncorrupted realm that preceded it. Laurel L. Cornell shows how what has typically been represented as the traditional Japanese house of sliding paper walls and tatami floors is a modern invention that reached its apogee at the beginning of the twentieth century.[70] Similarly, Sibel Bozdogan argues that the national or modern dualities associated with the "traditional Turkish house" are not inherent in the form, but socially constructed by institutions and agents in particular signifying contexts. There is, she writes,

> nothing that automatically links "good design" with the "old" . . . the traditional Turkish house is a relatively autonomous preoccupation of the architects, as well as a recurrent cultural construct within the discipline. It has, however, acquired historical significance and legitimacy only in the contexts of nationalism and postmodernity.[71]

Attempts to locate "tradition" within, rather than outside the spaces of capitalist modernity are perhaps at their most pointed in relation to the "heritage industry." On the one hand, the proliferation of world heritage sites, and the growing interest in historical preservation would seem to bring the arguments of the ethnographic pastoral to practical realization: the disappearing examples of traditional space are not simply preserved textually, but physically, at scales extending to that of entire neighborhoods or towns. At the same time, however, these articles reveal that the process of preservation almost inevitably forces out the occupants of the tradition environment being "saved." In a paradoxical trade-off described in locations as diverse as Jordan and Brazil,[72] the social space of tradition is simultaneously preserved and commodified by the intertwined processes of preservation, gentrification and global tourism.

Other recent research investigates tradition and heritage as practices of representation, or forms of urban rhetoric whose terms of reference become the site of political struggle between differently empowered social groups. In Kathryne Mitchell's discussion of Vancouver's Chinatown, "heritage" is not an innocent or disinterested process.[73] What counts as the official "past" and whether it should be preserved or allowed to change is first supported and then later rejected by the local Chinese community, as their class identity and connection to flows of transnational capital change. Whereas immigrants in the 1960s sought to preserve Chinatown from the city's urban modernization plans, the more recent and wealthy business immigrants of the 1990s have been anxious to lift preservation controls in order to permit new, Chinese-financed property development to take place. Mitchell reports, for example, that the Chinese Merchants' Association argued against the heritage designation by claiming that it presented an outdated and reductive image of the Chinese community that blocked their access to the benefits of modernization. The heritage designation was regarded as a form of racism in reverse.[74]

Mitchell's article also provides a valuable critique of "top-down" discourses of globalization, in which an abstractly defined "global economy" controls local events from above. Her article focuses attention on how transnational flows of capital have entered the Vancouver property market through local social networks, urban institutions and policies, and various forms of market regulation, among others. Her argument is part of a larger shift in research that has redefined globalization as transnationalism, and in doing so reasserted the role of various national, regional and local forms of regulation and social practice in mediating what has sometimes been constructed as the faceless operation of a marauding global economy.[75] Mitchell situates the production of "heritage" within the operations of the world economy, but in a way that discloses the crucial role of global actors operating in and through changing local discourses of place and identity.

CONCLUSION

My analysis of the *TDSR* has tracked the changing meanings of tradition. I have suggested that research on tradition has moved out of a bounded and timeless space where it was removed from larger social processes and into contact with issues surrounding the economy, globalization, tourism, and travel, among others. The shift has not simply been a question of placing objects already categorized as "traditional" in different contexts: analysis of the way tradition is written and represented has become central to its redefinition.

Recent debates on hybridity and heritage in the *TDSR* locate "tradition" within the contradictory operations of the world economy. The transformation nevertheless carries with it certain problems. The discourses of "manufactured traditions" and the "heritage industry" acknowledge that "tradition" is not disappearing but proliferating. Writing about the "heritage industry" describes the (post)industrialized production of tradition on a global scale, from theme parks and "new urbanism," to the gradual conversion of entire nation-states into vast outdoor museums. Yet representing heritage and tradition as forms of "commodification" recalls the very debates they seek to replace. For the discourses of "manufactured heritage" and "consuming traditions" simultaneously invoke their reverse: a heritage that is not manufactured, and traditions that are less alienated, more organic to human experience than their spectacular, commodified counterparts. These nostalgic reversals ironically recall the antimodern anxieties of the ethnographic pastoral, and redefine its narratives of loss on a global scale.

Assemblage, and more recently the *JSAH*, have argued in favor of forms of critically reflexive knowledge, in which not only the constitutive role of representations, but the influence of institutions and agents are woven into the research narrative. At the same time, both journals share a basis in what might be called the provincial space of the Euro-American academic system. It is this space – one that is collectively formed by the accumulation of places that authors write about, and the spaces that they write from – that the *TDSR* has attempted to move beyond. It is against this "Euro-American" interior that the increasingly global operations of both the *TDSR* and IASTE are constructed. Recent IASTE conferences were held in Cairo, Egypt (1998), Trani, Italy (2000), and Hong Kong (2002).

Yet the relation of the *TDSR* to this worldly space is ambiguous. Although I have been critical of the reductive and socially abstract representations of the ethnographic pastoral in this chapter, it is important to underscore the fact that despite this, these narratives contained a political vision of academic research. While problematic, it was nevertheless grounded in the world outside the academy in a way that is unique among the journals in this study. The early concern with preserving the environments of "ordinary people" and finding value in their "traditions" of building has not, as yet, been replaced with an alternative strategy to connect research in the journal with activist politics in the cities it now studies. If there is a silence in the more recent, critically reflexive *TDSR*, it is around this question of "praxis." It remains to be seen, as IASTE becomes bigger, better established, and more visible internationally, whether it can recognize the limit conditions imposed by its own expanding cosmopolitanism, and redefine a connection with the "ordinary" people who are now outside its research on "tradition."[76]

NOTES

Many of the ideas presented in this chapter were formulated when I was a Ph.D. student at Binghamton University. The chapter has been substantially revised and updated since then, first when a shorter version was published in the Spring 2000 issue of the *TDSR*, and subsequently for this book. I would like to thank the anonymous reviewers at the *TDSR*, whose comments were of great assistance in developing this chapter. I have also benefited from my involvement with IASTE since I began my employment at UC Berkeley in 1999, particularly through my participation in the 2000 and 2002 IASTE conferences in Italy and Hong Kong respectively.

1. See Amos Rapoport's classic text *House Form and Culture* (Englewood Cliffs, NJ: Prentice Hall Books, 1969), which he introduces by citing the research of Constantinos Doxiadis who concludes that less than 5 percent of buildings in the world are designed by architects, 2.
2. Nezar AlSayyad and Jean-Paul Bourdier (eds), in *Dwellings, Settlements and Traditions. Cross-cultural Perspectives* (Lanham, New York and London: University of America Press, 1989), 2.
3. The mission statement appears on the first inside page of each issue of the *TDSR*.
4. Although the majority of articles published in the *TDSR* are written by scholars based in US institutions, the demographic basis of recent IASTE conferences reflect a gradual change: at the 1996 IASTE conference for example, almost 20 percent of the papers were presented by scholars from newly industrializing nations of the former "third world" such as China and Indonesia, as well as from Turkey and Brazil, and African states such as South Africa and Guyana. The TDSR has a circulation of 350 readers. Sources: Ulrichsweb.com (2002) and IASTE.
5. The rapid adoption of the journal into national and highly competitive funding streams (such as the National Endowment for the Arts, and the Graham Foundation) together with what the editors regard as an overwhelming response to their first call for papers in 1987 (over 400 abstracts were submitted when fifty were anticipated) suggests that the *TDSR* and *IASTE* arrived on the US academic scene at a moment when discourses of the "other" began to achieve a high degree of institutional visibility and support.
6. Nelson Graburn, "IASTE 1996: Retrospect and Prospect," *TDSR* 9, no. 1 (Fall 1997): 61.
7. Eric Hobsbawm and Terrance Ranger, *The Invention of Tradition* (Cambridge: Cambridge University Press, 1997).
8. Ibid., 1.
9. Paul Rabinow, *French Modern: Norms and Forms of the Social Environment* (Cambridge, MA: MIT Press, 1989); Gwendolyn Wright, "Impasse and

Ambition" in *The Politics of Design in French Colonial Urbanism* (Chicago: University of Chicago Press, 1991).
10 Yasemin Aysan and Necdut Teymur, "Vernacularism in Architectural Education" in Mete Turan (ed.), *Vernacular Architecture. Paradigms of Environmental Response* (Aldershot: Avebury, 1990), 308.
11 Hilde Heynen, "Architecture as Critique of Modernity" in *Architecture and Modernity* (Cambridge, MA: The MIT Press, 1999), 79.
12 Ibid., 43–70.
13 Lawrence J. Vale, "Capital and Capitol: An Introduction" in *Architecture, Power and National Identity* (New Haven, CT: Yale University Press, 1992).
14 Aysan and Teymur, 309.
15 In 1969, when both Paul Oliver's *Shelter and Society* (London: Barry and Jenkins Ltd, 1969), and Amos Rapoport's *House Form and Culture* (Englewood Cliffs, NJ: Prentice Hall, 1969) were published, Oliver was Head of the Department of Arts and Art History at London's Architectural Association, School of Architecture, while Rapoport, originally from Australia, was a visiting professor at the Bartlett School of Architecture, University of London.
16 Felicity Scott, "Architecture without Architects: A Short Introduction to Non-pedigreed Architecture by Bernard Rudofsky," *Harvard Design Magazine* (Fall 1998): 69–72.
17 Ibid.
18 Bernard Rudofsky, *Architecture without Architects* (New York: The Museum of Modern Art, 1964).
19 Ibid., 6–7.
20 Ibid., 3.
21 Scott, op. cit.
22 Ibid.
23 Paul Oliver (ed.), *Shelter and Society* (London: Barry and Jenkins Ltd, 1969).
24 Oliver, "Documentation and Preservation": 13.
25 Paul Oliver, "Introduction": 7.
26 Amos Rapoport, *House Form and Culture* (Englewood Cliffs, NJ: Prentice Hall, 1969), 6.
27 Amos Rapoport, "On Cultural Landscapes," *TDSR* 3, no. 2 (Spring 1992) 36.
28 Ibid., 36.
29 Ibid.
30 Ibid.
31 Oliver, *Shelter and Society*, 28.
32 Ibid., 28.
33 Ibid.
34 Rapoport, "On Cultural Landscapes": 36–37.
35 Rapoport, *House Form and Culture*, 6.

36 James Clifford, "On Ethnographic Allegory," in James Clifford and George E. Marcus (eds), *Writing Culture. The Poetics and Politics of Ethnography* (Berkeley: University of California Press, 1986), 113.
37 Dominique Malaquais, "You are What You Build: Architecture as Identity Among the Bamileke of West Cameroon," *TDSR* 5, no. 2 (Spring 1994): 22.
38 Giancarlo Cataldi, Rasid Abdelhamid and Fabio Selva, "The Town of Ghardaia in M'zab, Algeria: Between Tradition and Modernity," *TDSR* 7, no. 2 (Spring 1996): 63.
39 Maria-Christina Georgalli, "The Morphology of Traditional Dwellings within an Insular Context: Amorgos, Greece," *TDSR* 2, no. 2 (Spring 1991): 50.
40 Joseph L. Aranha, "A Comparison of Traditional Settlements in Nepal and Bali," *TDSR* 2, no. 2 (Spring 1991): 35.
41 Saif-Ul-Haq, "Architecture within the Folk Tradition," *TDSR* 5, no. 2 (Spring 1994): 63.
42 Georgalli, "The Morphology of Traditional Dwellings": 50.
43 See, for example, Johannes Fabian, *Time and the Other. How Anthropology Makes its Object* (New York: Columbia University Press, 1983).
44 See, for example, Mary Louise Pratt, *The Imperial Eye/I. Writing and Transculturation* (London and New York: Routledge, 1992).

   A small number of articles published in the *TDSR* offer theoretical meta-analyses that are built upon a "documentary" base. The explanatory frameworks that underpin such analyses are based on Euro-American experiences of urbanism, space and architecture: Henri Lefebvre's model of "social space" is used by Anne Guernsey Allen to describe the Samoan attitude towards village hierarchy; Spiro Kostof's theory of spontaneous versus planned urban development forms the basis for comparing medieval towns in Thailand and France; Aldo Rossi's conception of architecture as an "unrepeatable phenomenon" is used to introduce an analysis of traditional dwellings in Greece; Guillermo Bonfil's theory of "cultural control" is used to determine the role ethnicity plays in the culture of "Indian groups" in Mexico; Martha L. Henderson interprets the settlement patterns of the "Chiricahua Apache Indians" of the American Southwest "geographically, by applying Robert Sack's theory of human territoriality."

   See: Anne E. Guernsey Allen, "Architecture as Social Expression in Western Samoa. Axioms and Models," *TDSR* 5, no. 1 (Fall 1993): 33–46; Sophie Clement-Charpentier, "New Towns in France and Thailand in the Middle Ages: A Comparative Analysis," *TDSR* 3, no. 1 (1991): 43; Georgalli, "The Morphology of Traditional Dwellings": 50–51; Amerlinck, "The Challenge of Change": 54; and Martha L. Henderson, "Duality in Modern Chiricahua Apache Settlement Patterns," *TDSR* 3, no. 2 (Spring 1991): 7.
45 Aranha, 42.
46 Allen, 34.

47 Ibid., 44.
48 Ibid., 34.
49 Malaquais, 22.
50 Ibid., 27.
51 Ibid., 33.
52 Allen, 44.
53 Aranha, 46.
54 James Steele, "The Translation of Tradition. A Comparative Dialectic," *TDSR* 7, no. 2 (Spring 1996): 19.
55 Ibid., 19
56 Ibid., 28
57 Amos Rapoport, "A Retrospective and Prospective Look at IASTE," *TDSR* 8, no. 2 (Fall 1996): 2.
58 Ibid., 1.
59 Gerard Toffin, "Ecology and Anthropology of Traditional Dwellings," *TDSR* 5, no. 2 (Spring 1994): 10.
60 Ibid., 9.
61 Ibid., 10.
62 Ibid.
63 Janet Abu-Lughod, "Disappearing Dichotomies: First World–Third World; Traditional–Modern" *TDSR* 3, no. 2 (Spring 1992): 9.
64 Dell Upton, "The Tradition of Change," *TDSR* 5, no. 1 (Fall 1993): 14.
65 Ibid., 9–19.
66 Duanfang Lu, "Ethnic Identity and Urban Form in Vancouver," *TDSR* 11, no. 2 (Spring 2000): 19–28.
67 Ananya Roy, "Traditions of the Modern," *TDSR* 12, no. 2 (Spring 2001): 7–20.
68 Ibid., 7.
69 Jyoti Hosagrahar, "Fractured Plans: Real Estate, Moral Reform, and the Politics of Housing in New Delhi, 1936–1941" *TDSR* 11, no. 1 (Fall 1999): 37–48.
70 Laurel L. Cornell, "House Architecture and Family Form: On the Origin of Vernacular Traditions in Early Modern Japan," *TDSR* 13, no. 2 (Spring: 1997) 21–32.
71 Sibel Bozdogogan, "Vernacular Architecture and Identity Politics: The Case of the 'Turkish House'," *TDSR* 12, no. 11 (Spring 1998): 16.
72 See Rami Farouk Daher, "Gentrification and the Politics of Power, Capital and Culture in an Emerging Jordanian Heritage Industry," *TDSR* 10, no. 2 (Spring 1999): 33–47 and Leonardo Castrioti, "Living in a World Heritage Site: Preservation Politics and Local History in Ouro Preto, Brazil," *TDSR* 10, no. 2 (Spring 1999): 7–20.
73 Kathryne Mitchell, "Global Diasporas and Traditional Towns: Chinese Transnational Migration and the Redevelopment of Vancouver's Chinatown," *TDSR*, 11, no. 2 (Spring 2000): 7–18.
74 Ibid., 14.

75 See, for example, Michael Peter Smith, *Transnational Urbanism. Locating Globalization* (Oxford: Blackwell, 2001).
76 See, for example, Bruce Robbins' discussion of a politicized cosmopolitanism that does not resort to leveling charges of elitism at academics simply because they are academics, but rather asks how professionals can contribute to transformative social change in a "world" context: "Here then the task is to drop the conversation dropping charge of privilege, and instead to discriminate degrees of complacency, degrees of service to the general welfare, within an overarching acknowledgement that the professional producers and transmitters of knowledge are of course not motivated solely if at all by pure disinterested altruism . . ." in "Comparative Cosmopolitanisms" in Pheng Cheah and Bruce Robbins (eds), *Cosmopolitics. Thinking and Feeling Beyond the Nation* (Minneapolis: University of Minnesota Press, 1998), 253–254.

Chapter 5: Economies of Representation

The "International Journal of Urban and Regional Research"

The next two chapters consider journals that are not part of the architectural worlds I have discussed so far. Although they are influential in their fields, neither the *International Journal of Urban and Regional Research* nor *Environment and Planning D. Society and Space* can claim academics from architecture as a significant part of their constituency of readers or contributors.[1] Nor does either pay much attention to individual buildings. The scale of analysis in both journals is considerably larger than anything examined in the previous three chapters, with the exception of some recent research published in the *TDSR*. Both take the neighborhood or urban district as their smallest scale of analysis. In the *International Journal*, where there has been a great deal of the debate about how to theorize the operations of the world economy, there is an entire genre of writing that examines the world as a single space, though this in most cases is an economic space.[2]

The rationale for including these journals here is related to the fact that together with the others I have discussed, they are part of a common field of spaces and processes in the contemporary city. Both aim to define and theorize the larger social and spatial context in which the previous three discourses are located. Although the city or the "urban region" is periodically mentioned in the other journals, the division of the academy into specialized disciplines and areas of professional activity means that the large-scale economic, political and social processes associated with the "urban question" have often been ignored in architectural research, just as the experiential, phenomenological, historical, formal and professional aspects of built form are largely absent from "urban research."

Society and Space and the *International Journal* are also important to consider because they have both played a leading role in examining the built environment in terms of Marxist-based political economy. Indeed, the impact of Marxist frameworks on spatial theory is arguably one of the central issues that both journals have struggled with. How do changes in the economy affect the production, use and experience of buildings? Is the economy the primary determinant of the built environment, or do other forces influence the way it is

Cover of the "International Journal of Urban and Regional Research," vol. 24, no. 1 (March 2000) courtesy of Blackwell Publishers.

produced and "lived" in a way that is not influenced by political and economic processes? And once the economy is admitted into the space of critical thought, how should it be defined? Is the economy so large and complex it can only be represented through the processes of scientific abstraction, or is it best analyzed as a set of cultural practices, grounded in particular national, regional and local institutions and social relationships?

However they are defined, discussions about political economy have been almost completely excluded from architectural culture. It is telling, for example, that while *Assemblage* invoked Marxism as one of the critical paradigms the journal's contributors would "transcode" into architectural terms, Marxist-based approaches were almost non-existent in the journal. Indeed, when Marxism has found its way into Euro-American architectural history and theory, it has done so largely on the terms of Frankfurt School ideology critique, where architecture stands as a constructed form of capitalist ideology. While these contributions, though valuable, are rare, they nevertheless have largely ignored the spaces of architectural production, property development, state and city policy, regulations, and education, and are focused like the rest of architectural culture on the transmission of meaning through built form. If the *International Journal* and *Society and Space* have not, to date, examined in sufficient depth the potential of buildings and urban spaces to transmit meaning, they are nevertheless both unique for the attention they draw to the wide array of capitalist processes that actually produce it.

Discussion of political economy remains largely marginalized in Euro-American architectural culture, in part because economic explanations are so powerful and "unitary" they can sometimes overwhelm all other considerations. Yet architecture, in all its forms, is dependent on economic forces for its very existence, and not to analyze buildings and professional culture in such terms constitutes a huge silence. It is clearly not a question of whether such analysis should take place, but how, and on what terms. The *International Journal* and *Society and Space* have both undertaken extensive research and theoretical experimentation in this area, and although they started with similar questions, each has arrived at very different answers. I will return to discuss *Society and Space* in greater detail in the next chapter. Although it differs from the *IJURR*, it also, to some extent at least, is built on similar Marxist foundations to the *IJURR*. Some of the major critical issues that shape the direction of *Society and Space* are set in motion by the earlier and path-breaking research on urban political economy pioneered by the *International Journal*.

The *International Journal* emerged out of debates in Western Marxism in the 1970s, and although it has undergone several major changes in emphasis it remains committed to a materialist critique of capitalism through the analyses of urban processes. It helped to pioneer scholarship that succeeded in establishing that the political economy of capitalism needed to be understood as *urban* political economy: that the way cities grew and were organized, both in terms of production and consumption, was absolutely central to the development of capitalism.

Research Committee 21 of the International Sociological Association (ISA) launched the *International Journal of Urban and Regional Research (IJURR)* in 1977. IJURR's roots in the ISA has meant that it has always had a significant number of contributions from various specializations within the social sciences, particularly sociology, but also geography, and to a lesser extent political science. The journal also attracts contributions from scholars in professional disciplines such as urban planning and architecture. When it began publishing, contributors were based in Europe, particularly the United Kingdom and France, and the United States. However, over the last decade, the journal has made significant efforts to broaden the geographic range of both writers and topics included in the journal. Among the journals studied here, in terms of both the country of origin of its writers and the geographic range of contexts analyzed, the *IJURR* is by far the most varied.[3]

In analyzing the *International Journal*, I focus attention on the way the "international" is defined and successively redefined in the journal, from the standpoint of material spatial practice, and institutional organization. The chapter follows these changing constructions in three major strands of writing. Each represents a distinctive historical shift in the discourse of urban political economy. When the journal began publishing, all its contributors were located in Western Europe, the United Kingdom, and the United States. Writing at the end of a long period of post-Second World War prosperity, these writers focused attention on the role of state intervention in urban economies, and the provision of elements of "collective consumption" (a term popularized by Manuel Castells, a prominent contributor to the urban political economy discourse) to refer to such facilities as roads, hospitals, schools, social housing – and the protest movements that arose to challenge their unequal distribution.

By the early 1980s, "advanced capitalist nations" were in the process of scaling back state intervention in the economy through austerity programs that demanded a return to "neo-liberal" forms of economic management. This is reflected in the journal by a shift towards the analysis of spaces and processes connected to "post-Fordist" industrial production. There is also a transformation in the scale of analysis. The discourse of "urban social movements" typically links the formation of protest groups in the city to the unequal distribution of resources by state or city policy. By contrast, discourses of the post-Fordist city attribute the social and spatial restructuring they describe to the "internationalization" of national economies, not least the shifting, by multinational companies, of international production to low labor cost countries: causality increasingly resides in international processes which are, to a greater or lesser degree, beyond the exclusive control of national governments. A third set of discourses considered in this chapter define a further break, both with prior conceptions of bounded, and self-regulating national economic systems and with international processes understood solely in terms of their national or Euro-American impact. Recent discourses of "world city formation" and "trans-nationalization" are organized within a "world" space that intertwines local, regional, national, and international economies, political systems and cultures in a "multi-centric" and interdependent "world economic system."

As the research in the journal shifts again to accommodate changing conceptions of a "world economic system" so too does the range of contributors expand. If the world outside the nation-states of the United Kingdom, France, and the United States is largely non-existent (or at least hardly recognized) in the early history of the journal, under what terms and conditions does it become visible in later discourses that stress the "world economic system" and "world economy?" How are "international" networks of contributors formed? Do they follow established lines of knowledge and power, or do they challenge them? Upon what basis, and according to whose terms, has the journal's geography of knowledge extended to more "global" levels of inclusion and exclusion? In short, how is this new domain of global knowledge defined, both from the standpoint of writing and institutions?

CITIES OF POLITICAL ECONOMY

Marxist-based urban research emerged in response to dramatic changes in large cities in Europe and North America in the 1960s and 1970s. The policies of the so-called Keynesian welfare state (based on the ideas of British economist John Maynard Keynes) involved Western governments spending heavily on new urban infrastructure as a way to stimulate and maintain economic growth and redistribute wealth.[4] From the end of the Second World War to the mid-1970s, governments spent large sums of money on the expansion of the highway system, hospitals, schools, housing, and universities or, in Marxist language, the elements of "collective consumption."[5] The proliferation and influence of these programs meant that relations of production could not be theorized simply in terms of an opposition between capital and labor: the rise of the state as the administrator or planner of capitalist societies (and the rise of an expanding professional managerial class, many of whom were directly or indirectly employed by the state) now had to be considered. For example, highways could be understood as indirect subsidies to the automobile industry. Highway construction not only carved up and reordered cities; it also reorganized the structure of the economy, helping to produce a new mass audience for the automobile.[6] In this light, urban policy and capitalist ideology were inseparable.

Throughout the late 1960s and 1970s scholars sought to develop a new set of paradigms that "connected city-forming processes to the larger historical development of industrial capitalism."[7] According to urban political economist and RC 21 member Elizabeth Lebas

> It was within a climate of relative affluence and political flexibility that a new school of urban and regional research was allowed an institutional place as a critical study which proposed to delve beneath the surface observation of social and economic issues and to offer new ways of explaining their occurrence and contradictions. For some researchers the objective went beyond academic study and political recommendations to include a political contemplation of the possibilities of, or impediments to, new forms of social organization and existence.[8]

The primary models of urban analysis in the Euro-American academic system up to the mid- to late 1960s were derived from the research of the "Chicago School" of urban sociology. Developed in the early part of the twentieth century, the Chicago School was based on assumptions of continuous economic growth, ecological adaptation and equilibrium. Manuel Castells' 1968 article "Y-a-t-il une Sociologie Urbaine?" was one of the first and most influential attempts to counter this approach with a materialist theory of urban processes under capitalism.[9] Castells criticized the research of the Chicago School for attributing causal properties to urbanism which, under Marxism, were considered to be fundamental aspects of the organization of capitalism itself.

Drawing upon the writings of the French structuralist Louis Althusser, Castells argued that the late capitalist state was a "structure in dominance" that sought to maintain the processes of capitalist production and reproduction through increasing penetration into the realm of everyday life. The unequal distribution of state-financed services such as highways, schools, hospitals, and housing gave rise to "urban social movements" that linked together different classes in protests against government policy.[10] Castells made the formation and effects of protest movements, rather than urban space itself, the primary object of study.

David Harvey's important 1973 book *Social Justice and the City* also played a pivotal role in helping to establish Marxist-based urban studies.[11] This early work adapts the central thesis of Marx's *Capital* and *A Contribution to the Critique of Political Economy* to urban studies by extending the concepts of "use value" and "exchange value" to urban land use theory. His book was influential not only for the clarity of its theoretical argument, but for the compelling way it turned Harvey's intellectual conversion to Marxism into a manifesto for a theoretically renewed urban studies. Laid out as a progressively unfolding, meta-critical move away from the technicist, empirical research that dominated the field at the time, Harvey's book encapsulated the ideological transformation of many other scholars concerned with urban research.

These pioneering works by Castells and Harvey were part of a groundswell in radical scholarship occurring at the same time, particularly in France and the

United Kingdom. Many of these efforts began to achieve institutional visibility in the 1970s.[12] At the time of the *International Journal*'s founding, many RC 21 members were active on several fronts simultaneously, editing collections of continental theory and organizing conferences that dealt with issues central to the emerging paradigms.

The membership of RC 21 played an important role in helping to foster these and other pioneering efforts. Formed at the World Congress of the ISA at Varna in 1970, the committee made its aims and intentions clear at its next meeting held at Budapest in 1972. In *Captive Cities,* an edited collection of papers presented at the World Congress held in Toronto in 1974, Michael Harloe, the future editor of the *International Journal* (and continuing in that role to the end of 1997), quoted the position of those who gathered in Budapest in 1972:

> Urban sociologists have been too frequently turned into the handmaidens of those practical professions concerned with making physical changes to the built environment. As a result many urban sociologists have become more concerned with the human relations of the city rather than the sociology of the city: it is as if industrial sociologists had turned themselves into personnel officers. We believe that an urban sociology cannot advance when it has abandoned the central issues, which have formed the central focus of the subject: only by a return to these issues can we see a possibility of moving forward in an intellectually fruitful way. It is our task to study society – its distribution of power and other resources, the structural limitations on life chances, and the patterns and processes of conflict inherent in the nature of society. We, of course, in this Research Committee, are limited to the manifestations of the social processes as they occur in a spatial context.[13]

Between 1975 and 1979, Michael Harloe organized annual conferences in London through the now defunct Center for Environmental Studies under the heading of "Urban Change and Conflict."[14] These were significant in promoting a forum for materialist discourse, as well as introducing the research of Castells and other theoreticians to a British audience. In 1976, Chris Pickvance, a founding member of RC 21, and a regular contributor to the *International Journal* since its inception, edited a highly influential collection of essays entitled *Urban Sociology. Critical Essays*.[15] The collection provides one of the first surveys of Marxist structuralist approaches to urban studies and also contained the first English translation of Castells' 1968 article "Y-a-t-il une Sociologie Urbaine?" John Walton, an American sociologist, was the first among this group to address urban processes in an explicitly "international political economy perspective" through research he conducted in the 1970s that culminated in his chapter "Political Economy of World Urban Systems," in the 1981 collection he edited with Louis Massotti entitled *The City in a Comparative Perspective*, and later a

1981 book written with Alejandro Portes entitled *Labour, Class, and the International System*.[16]

Manuel Castells was one of the original members of RC 21, and a founding member of the *International Journal*'s advisory board. He was also influential in the establishment of various Paris-based CNRS programs, and several CNRS researchers became frequent contributors to the journal, including Jean Lojkine, Edmond Preteceille and later Christian Topolov. Lojkine and Preteceille attempted to build upon the insights of Castells' work into state intervention and urban social movements. Research committee members from Italy included Enzo Mingione and Piero Della Seta, both of whom taught at the University of Milan at the time of the journal's founding. Mingione's early contributions to the *International Journal* are among the first to address the emergence of the "dual city" and related themes of informalization, and economic restructuring, while Della Seta adapted Castells' thesis on urban social movements to "urban struggles" over housing and municipal services in major Italian cities. Ivan Szelenyi, an emigre from Hungary first to the United Kingdom, and then to the United States, played an important role in developing debates in the journal over the role of communist states in urban and regional development. Partly through Szelenyi's efforts, the *International Journal* played a pioneering role in studying the impact of the reunification of Germany and the restructuring of the Eastern bloc under capitalism after the fall of the Berlin wall.

Early issues of the *International Journal* reflect the sense of hubris and debate that accompanied the incorporation of Marxist frameworks into urban studies in the late 1970s. Indeed, the initial importance of the journal resides in its status as a point of convergence for a reinvigorated "Western Marxism" and a theoretically renewed field of urban studies.[17] From the first issue in 1977, through the first five years of publication, the pages of the journal are dominated by lively debates about recent developments in Marxism, particularly theories of the state by Louis Althusser and Nicos Poulantzas, and their possible relationship to urban studies. Simply stated, these authors tried to understand the changing role of the state policies in transforming the growth of capitalism.

A network of international contributors including Jean Lojkine (France), Chris Pickvance (United Kingdom), Richard Child Hill (United States), and Enzo Mingione (Italy), all write articles in the first issue that consider how the emergence of a powerful, technocratic "state apparatus" challenged the opposition between capital and labor typical of "industrial capitalism." The state is represented as a "structure in dominance," intervening not only in the workplace, but the realm of everyday life. Lojkine argues, for example, that a "theorization of the state apparatus" is needed to "grasp in all its contradictory aspects, the intervention of the capitalist state into the processes of production-consumption."[18]

These articles established the urban basis of social change under "state-managed" capitalism. Writers such as Manuel Castells explored the emergence and impact of political movements that sought to challenge the direction and outcome of such change. Castells and others argued that the intervention of the state in urban processes helped to initiate political movements that were specifically urban in character. These movements contested the state's unequal distribution of elements of "collective consumption," or the large-scale investments in the infrastructure of postwar capitalism. The discourse of urban social movements constituted a striking departure from class-based Marxist analysis by considering the spaces of "everyday life," as well as the industrial workplace, as a potential fulcrum for revolutionary politics. Part of its initial appeal resided in its "theoretical openness" to a wider range of experiences and spaces than conventional Marxist approaches could accommodate at the time.[19] Precisely because huge infrastructure elements like highways were not targeted at one class, attempts to stop their construction, or place them in a different location, could form the basis of protest movements that were organized less around specific class identities, than urban issues that linked different classes together. As Gillian Rose has noted, the paradigm

> ... spoke of "social" struggles rather than immediately requiring all urban movements to become "class" antagonisms and "class struggles" [and] offered a prospect of making the connections between struggles within both the work place and the living place.[20]

The innovation of the urban social movement thesis was to redefine the city as a site of conflict, and to make the study of such conflict an accepted part of urban studies. The *International Journal* played a pivotal role in advancing research on both sides of postwar capitalism of "advanced industrial societies": from the "top down" perspectives which examined urban policies and planning initiatives of the state, and from the "grassroots," through detailed studies of how social groups form into political movements to challenge these practices. These areas of study linked political events in the world outside the academy to the formation of new domains of knowledge within it. The question of how this research is represented, who it is ultimately for, and what happens to it once it is complete, is key to any discussion of Marxist-based urban research and how it has changed over time.

GLOBAL DISPLACEMENTS

Writing on urban social movements in the *IJURR* begins by examining the issues surrounding housing for lesbians. That the *IJURR* published E. M. Ettorre's article about the "lesbian ghetto" soon after it began publishing is evidence not only of the openness of the paradigm that Rose describes above, but of the visionary stance of the journal at its inception.[21] Like the subsequent articles in the genre, this one is less concerned with spatial qualities than with the analysis of a protest movement concerned with organizing access to housing. In subsequent articles, not only housing, but everything from heath services, schools, and community services, to parks, roadways, and streets, are evaluated primarily for the politics of their distribution rather than for the spaces they form, and the meanings they might hold for their occupants or users. Housing and other forms of collective consumption acquire an instrumental status: "Housing struggles," write Guido Lagana, Mario Pianta, and Anna Segre, have "the objective of social management of housing stock."[22]

The writing is rigorously empirical, and exemplifies Richard Child Hill's definition of Marxism (presented in the first issue) as "a method of scientific investigation" that abstracts "out of the social totality the laws of motion of the mode of production in the purest form. These laws then become tools for explaining concrete events in a totality through a process of successive approximation."[23] In what follows, I suggest that it is this form of abstraction that has enabled the paradigm of urban social movements to travel internationally and remain largely unchanged. Another area of research into collective consumption in the *International Journal* is more frankly class-based, and examines how the consumption of "social" or "public" housing contributes to, or impedes, the construction of class identity and class stratification. While most of this research is linked to a much more economistic reading of Marxist theory than what is presented in the discourses of urban social movements, it also includes a range of approaches inspired by "non-Marxist" theorists of social stratification. Indeed, much of the writing published by the British sociologist Peter Saunders in the journal is concerned with the "sociological significance of private property rights in means of consumption."[24] Ray Pahl, another prominent Weberian who writes for the journal on housing issues, examines "employment, work and the domestic division of labor," thus opening up unpaid domestic labor to a larger, more complex theorization of the working class.[25]

However, the majority of these articles consider "public" housing as an ideological mechanism of the state intended to limit the revolutionary potential of the working class. These studies are characteristically focused on British contexts. Early articles deal with "class analysis and domestic property,"[26] "housing classes and housing policy"[27] and "the differential rate of capital gain from owner occupation for the formation of housing classes."[28] They also begin to address the impact of housing privatization on class consciousness and "socio-tenurial polarization," as the sale of council housing (i.e. social housing) in the United Kingdom reaches a peak in the Thatcherite mid-1980s. Articles begin to emerge with titles such as "Marginalization and subsidized individualism: the sale of council housing in the restructuring of the British welfare state."[29]

The Euro-American urban social movements studied in the journal are closely tied to state-managed consumption of urban space in "advanced capitalist" nation-states. When that stage was perceived to end in the West so too did writing on urban social movements. The paradigm did not die out, however. It was displaced to other contexts which were perceived to be entering the particular form of state-managed capital that the West had left behind. Acting in response to a global recession in the early 1980s, industrialized states began to withdraw from the provision of services and spaces of collective consumption. Articles appear in the *IJURR* that describe a growing "crisis of French urban research."[30] Indeed, one of the few contributions to reflect critically on the institutional status of the discourse argues that research into urban social movements had, by the early 1980s, become so dependent upon state funding for its survival (particularly in France where the discourse originated) that its future was completely tied to the state apparatus it originally sought to analyze and challenge.[31]

In the mid-1980s some of the scholars who played a key role in introducing "the French School" of urban sociology to Euro-American academic systems begin to consider other contexts around the world where the discourse might be applied. In a 1985 article entitled "The Rise and Fall of Urban Movements and the Role of Comparative Analysis" Chris Pickvance argues that scholars needed to recognize the "uneven development of urban social movements"[32] in which "decline in the West is compensated for by the growth of urban movements elsewhere."[33]

When introducing a special issue of the journal on African cities in 1988, Pickvance argues that the geographical transfer of the discourse to the "third world" requires changes in method: theoretical operations need to be performed on "third world" cities before the structural causes of urban protest can be properly analyzed. He suggests that the consideration of "culture" must be repressed in order to constitute conditions similar enough to allow both the application of the discourse and the comparison of its results on an international basis. He endorses the "third world city" as a category of analysis precisely because it ignores "cultural specificity" and allows comparison between disparate cultural conditions and geographical locations:

> A major theme of much of the previous work on the subject has been the cultural specificity of the Islamic City . . . by choosing the third world city as the frame of reference [these writers] are implicitly rejecting a culturalist perspective . . . all the papers concern the economics of housing and land development and the access of different groups to land.[34]

While stressing economic practices allows the comparison of "third world cities," it also eliminates consideration of the role of cultural identity (and many other aspects of difference) in shaping urban politics – the very characteristic that served to differentiate the discourses of urban social movements from other more economistic debates in the first place. At this point in time, Pickvance's argument is predicated on the assumption that economic processes exist somewhere outside of "cultural specificity."

Concerns about the latter assumption are voiced as early as 1981 in Michael Harloe's contribution to an important survey of Marxist urban studies edited by Michael Dear and Alan J. Scott.[35] Harloe argues that the methodology of the "French School" was derived from French experiences of state intervention and then generalized to other European and North American contexts. He suggests that the long history of welfarism in the United Kingdom produced a mode of state intervention based on an elaborate bureaucracy that frequently inhibits, rather than supports, the instrumental rationality Castells discovered in the French state. Thus attempts to retreat into the realm of economic determination to avoid the confusions of "culture," as suggested by scholars such as Pickvance, may simply result in a failure to recognize the cultural determination of economic systems.

Similar criticisms are raised again in 1987, when Harloe writes a strong editorial in the *International Journal*, suggesting that not only the confined geography of the paradigms of the "French School," but the underlying assumptions about economic change needed to be re-examined. He writes that the

> "IJURR" was the product of the so-called new urban sociology and of the relatively small network of researchers [mainly based in Western Europe] associated with the development of this new paradigm . . . far-reaching economic changes of the past few years, together with the associated political and ideological shifts, have shown that many of the . . . assumptions are incorrect or too superficial . . . in the minds of many, the "IJURR" continues to be identified with a limited range of issues and perspectives with which we were concerned in the 1970s.[36]

The changes Harloe and the editorial board announce include the establishment of a panel of contributing editors based in "countries/regions not represented on the editorial board," to assist in the development of the contents of the journal, and a much more sustained effort to "involve a wider range of countries and regions than we have concentrated upon in the past."[37]

Despite these proposals, the discourse of urban social movements continues to be represented in the journal. If anything, Castells' early writings on the subject (which he has increasingly distanced himself from) have been elevated to almost canonical status. Writers based in such disparate locations as Brazil, Mexico City and Hong Kong begin their papers by citing the centrality of Castells' research from the late 1970s and early 1980s to their research. Writing from South Africa in 1995, Claudia N. Reitgnes notes, "the species of the urban social movement is very much alive and kicking."[38] The international displacement of the paradigm suggests that when theories become obsolete in one place, they may travel via a circuit of academic influence to other, more viable locations. To borrow Arjun Appadurai's phrase "our past becomes someone else's future."[39]

The paradigm has also re-emerged in relation to contexts in the "West." For example, almost twenty years after the publication of E. M. Ettorre's first (and until then only) research into lesbian feminist politics in London, an article is published in 1992 by Sy Adler and Johanner Brenner entitled "Gender and Space: Lesbians and Gay Men in the City."[40] Like the contributions dealing with locations outside Europe and North America, the authors begin by citing the centrality of *The City and the Grassroots* to their research, and their article locates their argument within the urban social movements paradigm.

The somewhat mechanistic recuperation of the urban social movements paradigm here and elsewhere in recent issues of the journal also attests to the inward turn of the *IJURR*'s discourses. While contributors to the journal have been successful in appropriating and transforming highly theoretical forms of Marxism to the study of urban space, there have been few comparable efforts to relate the (now vast) literatures on "identity" to the analysis of urban and regional space. Adler and Brenner's article is emblematic of this lacunae. When referring to the "literature on the difference between gay men and lesbians in relation to urban space" the authors cite only Castells' 1982 book and research into the political economy of gay neighborhoods by Lawrence Knopp. They do not refer to literature from the emerging field of queer studies that developed during the same period, much of it related directly or indirectly to the question of "sexuality and space."[41] An important exception is Gill Valentine's 1995 article on "lesbian geographies," which cites much of this literature. While acknowledging the contribution of the urban social movements paradigm, she also attempts to move beyond it. Valentine examines how "lesbian spaces are also produced or claimed through collective imaginings and sometimes fantasies focused upon social networks, individual celebrities, and specific sites." Her article is a rare attempt within *IJURR* to theorize the role of images and representation in the production of physical space, outside the framework of political economy.[42]

The continuing influence of discourses of urban social movements therefore holds a contradictory meaning: on the one hand, it may signal the beginning of an important effort on the part of the journal to deal with the increasingly volatile "politics of cultural difference" in cities internationally, rather than to submerge them in homogenizing arguments about economic determination. At the same time, however, the fact that scholars have returned to the urban social movement paradigm largely in isolation from other discourses on cultural identity also suggests a form of disciplinary introversion that the journal originally hoped to challenge.

THE CRISIS WITHIN

If the global displacements of writing on urban social movements constitutes one side of the transformation of urban theory in the *International Journal* during the turbulent years of the late 1970s, the discourses of "crisis" and "informalization" are the other. When the *International Journal* began, the image of the sometimes brutal interventions of the state against a backdrop of protest occurred within the context of sustained economic growth. Yet it is precisely the sudden end to this growth that brought about a major shift in the journal. The state, initially posited as a mediating influence between corporate capital and the working class, is de-emphasized, and the prior antimony between capital and labor is restored, but in a different form.

The events leading to this "crisis" in the structure of advanced capitalism actually begin with the oil shocks of the early 1970s, before the *International Journal* started publishing. The global recession that followed marked the beginning of a period of dramatic reorganization in which models of state-managed economic growth were gradually replaced with neo-liberal strategies that favored public/private partnership. The changes initially register in the *IJURR* through studies of the "urban fiscal crisis" in large US cities, many of which suffered from declining tax revenues in the late 1970s, with some verging on bankruptcy.[43]

By the late 1980s the "restructuring" associated with the period is increasingly subsumed under the heading of "post-Fordism."[44] By stressing the transformation of labor patterns, industrial location, and later, the breaking up of a standardized "Fordist" mode of production, this research marks a shift away from "everyday spaces" and housing previously considered in the discourse of urban social movements. At the same time, the optimistic assumption that urban social movements might act as a bridge to potentially revolutionary political actions all but disappears. With a few notable exceptions, discussions about the growing "crisis" do not document the presence of political opposition. Instead, they focus on describing new structures of exploitation targeted at a "post-industrial" working class.

The "crisis" also brings conditions previously associated in the journal with the "underdeveloped" nations of the "third world," into the center of the so-called first world through rapid increases in legal and illegal non-European immigration, and the emergence of a so-called "informal economy." Thus Michael P. Smith *et al.* write of "ethnic group class formation" in relation to "new Asian" households in California.[45] "Immigrant women workers" in London are examined in order to reveal the links between "productive and reproductive labor";[46] the labor practices of "Dominican women in the New York apparel industry" are analyzed to determine whether migrant women's incorporation into the "waged economy" improves their status with respect to "patriarchy and female subordination in the household."[47]

These articles bring an exteriorized international into national contexts through the embodied figure of the economic migrant. As such they begin to erode the conception of what previously has often been represented as an autonomous, self-determining national economic space. At the same time, however, because the migrant groups are ultimately constituted as supplements or complications to class structures, their impact on the city is often theorized in terms of abstractions such as "labor patterns" and "wage differentials." The complex transformations in the signifying processes of urban space brought about by the formation of "hybrid" national cultures (as referenced through the proliferation of everything from street markets and bodegas to political murals and foreign-language neighborhood newspapers) in large metropolitan centers remains largely unexamined.[48]

A clearly defined model of historical periodization also informs the writing of "urban crisis." Whether described in terms of restructuring within a primarily white working class or in terms of the super-exploitation of "economic refugees," the emergence of informalization is linked to changes in the structure of "advanced industrial economies" that begins following the Second World War. This limited time span cannot recognize the complex history of forced migration through slavery to the United States and its relation to a historic "underclass" in the US, or the equally complex forms of class stratification that occurred in colonial societies.[49]

THE POST-FORDIST CITY

By the late 1980s, terms that were previously used to describe scattered symptoms of a "crisis" (informalization, the re-emergence of sweatshops, the increased prevalence of part-time and subcontracted labor, the "deregulation" of industrial production, and the "geographical transfer of value" or off-shoring of production capacity to cheaper labor markets) all find their place in a larger theoretical framework that understands "advanced capitalism" as a whole and is undergoing a large-scale shift to a "post-Fordist regime of accumulation."

As its name implies, "post-Fordism" grows out of the detailed analysis of changing labor practices and employment patterns in industry, the epitome of which is the mass-production automobile plant. The paradigm has its origins in research undertaken by a group of European Marxists collectively known as the "regulation school." Influential figures in this movement include Alain Lipietz and Michel Aglietta. *A Theory of Regulation*, a pioneering 1979 text by Aglietta, has played a foundational role in the discourse.[50] Lipietz published a series of influential articles in the mid-1980s[51] that develop the theme of a "post-Fordist" mode of regulation. Lipietz defines a "mode of regulation" as a materialization of a regime of accumulation taking the form of norms, habits, laws, regulating networks and so on, that ensure the unity of the process, i.e. the appropriate consistency of individual behaviors within the scheme of reproduction.[52]

As with earlier forms of Marxist analysis, the contribution of the *International Journal* to this area of theory has been to explore its specifically urban dimensions. The most salient aspects concern what is called "the geographical displacement of production," or what David Harvey famously called the "spatial fix" of post-industrial capitalism, by which industries formerly centralized in one place are broken up and scattered around the globe according to the location of cheaper labor markets. David Harvey's important 1978 article[53] in the *International Journal* anticipates the later links that he and other scholars form between urban studies and the regulation school. In this article, Harvey classifies periods of capitalist development according to the differing "regimes of accumulation" that predominate in each. He argues that "advanced capitalism" is undergoing a "shift" but does not spell out the characteristics of the new regime of accumulation. The question is answered in his 1989 book *The Condition of Postmodernity*, where the "transition" from Fordism to "flexible accumulation" becomes the centerpiece of his argument. Harvey considers flexible accumulation, or "post-Fordism," as part of an epochal shift embracing not only labor patterns and modes of industrial production in the West, but changes in the realm of ideology and cultural production.[54]

The *International Journal* remains primarily concerned with producing the hard empirical evidence of changing patterns of labor and industrial location. Its focus has been resolutely on the industrial workplace.[55] The technical and highly abstract terminology of the writing leads the reader into the world of human labor redefined as "national units and regional aggregates" and the sometimes brutal processes of domination are described as the "facilitation of the accumulation of capital by an international capitalist class."[56] Urban struggles are redefined as "community protest in a metropolitan control center."[57]

Harvey and other Marxists concerned with post-Fordism have considered (however problematically) the manifestations of post-Fordist culture at the level of films, television, art and architectural production, and this debate has gradually filtered into more recent issues of the *International Journal*.[58] The post-Fordist consumer city has become the primary (and in fact only) site of an emerging discourse of urban culture in the journal. Perhaps the best example of this is David Clarke's 1997 article entitled "Consumption and the City, Modern and Postmodern," the first systematic attempt published in the *IJURR* to relate the insights of Jean Baudrillard's thesis on signification to urban studies.[59] Clarke argues that the "modern city" has been replaced by its postmodern alternative, which "amounts to a living on [sic] in a city that continues its existence in a fractal form."[60] The hypermarket (itself a term that is specific to French shopping culture) provides the dominant metaphor for social relations in a "postmodern" world:

> The specificity of the [consumer] object thus becomes generalized and reinscribed across postmodern society as a whole. . . . Henceforth we will have experienced a "perpetual testing" by the system. . . . the entire sphere of consumption possesses the character of an indefinite referendum, constituting the "space-time" of a whole operational simulation of social life.[61]

Clarke suggests that we no longer understand objects on their own terms, but rather through elaborate systems of meaning that are constructed for them through marketing campaigns and advertising. These precede the object, which is meaningless and empty without them. Thus to enter into consumption is to simultaneously enter into a series of tests, where we are solicited to play a part. The test determines whether we know our lines or not.

This state of hyperconsumption absorbs all of social life into the fabricated narratives of marketing campaigns, and replaces the "real" with the "simulated real" as the origins of the meaning.[62] It is without question a vital part of consumption practice in certain locations. Yet to suggest that the practices described here define an entire social world called "postmodern life" ignores the geographical, cultural and class specificity of such practices. As a mode of analysis, it follows the same model of periodization that structures the journal as whole, and implicitly assigns locations that have not passed through the postmodern/post-Fordist transition to an invisible and "non-cultural" status.

Lila Leontidou's article entitled "Alternatives to Modernism in (Southern) Urban Theory: Exploring In-Between Spaces," questions and then departs from this position.[63] She describes postmodernism as a "retrieved, subordinate position, alternative to modernism, rather than a previously inexistent condition."[64] She argues that Mediterranean cities and, more broadly, "Southern" cities, which are typically not included in paradigmatic formulations of modernity, are "formidable fields" for such arguments. Not only does she question the limited geography of the post-Fordist thesis on (postmodern) culture, she also questions its periodization. Postmodernism is redefined as all that is marginalized by hegemonic conceptions of modernity. It is a discrepant reading of modernity that has not, as yet, been pursued in subsequent issues of the journal.

Leontidou's article also opens the door, if only slightly, on interpretations of urban culture outside the "first world city." Yet in all of the writing I have discussed so far, the "non-Western" or "third world" city becomes visible because it begins to approximate conditions in the "West," or is the target of changes initiated as part of "post-industrial restructuring" in Europe, the United States, and the United Kingdom. Although the world outside these spaces comes into view, it continues to do so as an economic hinterland subordinated to various crisis conditions in the "West."

WORLD CITY FORMATION

A different picture of the world emerges from a parallel strand of research that begins to develop in the journal with the publication in 1982 of John Friedmann and Goetz Wolff's now classic article entitled "World City Formation. An Agenda for Research and Action."[65] This article lays out an important new research direction in the journal. I discuss this in somewhat more detail here because it constitutes a significant break with previous conceptions of the "international" in urban studies.

The article begins by describing the emergence of the "world city," a phenomenon that they link to capitalist expansion following the Second World War. A detailed description of what are seen as some of the common attributes of the world city is followed by a discussion of the growth of the world economic system. The engines of this expansion include transnational corporations, the rise in new technology, changes in production, "sectoral employment shifts" including informalization, a "new international division of labor," and the "differential mobility" of capital, labor, and land.[66]

Many of these terms recall the discourses of the "post-Fordist mode of production." Indeed, the world city paradigm and theories of post-Fordism share the same epochal conception of capitalist development that links progressive jumps in the compression of space and time to the crisis conditions of capitalism. Both paradigms describe a shift away from constraints that emerged following the Second World War. Under post-Fordism, it is the constraints of the rigid patterns of Keynesian economic regulation from which capitalism frees itself. Under the world city paradigm, it is national economic constraints that are overturned:

> Since the Second World War, the processes by which capitalist institutions have freed themselves from national constraints and have proceeded to organize global production and markets for their own intrinsic purposes have greatly accelerated. The actors principally responsible for organizing the economic map of the world are transnational corporations. . . . The emerging global system of economic relations assumes its material form in particular, typically urban localities that are enmeshed in the global in a variety of ways.[67]

Post-Fordist discourses imply the presence of an integrated world economic system, but discuss only metropolitan centers in Europe and North America where "advanced capitalism" is in crisis. By contrast, the world city paradigm understands urban contexts as "nodes" in an interconnected "network" of "world cities," which are classified according to their mode of integration into the world economy. The result is a system of world city "typologies" based on their spatial location within the world economy.[68] The authors argue that the world city is a recent phenomenon, and as a result they claim that no landmark studies exist on the subject. Nor, they claim, is there an "integrated" or common framework "that would enable us to relate individual city studies to the larger vision of process and structure in the formation of human settlements."[69]

Friedmann and Wolff's world city represents global flows coming together within the jurisdictional boundaries of cities such as New York, Los Angeles, Paris, or Tokyo. The result is to localize highly mobile, transnational processes. When considered in relation to the transnational flow of goods and services, the "inside" of the world city tends to assume the designation of "here" and the rest of the world as "there." Localities are essentialized as "regional characteristics of labor pools" just as transnational migrants are defined as "economic migrants" who bring their enduring "cultures" and "identities" with them to the world city, resulting in its "creolization" and "informalization." Yet the internal structure of the world city is also dichotomized: the initial image in 1982 is of the "citadel" alongside the "ghetto."[70] Office towers and the "amenity spaces" of global "command and control centers" look down upon an increasingly segregated informal labor force, effectively eliding Enzo Mingione's earlier conception of the "dual city" with that of the "world city." The result is to transform the world city into a metonym for the world economy itself: an outer boundary limits the edge of a "complex life world" arranged according to dependent but polarized social relations.

There is something truly heroic in attempting to correct all the problems of urban research by moving to the final and most absolute scale of analysis, that of the entire world. In as much as the world city paradigm calls for a re-organization, not only of urban studies, but the entire academy, it necessarily subordinates everything to its grand (re)visions: there is no middle ground, and as such it is also very polarizing in its effects. The claim to discover, rather than construct a "world system" expands the claim for disciplinary territory across the academy, and at the same time removes such academic imperialism from critique because of the putatively objective status of the research.

Though the discourses on world city formation have not led to the reformulation of disciplines in the way Friedman and Wolff suggest, it has exerted a powerful influence on the writing published in the *International Journal*. Many of their key ideas continue to inform research in the journal up to the present. The "world city" has emerged as an ideal type against which all other cities are measured and compared, in much the same way that Chicago was interpreted as an archetypal model of the city of capitalist modernization in the first part of the twentieth century. And indeed one of the subtle ironies of the emergence of the world city as an ideal type is that, in some cases, its "inner life" has been plotted according to a revised version of urban ecology – the very paradigm that Marxists rejected when the *IJURR* began.

Before turning to a more detailed discussion of the representation of the world city as an ideal type, I want to briefly discuss several strands of research that have challenged some of the presuppositions of the paradigm. These debates, though effectively bypassed by subsequent research in the journal, nevertheless constitute important alternate visions of the world. I treat them here together, first discussing emerging theories of transnational urbanism, and second, attempts to position the world city historically.

TRANSNATIONAL CROSSINGS

The world cities paradigm imagines a network of cities that are to various degrees abstracted from the nation-state and its regulatory boundaries. World cities thus operate in a frictionless, interconnected "space of flows."[71] The idea of "global" or "world space" as separate from (or above) that of the nation-state is questioned in the first major attempt in the *IJURR* to trace the impact of "transnationalization" on the post-Second World War economy and urban processes. This occurs in a special issue entitled "Transnationalization and the Pacific Rim" edited by Mike Douglass and published in September 1988. The issue is a "first" in the journal, not only for its emphasis on the theme of transnationalization, but for its focus on South East Asia.[72]

Though the word is as cumbersome and potentially as reductive as its global counterpart, transnationalization is intended to signal a different, more socially situated interpretation of "world" space. As Michael P. Smith has argued, transnational analysis reintroduces the nation-state as an important mediating force in global flows, through specific forms of regulation, national traditions of business practice, and the distinctive social, economic and political histories of nation-states.[73] Transnational production and investment is strategically broken up and spread across several nations at once in a manner that exceeds the simple core/periphery binary common to prior arguments about globalization. Indeed, in transnational urban theory, the global only becomes understandable through "situated social practices" that are bound up with the national contexts in which they occur.[74] The so-called world city does not exist as a deregulated, free floating island surrounded by the nation, but operates within overlapping networks of agents and institutions that are "embedded" directly or indirectly in cultural ideas and practical operations of the nation-state.

From a spatial standpoint, perhaps the most radical assertion of transnational theory is the idea that the nation is becoming "deterritorialized."[75] This does not mean that nation-states are disappearing, but rather, that the idea of nation is being de-linked from the possession of territory. Global flows of migration mean that the boundaries of the nation as "imagined community" no longer necessarily align with the geographical boundaries of the formal nation-state. For example, Aihwa Ong writes of the cultural practices of "flexible citizenship" where Chinese capitalists may engage in "self-orientalization" in some contexts, while assimilating to national norms in others. Here different forms of nationally defined business practices are understood and analyzed by Ong as forms of embodied cultural practice, and not simply the anonymous, technical operations of a transcendent world economy.[76]

In the *International Journal*'s special issue on transnationalization, emphasis is placed on examining the emergence of a regional economic system that operates outside the core periphery dichotomy of the world system perspectives. Douglass defines the transnational process as "the buying of labor power as an international act on the part of the firm."[77] Despite this apparently economistic focus, he is careful to argue against assigning too much power to transnational corporations: they must not be considered omnipotent, or "ultimately in control of the capitalist system."[78] Instead, he argues that researchers should seek to understand "territorial and locational difference in cultural, social, and economic relations, which subject them to interpretation and modification."[79]

Douglass's exhaustive analysis of the conditions of everyday life in the Tokyo region and Peter Rimmer's article on the impact of multinational construction companies in Japan come the closest to these aims. Douglass's article, though focusing on a "first order" world city by Friedmann's definition, avoids the dichotomized representation of an underclass and a privileged elite. Instead, he focuses on the conditions experienced by a vast population of mid-level workers who spend several hours commuting across an "agglomeration" landscape of capitalist industrialization.[80] A detailed analysis of how urban land rents in Tokyo have been monopolized by several large transnational corporations since the Second World War is balanced with an account of domestic life that includes a description of gendered roles within various strata of the middle class.

Peter Rimmer, though concentrating on the activities of "multinational Japanese construction companies" and the underlying capitalist logic of their maneuvers, focuses his article primarily on their impact on the built environment. He examines several massive (and unnecessary) infrastructure projects designed and sold to the Australian government by a large Japanese construction company seeking "investment opportunities" for surplus capital outside Japan where the market for such projects is saturated and the returns minimal. Although the underlying economic argument is clear, like Douglass's article, it is balanced by attention to the effects – both symbolic and practical – on the urban structure of Sydney. Indeed, these two articles are among the very few published in the *IJURR*'s history that descend from a planetary position of overview to examine the impact of massive abstractions as the "world economy" on everyday life.[81]

SPACES OF WORLD HISTORY

If abstraction from the social, economic and political space of the nation-state is one of the critical issues raised by the discourse on world cities, the transcendence of history is the other. The next major contribution to the debate on world cities is a special issue in 1989 guest edited by Anthony King that examines the relationship between "colonialism, urbanism, and the capitalist world economy."[82] The innovation of this issue is to consider how the study of colonial urban development might inform an understanding of the contemporary world city. The issue constitutes the only significant attempt in the journal's history to place urban development in a historical context that precedes the Second World War. King begins his introduction by challenging Friedmann and Wolff's assertion that it is only since 1980 that the study of cities has been linked to the world economy. He argues that

> fundamental to the development of the world economy (the term was already in use in the 1880s) and the world system in general, was the emergence of modern industrial colonialism, the cities that it created and through which it operated. Hence the study of cities as "directly linked to colonialism" is the immediate and necessary prerequisite for understanding cities as "directly linked to the world economy."[83]

Three of the articles included in this issue extend Marxist political economy to the analysis of the colonial city in Africa, Brazil and India. While successfully challenging the "presentism" that characterizes much of the writing in the journal, they do so from within the urban political economy perspective. The colonial city, though "culturally and environmentally modified" and invested with "social and spatial conflicts and contradictions," is nevertheless largely a reflection of the "colonial mode of production" that it serves. Indeed, when comparing José Ribeiro's research on Rio de Janeiro to recent scholarship on Latin American urbanization King remarks that "the spatial structure of urbanization in Latin America can be 'read off' from prevailing modes of production."[84]

Yet in his concluding remarks King also draws attention to an entirely different conception of power that is not connected to Marxian "mode of production" narratives:

> It might be (editorially) added here that in Africa, as elsewhere to varying degrees, colonial state ideologies persist in urban centers, encoded in a hundred different practices: legislation, regulations, bylaws, building codes, surveillance procedures, institutional roles, educational and professional practices (not least in planning), the enforcement of standards which continue to reproduce the institutions and environments of colonialism even though the phenomenon itself has long disappeared.[85]

It is this notion of the "institutions and environments of colonialism" as a "disciplinary terrain, a mechanism for inducing new practices, an arena around which new discourses are created"[86] that Paul Rabinow's article entitled "Governing Morocco: Modernity and Difference"[87] explores. Rabinow's article differs from the other contributions in this issue (and much of the research published in the journal as a whole) by focusing on planning as a historically determined discourse, grounded in socially specific institutions. Unlike other research in this issue that addresses colonial planning as a reflection of the "colonial mode of production," he considers how power is constituted in and through the "norms and forms" of "modern" planning disciplines and discourses.

THE WORLD CITY AS AN IDEAL TYPE

Attention to the historical specificity of world cities, and the mediating role of the nation-state largely disappear from the subsequent issues of the *International Journal*, although both debates continue to exert a major influence on the discussions of the world or global cities outside the journal. Instead, the *IJURR* has focused increasingly on the model of historical periodization outlined in Friedmann and Wolff's article, and the dyadic construction of epochal change that accompanies it. Yet even here the nation returns, if in an unacknowledged manner. Though the world cities paradigm claims to define conditions that transcend national barriers, the representations of cities that result are often unintended narratives of national history. Robert Beauregard's 1991 essay entitled "Capital Restructuring and the New Built Environment of Global Cities: New York and Los Angeles" provides an example of how US-based experiences of urbanization and capitalist restructuring can be universalized into a normative model of the world city. Beauregard describes the world city as a "novel urban form," a "new capitalist metropolis" and part of the "new built environment of global cities."[88] At the same time, this "new" condition is presented as a result of a "transition" from the "Keynesian" or "Fordist" city, whose processes and spaces it "restructures." He claims that

> theorists of urban restructuring generally agree on qualitative change in the earlier form of the postwar city. The high-density central city with its low-density, residential suburban ring has been replaced by a multi-nodal, sprawling built environment with the central city less and less distinguishable from its competitive "outer cities."[89]

The characteristics Beauregard attributes to the Fordist city draw upon the urban rhetoric of the Chicago School of sociology, where the concept of "agglomeration" and "ring development" around a "central city" was generalized as a universal type by Wirth from the study of Chicago in the early twentieth century. Beauregard's representation of the world city is essentially a more complex, multi-nodal version of Wirth's industrial city. The industrial city (and its later development into the Fordist, or "postwar city") and the "world city" are represented as (US-based) ideal types, with the latter being the progressive transformation of the former.

From 1992 onwards, the notion of "transition" disappears from articles on the world city, while the descriptive vocabulary of nodes, districts, and sprawl remains. An invariant ideal type emerges, characterized by a relatively limited repertoire of formal characteristics. The dominant spatial image is the "node," often less a material form than a concentration or "agglomeration" of particular "command functions" in a specific location.[90] For example, a 1992 article on Tokyo describes the world city as a location for "the formation of space for global control functions" and the expansion of "space for domestic control functions in urban central areas and urban sub-centers . . . the relocation of regional control functions from the central area to subcenters."[91] The language of nodality, centralization and dispersion is developed further in subsequent articles in the journal by Ann Markusen and Vicky Gwiasda. Their 1994 article entitled "Multipolarity, and the Layering of Functions in World Cities: New York Struggles to Stay on Top"[92] explores the New York City's "multi-nodality" within a larger system of global command and control nodes.

The image of a multi-nodal world city characterized by multiple centers and peripheries that operate simultaneously at local, regional, national, and global scales becomes the basis for a conference staged by RC 21 in Los Angeles in 1992 entitled "A New Urban and Regional Hierarchy? Impacts of Modernization, Restructuring and the End of Bipolarity."[93] A review of the conference by Hilary Silver published in the *International Journal* reveals the degree to which the paradigm of the world city has become a unified system capable of absorbing vastly different contexts into a common theoretical proposition:

> I suspect that this concept will continue to be a subject of controversy in the future. The systems approach characterizing "global cities" perspectives, in which specialization in multinational service industries or corporate command looms so large, flirts with functionalism. It draws heavily on neoclassical analyses of international finance markets, which according to flexible accumulation and flexible specialization models are incidental to the true engines of capitalist growth . . . the approach largely neglects political and cultural rationales for location decisions. Half in jest, someone suggested that the very term "global cities" was a public relations gimmick taken over wholesale from urban economic development efforts.[94]

Silver praises the geographical variety of presentations, but expresses concern about the underlying homogeneity of their observations and the demotion of issues related to race, ethnicity, gender and sexuality to the status of "secondary themes" in the conference. She suggests that a self-reinforcing, closed theoretical world has taken hold that is distinctly at odds with the day-to-day lived experiences of cities such as Los Angeles where race plays a primary role in structuring social and spatial relations of power:

> In retrospect the global hierarchy theme of the conference was overshadowed by subsequent events which highlighted the secondary theme of racial and ethnic relations. Within a week of the conference, riots broke under the Southern California sun so enjoyed by the conference participants. With its strong emphasis on political economy RC21 has typically given short shrift to racial or ethnic inequality, or has reduced it to yet another aspect of class struggle, social movement or postmodernism. [95]

She adds that

> as one who happened to be in South Central LA just hours before the Rodney King verdict and the subsequent disturbances, I can only recommend that future conferences highlight such sessions and encourage guided, inconspicuous visits to such neighborhoods.[96]

The suggestion of "guided inconspicuous tours" through areas of "disturbance" and "urban unrest" may help committee members to confront the importance of race and the differential role it plays in establishing social relations of inequality. At the same time, the uncritical promotion of "academic tourism" as a means to discover "authentic" unrest, underlines the lack of attention given in the journal to the way in which the privileged position of the researcher is shaped by the very object of "urban unrest" s/he studies.

CONCLUSION: SPACES OF (IN)DIFFERENCE

In its quarter of a century history, the *International Journal* has played a leading role in supporting an increasingly sophisticated range of discourses that relate the study of urban and regional development to various conceptions of political economy. One of the central achievements of the journal has undoubtedly been to recognize the emergence of a new phase of international capitalist urban development and to support research that attempts to follow and diagnose the social and spatial consequences that result from it.

One of the important questions raised by the journal's shift towards "international" objects of analysis concerns "positionality": from whose position will the history of "global economic restructuring" be written? A recurring critical issue identified in this chapter suggests that writing in the *IJURR* persistently identifies changes in the structure of Euro-American economies as the point of origins for the international processes it seeks to theorize. The discourses of the *International Journal* share a common historical datum that links each conceptualization of the international, whether "state-centric" or "multicentric," to crisis conditions emerging in the "West" since 1945. In the urban social movements paradigms, the mode of production in crisis is "state managed capitalism." The "international" is defined largely by contexts studied in Europe and North America where similar forms of state intervention in the economy predominate. Though the range of contexts expands in the mid- to later 1980s to include Latin America, South America, and Africa, the theoretical framework, developed through European (primarily French) experiences of state intervention remains largely unchanged.

The theory of transition embodied in the shift from Fordism to post-Fordism is also tied to "crisis conditions" observed in "advanced industrial economies." In this case, soaring debt loads, high levels of "liquidity," and saturated domestic markets require a system-wide "restructuring of the materialization of the regime of accumulation," or the "mode of regulation." Like the urban social movements paradigm, the post-Fordist regime is a "spatial fix," but one that brings a much broader range of contexts and social structures into view by virtue of the increased mobility of capital, labor and ideas.

Whereas the crisis is resolved in urban social movements paradigms through investment in the spaces and services of the "advanced industrial city," in the post-Fordist regime the spatial fix involves the off-shoring of productive capacity to the "third world." Despite this, the research emphasizes the impact of restructuring in the West. Newly industrializing countries of the former third world are discussed primarily as destinations for jobs and capital, rather than as objects of study in and of themselves.

Another principal category of analysis discussed in this chapter, that of the "world city," can be understood as an epistemological break with prior conceptions of political economy in as much as the understanding of the underlying mode of production no longer grows solely out of the response to crises in "advanced capitalist nations." Instead, the paradigm begins with the assertion of a "world economic system" that is "multi-centric," and engaged in a set of interdependent economic relations. However, the emergence of a "world economic system" is theorized as the outcome of a shift from a spatially closed phase of capitalist accumulation stressing national development to one that is multinational in character. The shift is explained by the same structural "crisis conditions" that underpin both urban social movements and post-Fordist restructuring. This interpretation of the international tends to ignore the extensive literature on the history of imperialism and related research into colonial urban development, as well as the complex field of political economy that treats the capitalist world economy as a historical phenomenon dating at least from the late sixteenth century, and even beyond.

A second limitation that all the paradigms in the journal share concerns the way in which space is defined and represented. Although the conception of urban political economy has changed substantially over the journal's history, the way in which space is related to political economy has not altered significantly. Space has remained a material abstraction that is epiphenominal to the economic processes that are presumed to produce it. Space is discussed only in as much as it leads back to a fuller understanding of the changing structure of capital accumulation.

Three representations of space predominate. In the first of these, buildings are represented through the public policies and government regulations that allocate their distribution and define their characteristics. This is particularly true of the writing associated with state management and urban social movements. Hospitals, housing, schools, expressways, even rainforests and lesbian ghettoes are defined or delimited largely in relation to government policy. Protest movements develop – not because of the symbolic content or the forms of social organization urban spaces engender – but rather, because in very different ways they represent what are described as "scarce resources" that are distributed unequally among a population. They are the reified equivalent of money, and unequal access to them helps to reproduce dominant relations of power in the nation-state.

In the post-Fordist city, "space" becomes visible primarily through "labor patterns" and their location. The industrial workplace is represented as a container for a particular set of labor practices produced through changes in management and state regulation. While there are discussions of the "secondary circuit" of capital accumulation (as manifested through property development), these are concerned with patterns of financial investment in speculative office development, rather than the role such buildings play once they are constructed in reproducing or contradicting dominant relations of power in the city. Other areas of research have started to develop in relation to post-Fordism that stress, for example, the role of imagery and symbolism in the reproduction of capitalism, but these reproduce the epiphenominal role assigned to buildings and culture elsewhere in the journal.

In the world city paradigm "space" is also a container where capitalist "flows" are concentrated or dispersed. As noted above, the image of the city as a set of nodes, agglomerations, centers, and peripheries is derived from the empirical analysis of tax policies, fiscal and investment flows, land-use data, labor migration and accumulated labor patterns, population counts of "salaried mental laborers," office tower rental rates, and "functional distributions." The world city is a space that is defined through opposition between the local and global, where the local becomes a space of fixity determined by the dynamism of the "metropolitan command and control center."

The links between these representations of space is the scientific and interpretive position of detachment they construct for both the research scholar and the reader. Though the conditions described in the *International Journal* are often associated with extreme forms of exploitation, they are described in a way that allows them to be read as part of a larger "objective" understanding of the development of capitalism. It is the rigorous commitment to a highly technical, empirical description of the machinations of global capitalism that makes it possible for scholars from around the world to meet at conferences and speak the same language. At the same time, however, it is the homogenizing, reductive potential of these generalizing techniques that make cultural difference and contradiction difficult, if not impossible to acknowledge.[97] The stress on economic structures, empirical analysis of public policy and its impact, comparisons of "like conditions," and on "nodes within a common world system" all help to transform the globe into a common theoretical space in which social, cultural, or even political difference have relatively little impact.

Indeed, the language and methodology of the journal's urban political economy paradigms have now been refined to the point where they operate in a quasi-mechanistic manner. An analysis of the most recent summary of research interests of active RC 21 members (undertaken in 1995) reveals few attempts to depart from the major research paradigms discussed in this chapter.[98] As longstanding research committee member John Walton notes,

> Two problems have overtaken the field. First is the problem of overconfidence; the accumulation of a sufficiently impressive body of theory and research that allows practitioners to prefigure answers to new questions. A cocksure analytical style begins to enter the writing in which developed theory is used to implicitly "read off" interpretations for empirical events. A genuine sense of puzzlement is seldom encountered. The second is the problems of economism: the tendency for political economy to become enamored of the seeming causal potency of economistic analyses to collapse social issues into exclusively technical and organizational terms.[99]

These criticisms are echoed in a 1994 issue of the RC 21 *Newsletter* edited by John Logan, another long-time member of RC 21 and its President at that time. Citing with concern recent articles by committee members Mark Gottdiener and Joe Feagin that declare the urban political economy paradigm as the "dominant one in the field," Logan calls for a note of caution and a sense of critical distance:

> I would like to organize sessions at our upcoming conferences with the specific purpose of rethinking the political economy perspective, where it has led us, and where it is insufficient. I would specifically like to stimulate comments from our colleagues in the third world and former socialist countries to reflect on how their worlds have changed and what kind of theory is needed to be ambitious again, and not only to enjoy one another's company.[100]

The paradigms that have taken hold in the *International Journal* were first developed by scholars working in western Europe or the US. As a result, the homogeneous theoretical space the *IJURR* and RC 21 have constructed is a Euro-American invention, based on a model of historic periodization derived from the experiences of "crisis" primarily in the United States, the United Kingdom and elsewhere in Europe. From here, the paradigms have been diffused, either through the global activities of the RC 21 and its annual conferences, the *International Journal* (now published and distributed by a multinational press) and the migratory paths of its writers, some of whom have studied in Great Britain or the United States under leading RC 21 figures and then returned, together with political economy paradigms they have studied, to their countries of origin.

Despite the comments of longstanding members of the *International Journal* like Logan, the editors appear to be unwavering in their commitments to the journal's objectivist language, and structuralist models of research. The most recent assessments of the journal's mission occurred in 1998, when Michael Harloe stepped down as editor. He and three other longstanding members of the editorial board who have been involved with the journal since its founding published a retrospective overview that argues in favor of the journal's scientific approach to urban studies. They claim that a common language provides the only way to successfully contest the authority of state- orchestrated planning ideologies and capitalist urban development. They sought to foster a separate but equally powerful language, which would be capable of objectively revealing the forces at work in "urban change":

> . . . theoretical statements were made explicit, and subjected to controlled empirical investigation. By acting as an instrument of debate and circulation of ideas, but also mutual scientific control, the journal thus became part of the construction of an international urban research community.[101]

As I have argued, it is also the journal's commitment to scientific method that has led to an increasingly self-referential discourse. Because its methods are viewed as "scientifically" determined rather than "culturally constructed," it is impossible to assess how the practices of "controlled empirical investigation" shape the object investigated. Yet even as the journal stagnates methodologically, it continues to expand its readership internationally. Walton's comments suggest that the journal's continued growth depends on formulaic methods and languages of investigation. The *IJURR* has apparently developed a portable analytic system that reproduces the world in its image.

If a mode of cultural interpretation has emerged in the journal that is not tied to political economy, it is ironically one that leads back to the very paradigms the journal contested when it began: urban ecology and the traditions of the Chicago School of urban sociology. The most complete example of this approach so far appeared in the December 1998 issue on "symbolic ecology," which immediately followed the journal's change in editorship.[102] The issue largely avoids conceptions of urban political economy, and instead proposes a taxonomy of urban memory (collective, historic, projective, and cultural) as a way to consider the construction of urban meaning. Yet in doing so, the issue seems to suggest that urban memory constitutes a domain that is bounded by the geographical limits of the city, and whose specific history defines the relationships between these categories. Not only does this model tend to subsume cultural differences between "city dwellers" under a common urban identity, it also constitutes that identity as distinct, even autonomous from other cities, and is completely at odds with the ideas of global interdependence that otherwise predominate in the journal.

The return to urban ecology as a way to understand "culture" in the *International Journal* is probably more significant for the questions it raises about the journal's larger critical project than what the theory itself has to offer. In turning towards symbolic urban ecology, the *International Journal* turns backward, reclaiming a model of analysis previously abandoned for its mystification of capital. Even as this paradigm returns, the commitment to political economy is renewed, as if to say that "culture" will be acknowledged, but in a manner that separates it from other research. And while the return to urban ecology may seem contradictory, its construction of an urban subject, while "classless," is not "fragmented" by considerations of cultural differences and their urban consequences. While not acknowledging the primacy of class determination, the discourse of symbolic ecology does not directly challenge it either.

While the outgoing editors mention gender, sexuality and race as topics that have been studied in the *IJURR*, they have been examined as supplements to the underlying foundation of class identity. It appears that this position will be maintained for the foreseeable future. A policy statement by the incoming editors that follows the comments by Harloe *et al.* in the same issue argues that the journal will move forward by developing "a cultural political economy approach, including putting identity and discourse into the political economy of cities."[103] Their goal is to develop a "more open" and "revised political economy tradition" without succumbing to "negative individualism" which is the "name for the risk of society's disaggregation and fragmentation."[104] Like the departing editors, who apparently concluded after discussions with readers and contributors that "the policy that gave *IJURR* its identity should be maintained," they believe that there is "no need for a radical change in direction."[105]

NOTES

1 According to data provided by the Journal Citation Reports of the Institute for Scientific Information (ISI), *IJURR* has the highest "impact factor" of journals listed in the field of urban studies, while *Society and Space* is ranked fourth amongst those listed in geography. According to the ISI, the impact factor is "a measure of frequency with which the 'average article' in a journal has been cited in a particular year." The impact factor is used by institutions

institutions and academics to evaluate a journal's relative importance when compared to others in its field. There is no comparable measure for journals in the humanities. Source: ISI web of science 2001, JCR Social Sciences Addition, ISIknowledge.com

2. This is different from the influential model of analysis pioneered by Roland Robertson, which argues the world has become a single space, but through cultural relationships which precede (and hence make possible) those that are primary economic.

3. Based on an analysis of 367 articles published in the *IJURR* between 1977 and 1991.

4. See, for example, David Harvey, "From Fordism to Flexible Accumulation" in *The Condition of Postmodernity* (Oxford: Blackwell, 1989), 140–172.

5. See Castell's classic collection of case studies on struggles over the distribution of collective consumption in Manuel Castells, *The City and the Grassroots* (Berkeley: The University of California Press, 1983).

6. Stephen Graham and Simon Marvin, "Constructing the Modern Networked City, 1850–1960," and "The Collapse of the Integrated Ideal" in *Splintering Urbanism* (London and New York: Routledge, 2001), 38–137.

7. John Friedmann, "The World City Hypothesis," *Development and Change* 17, no. 1 (1986): 69.

8. Elizabeth Lebas, "Introduction" in Michael Harloe (ed.), *Captive Cities: Studies in the Political Economy of Cities* (London and New York: Wiley, 1977), ix.

9. Manuel Castells, "Is there an Urban Sociology?" in Chris Pickvance (ed. and trans.), *Urban Sociology. Critical Essays* (London: Tavistock Press, 1976), 33–59.

10. Castells states that ". . . we wish to understand some aspect of a system of historical action, e.g. a social movement, it would be pointless to search for social classes in *grand ensembles*. Rather the object of the social movement (e.g. social class on which it is based) must be defined beforehand in relation to the issue one wishes to study, and then reconstructed in reality . . ." Ibid., 56–57.

11. David Harvey, *Social Justice and the City* (London: Edward Arnold, 1973).

12. By 1977, a group of Marxist researchers within the Centre Nationale de la Recherche Scientifique (CNRS) were accorded official recognition by the "Recherche Coordinée Programme", and in 1979 the Société Française de Sociologie sponsored a meeting at the University of Bourdeaux whose theme was " Crisis Avenir des Sociologies Specialises" which focused on the specificity of urban research in relation to protest movements and state intervention. In the United Kingdom, the Conference of Socialist Economists (CSE), a national network of academics and activists, began a "Political Economy of Housing" workshop in 1973 which occasionally published its own collection of papers. Beginning in 1977, the CSE's journal, *Capital and Class*, published

relevant reviews and articles. At the same time, the Bartlett School of Architecture and Planning at the University of London, organized a summer school on the "Production of the Built Environment," examining issues of housing provision, design, and construction from a political economy perspective. The Graduate Planning School of the Architectural Association, along with the Centre for Urban and Regional Studies at the University of Birmingham, also offered courses and seminars with materialist content.

See Elizabeth Lebas, "Trend Report. Urban and Regional Sociology in Advanced Industrial Societies: A Decade of Marxist and Critical Perspectives," *Current Sociology* 30, no. 1 (Spring 1982): 17–20.

13   Michael Harloe, *Captive Cities: Studies in the Political Economy of Cities* (London and New York: Wiley, 1977), 312.
14   Lebas, "Trend Report": 19.
15   Chris Pickvance, *Urban Sociology*, Critical Essays (New York: St Martins Press, 1976).
16   John Walton and Louis Massotti, *The City in a Comparative Perspective* (New York, Wiley, 1976); and John Walton and Alejandro Portes, *Labour, Class, and the International System* (New York: Academic Press, 1981).
17   For a summary of theoretical developments in Western Marxism from the end of the Second World War, see Perry Anderson, *Considerations on Western Marxism* (London: New Left Books, 1976). Anderson concludes his book with a call for Marxist research that overlaps with the early agenda of the *IJURR*:

> after the prolonged, winding tour of Western Marxism, the questions left unanswered by Lenin's generation . . . continue to await reply . . . First and foremost, what is the real nature and structure of bourgeois democracy as a type of state system, that has become the normal mode of capitalist power in advanced countries? What type of revolutionary strategy is capable of overthrowing this historical form of state – so distinct from that of Tsarist Russia.
>
> Anderson, 1976, 103.

18   Jean Lojkine, "L'Analyse Marxiste de l'Etat," *IJURR* 1, no. 1 (March 1977): 19.
19   Gillian Rose, "In Practice Supported, in Theory Denied: An Account of an Invisible Urban Movement," *IJURR* 2, no. 1 (March 1978): 522.
20   Ibid., 522.
21   E. M. Ettorre "Women, Urban Social Movements and the Lesbian Ghetto," *IJURR* 2, no. 3 (October, 1978): 499–520.
22   Guido Lagana, Mario Pianta and Anna Segre, "Urban Social Movements and Urban Restructuring in Turin 1969–1975," *IJURR* 6, no. 2 (June 1982): 223–245. See also Hugo Priemus, "Squatters in Amsterdam: Urban Social Movement, Urban Managers or Something Else?" *IJURR* 7, no. 3 (September 1983): 424.
23   Richard Child Hill, "Two Divergent Theories of the State," *IJURR* 1, no. 1 (March 1977): 39.

24 Peter Saunders, "Beyond Housing Classes: The Sociological Significance of Private Property Rights in the Means of Consumption," *IJURR* 8, no. 2 (September 1984): 202–227. Elsewhere Saunders has adopted an antagonistic position towards Marxist research, decrying its hegemony in urban studies as reductive and "unscientific." See P. Saunders and P. R. Williams, "For an Emancipated Social Science," *Environment and Planning D. Society and Space* 5 (1987): 427–430.
25 See, for example, R. E. Pahl, "Employment, Work and the Domestic Division of Labour," *IJURR* 4, no. 1 (March 1980): 1–21.
26 Geraldine Pratt, "Class Analysis and Urban Domestic Property. A Critical Reexamination, "*IJURR* 6, no. 4 (December 1982): 481–502.
27 Josef Hegedus and Ivan Tosics, "Housing Classes and Housing Policy: Some Changes in the Budapest Housing Market," *IJURR* 7, no. 4 (December 1983): 467–495.
28 David C. Thorns, "The Implications of Differential Rates of Capital Gain from Owner Occupation for the Formation and Development of Housing Classes," *IJURR* 5, no. 2 (June 1981): 205–217.
29 Ray Forrest and Alan Murie, "Marginalization and Subsidized Individualism: The Sale of Council Housing in the Restructuring of the British Welfare State," *IJURR* 10, no. 1 (March 1986): 46–66.
30 On the one hand, the researchers observe that the study of protest movements has increasingly been absorbed into the government policy-making departments who provide financial support for the research, while subverting its aims to serve the needs of "urban management." See Jean-Claude Kaufmann and Monique Laigneau, "The Crisis of French Urban Research," *IJURR* 9, no. 2 (June 1985): 155–163. On the other hand, there is an acknowledgement that the "historical conjuncture" that brought urban social movements into being is about to pass. See Christian Topalov, "A History of Urban Research: The French Experience since 1965," *IJURR* 13, no. 4 (December 1989): 625–651.
31 Ibid.
32 Chris Pickvance, "The Rise and Fall of Urban Movements and the Role of Comparative Analysis," *Society and Space* 9, no. 1 (March 1985): 31–53.
33 Ibid., 33.
34 Chris Pickvance, "Introduction: Land and Housing Development in Middle Eastern and North African Cities," *IJURR* 12, no. 1 (March 1988): 1.
35 Michael Harloe, "Notes on Comparative Urban Research" in Michael Dear and Alan J. Scott (eds), *Urbanization and Urban Planning in Capitalist Society* (London and New York: Methuen, 1981), 184.
36 Michael Harloe, "In this Issue . . . ," *IJURR* 11, no. 1 (March 1987): 1–4.
37 Ibid., 3
38 Writing from South Africa in 1990, Claudia M. Reintges states that "the starting point for this discussion is Castells' *The Urban Question* (1977) . . .

the species of urban social movements is very much alive and kicking in South Africa's urban areas." Claudia M. Reintges, "Urban Movements in South African Black Townships: A Case Study," IJURR 14, no. 1 (March 1990): 109–134; Susan Eckstein summarizes her extensive research into the "inner-city slum in Mexico City in 1967–68, 1971–72" and "some follow-up work" in 1987 by claiming that "Marxists (Castells, 1983) have correctly interpreted squatter mobilization as social protest movements . . ." Susan Eckstein, "Poor People versus the State and Capital: Anatomy of a Successful Community Mobilization for Housing in Mexico City," IJURR 14, no. 3 (June 1990): 274–296; Alejandro Portes and Jose Itzigsohn write an article entitled "The Party or the Grassroots: A Comparative Analysis of Urban Political Participation in the Caribbean Basin." The title pays homage to the centrality of Castells' 1983 book *The City and the Grassroots* to their research. Indeed, their emphasis on gathering empirical data related to protest movements within a delimited urban region recalls the first article Castells published in the journal; whereas Castells documented 180 social movements in the Paris regions over five years, Portes and Itzigsohn examine "popular participation" by "new social actors" in "new movements" through "data collected from surveys conducted simultaneously in five Caribbean Basin countries during 1992." IJURR 18 no. 3 (September 1994): 491–509.

39 Arjun Appadurai, *Modernity at Large. Cultural Dimensions of Globalization* (Minneapolis: University of Minnesota Press, 1998), 30 .

40 Sy Adler and Johanner Brenner, "Gender and Space. Lesbians and Gay Men in the City," IJURR 16, no. 1 (March 1992): 24–34.

41 Key texts to emerge in this area that deal with sexuality and space in the 1990s include: Nancy Duncan (ed.), *Bodyspace* (New York and London: Routledge, 1996); Elizabeth Wilson, *The Sphinx and the City* (Berkeley: University of California Press, 1991); Alison Blunt and Gillian Rose, *Writing Women and Space. Colonial and Postcolonial Geographies* (London and New York: The Guildford Press, 1994); George Chauncey, *Gay New York. Gender, Urban Culture and the Making of the Gay Male World* (New York: Basic Books, 1994); Charles Kaiser, *The Gay Metropolis* (New York: Houghton Mifflin and Co., 1997); Gordon Brent Ingram (ed.), *Queers in Space* (Seattle: Bay Press, 1997); Doreen Massey, *Space, Place and Gender* (Minneapolis: University of Minnesota Press, 1994), 191–211; Beatriz Colomina, *Privacy and Publicity. Modern Architecture and Mass Media* (Cambridge, MA: The MIT Press, 1996); Francesca Hughes (ed.), *The Architect. Reconstructing her Practice* (Cambridge, MA: The MIT Press, 1996), 2–25.

42 Gill Valentine, "Out and About: Geographies of Lesbian Landscapes," IJURR 19, no. 1 (March, 1995): 97.

43 The discussion begins in the first issue with Richard Child Hill's article: Richard Child Hill, "State Capitalism and the Urban Fiscal Crisis in the United States," IJURR 1, no. 1 (March, 1977): 76–100. See also, James O'Connor, "The

Meaning of Crisis," *IJURR* 5, no. 3 (September 1981): 303; Desmond S. King and Ted Robert Gurr, "The State and Fiscal Crisis in Advanced Industrial Economies," *IJURR* 12, no. 1 (March, 1988): 87; Mark Gottdiener, "Crisis Theory and State-Financed Capital: The New Conjuncture in the USA," *IJURR*, 14, no. 3 (September, 1990): 383.

44 See, for example, Josef Esser and Joachim Hirsch, "The Crisis of Fordism and the Dimensions of a 'Postfordist' Regional and Urban Structure" in Richard Child Hill, "State Capitalism and the Urban Fiscal Crisis in the United States," *IJURR* 13, no. 3 (September, 1989): 417.

45 Michael Peter Smith, Bernadette Tarallo and George Kagiwada, "Coloring California: New Asian Immigrant Households, Social Networks and the Local State," *IJURR* 15, no. 2 (June 1991): 276–287.

46 Wenona Giles, "Class, Gender and Race Struggles in a Portuguese Neighborhood in London," *IJURR* 15, no. 3 (September 1991): 432–442.

47 Patricia R. Pessar, "Sweatshop Workers and Domestic Ideologies: Dominican Women in New York's Apparel Industry," *IJURR* 14, no. 1 (March 1990): 127–142.

48 Until now, there have been few attempts to question the bipolar construction of interior/exterior, national/international that characterizes much of the research in the Journal. One of the rare exceptions is Christina Marouli's 1995 article, "Women Resisting (in) the City: Struggles, Gender, Class and Space in Athens," *IJURR* 19, no. 4 (December, 1995): 534–548. While clearly grounded in orthodox sociological methods, this article is notable because it is one of a very few that attempts to acknowledge and challenge their ethnocentricity:

> Since sociology is mostly Euro- and North American-centric, its concepts should not be adopted blindly since they can obfuscate women's realities in other socio-economic contexts, such as Greece, which does not fit comfortably into any of the habitual categories: north/south, first/third world, developed/underdeveloped world etc.
>
> Marouli, 1995, 535

Her solution is to let "Athenian women" speak for themselves: "For this reason I have chosen to use open-ended, in-depth interviews as the method of study on Athenian women's agency" (535). By invoking the category of the "authentic" Athenian woman that exists outside the "habitual categories" of sociological representation, the author is able to avoid considering how her own position as a benevolent "first world social scientific woman" who ultimately defines the "Athenian women" she analyzes. She allows the "Athenian women" to speak, but on terms that have been decided in advance: the "open-ended interview" involving a "snowball sample of 75 women." The critique of representational practices (the ethocentrism embedded in "Western" sociology) results in an attempt to move beyond represen-

tation itself. However, the critical response displaces the problems to a different set of sociological techniques, leaving unexplored the question of how the subject and object of knowledge are constructed in representation.
49 As Edward Said and post-colonial critics have noted, the concept of "class" itself is developed as a conceptual category through the analysis experiences and histories of the industrial working class in Europe and North America.
50 M. Aglietta, *A Theory of Regulation* (London: Verso, 1979).
51 See, for example, Alain Lipietz, "New Tendencies in the International Division of Labor: Regimes of Accumulation and Modes of Regulation" in A. Scott and M. Storper (eds), *Production, Work, Territory: The Geographical Anatomy of Industrial Capitalism* (Boston: Allen and Unwin, 1986), 16–40.
52 Ibid., 19.
53 David Harvey, "The Urban Process under Capitalism: A Framework for Analysis," *IJURR* 2, no. 1 (March 1978): 101–132.
54 The book has been both praised and criticized for the synthetic links it forms between postmodern culture and the shift to a "flexible" mode of capital accumulation. See David Harvey, *The Condition of Postmodernity. An inquiry into the origins of cultural change* (Cambridge, MA and Oxford: Blackwell, 1989).
55 A. J. Scott, "Flexible Production Systems and Regional Development: The Rise of New Industrial Spaces in North America and Western Europe," *IJURR* 12, no. 2 (June 1988): 171.
56 Elizabeth Lebas, "The Role of National Boundaries in a Cross-National Labour Market," *IJURR* 4, no. 2 (June 1980): 157.
57 David Lovatt and Brian Ham, "Class Formation, Wage Formation, and Community Protest in a Metropolitan Control Center," *IJURR* 8, no. 3 (September 1984): 354.
58 A conference organized with the multidisciplinary program of research on cities of the CNRS in Paris, France, was held in Lille, France, on the topic in 1995, entitled "Cities, Enterprises and Society on the Eve of the 21st Century: A Fordist Conference on Cities in the Era of Flexible Production," Lille, March 1994. A review by Pavlos Delladetsima and Frank Moulert in *IJURR* 19, no. 2 (March 1995): 319–322.
59 David Clarke, "Consumption and the City, Modern and Postmodern," *IJURR* 21, no. 2 (June 1997): 218–237.
60 Ibid., 233
61 Ibid.
62 See Jean Baudrillard, *Simulacra and Simulation* (Ann Arbor: University of Michigan Press, 1994); see also Mark Gottdiener's discussion of Baudrillard's ideas in relation to the branding and theming of the built environment in Mark Gottdiener, "The Mirror of Production," and "Themed Culture and Themed Environments" in *The Theming of America* (Boulder, CO: Westview Press, 2001), 41–103.

63 Lila Leontidou, "Alternatives to Modernism in Southern Urban Theory: Exploring In-Between Spaces," *IJURR* 20, no. 2 (June 1996): 178–195.
64 Ibid., 178.
65 John Friedmann and Goetz Wolff, "World City Formation. An Agenda for Research and Action," *IJURR* 6, no. 3 (September 1982): 309–343.
66 Ibid., 313–319.
67 Ibid., 310.
68 Ibid., 319.
69 Urban studies is characterized as an overspecialized field, resulting in a lack of synthesis between two important areas of Marxist research: the world system approach of Wallerstein, Samir Amin, and André Gunder Frank on the one hand, and Marxist urban studies influenced by Henri Lefebvre, Manuel Castells, and David Harvey on the other. The only book the authors suggest has begun to initiate a synthesis between these approaches is by RC 21 committee members John Walton and Alejandro Portes, entitled *Labour, Class, and the International System* (1981), which applies the world system perspective to the study of international migration, the informal sector, and class formation.
70 Friedmann and Wolff: 325.
71 See Manuel Castells' influential account in "The Space of Flows," Chapter 6 in his book *The Rise of the Network Society* (Oxford: Blackwell Publishers, 1996), 376–428.
72 Mike Douglass, "Transnational Capital and Urbanization in the Pacific Rim: An Introduction," *IJURR* 12, no. 3 (September 1988): 343–355. Until this point, only one article had been published on the subject of urbanization in South East Asia. See Amy K. Glasmeier, "The Japanese Technopolis Programme: High-Tech Development Strategy or Industrial Policy in Disguise?" *IJURR* 12, no. 3 (September 1988): 268–284.
73 M. P. Smith, "From Globalization to Transnational Urbanism" in *Transnational Urbanism. Locating Globalization* (Oxford: Blackwell, 2001), 165–183.
74 Ibid., 166.
75 See Arjun Appadurai, "The Production of Locality," op. cit., 178–199; Ayse Oncu and Petra Weyland, "Introduction: Struggles over Lebensraum and Social Identity in Globalizing Cities" in A. Oncu and P. Weyland (eds), *Space, Culture and Power. New Identities in Globalizing Cities* (London and New Jersey: Zed Books, 1997), 1–20; Doreen Massey, "A Global Sense of Place" in D. Massey, *Space, Place and Gender* (Minneapolis: University of Minnesota Press, 1994), 146–157.
76 Aihwa Ong, "Introduction" in A. Ong, *Flexible Citizenship: The Cultural Logics of Transnationality* (Durham, NC: Duke University Press, 1999), 1–26.
77 Douglass, "Transnational Capital": 343.
78 Ibid., 345.
79 Ibid.

80 Mike Douglass, "The Transnationalization of Urbanization in Japan," *IJURR* 12, no. 3 (September 1988): 425–454.
81 Peter Rimmer, "Japanese Construction Contractors and the Australian States: Another Round of Interstate Rivalry," *IJURR* 12, no. 3 (September 1988): 404–424.
82 Anthony D. King, "Colonialism, Urbanism and the Capitalist World Economy," *IJURR* 13, no. 1 (March 1989): 1–18.
83 Ibid., 3.
84 Ibid., 13.
85 Ibid., 14–15.
86 Ibid., 15.
87 Paul Rabinow, "Governing Morocco: Modernity and Difference," *IJURR* 13, no. 1 (March 1989): 32–46.
88 Robert A. Beauregard, "Capital Restructuring and the New Built Environment of Global Cities: New York and Los Angeles," *IJURR* 15, no. 1 (March 1991): 91.
89 Ibid., 90–91.
90 The seminal account in this area is Saskia Sassen, *The Global City. New York, London, Tokyo* (Cambridge: Cambridge University Press, 1988).
91 Takashi Machinura, "The Urban Restructuring Process in Tokyo in the 1980s: Transforming Tokyo into a World City," *IJURR* 16, no. 1 (March 1992): 114–128.
92 Ann Markusen and Vicky Gwiasda, "Multipolarity, and the Layering of Functions in World Cities: New York's Struggle to Stay on Top," *IJURR* 18, no. 2 (June 1994): 167–193.
93 Hilary Silver, "A New Urban and Regional Hierarchy? Impacts of Modernization, Restructuring, and the End of Bipolarity: Conference, Los Angeles, April 1992," *IJURR* 16, no. 4 (December 1992): 651–653.
94 Ibid., 651.
95 Ibid., 653.
96 Ibid.
97 When the *International Journal* began publishing in 1977, its writers were primarily located in the United Kingdom or elsewhere in western Europe, particularly in France, Italy, and West Germany. Nearly twenty years later, the Research Committee continued to be dominated by scholars from these three locations: taken together, they comprise over 70 percent of the active membership.

However, both the journal and RC 21 have made substantial advances in developing links with scholars in institutions in the former Soviet bloc, who now represent 15 percent of the active membership, and approximately 10 percent of the regular contributors to the journal in 1995. The geographic range of article topics has also changed dramatically since the journal began publishing: between 1987 and 1997, the journal has regularly devoted at least 30 percent of its coverage to rapidly industrializing regions and continents such as South America, Korea, India, the Middle East, and Central America, as well as Africa and the Caribbean. This differs starkly from the first decade of publication, when the number of articles dealing with such locations varied between 5 and 10 percent of the total.

Based on my analysis of "Active Member's addresses and Research Interests at 01.07.1995," International Sociological Association Research Committee on Sociology of Urban and Regional Development (Essex, 1995).

98 Ibid.

The most popular research category concerns state-sponsored urban "managerialism" and urban social movements. Most researchers in this category describe themselves as being concerned either with the study of "urban politics" and "protest movements," or with the analysis of "state policy," "state intervention" and "collective consumption." Taken together, this accounts for the research of 40 percent of the active members.

Research concerned with industrial labor regulation, informalization, urban restructuring and the various themes associated with the post-Fordist city occupy 15 percent of the membership, while a comparatively small number (8 percent) list research into the world economy, or world city formation as their primary interest. Only one researcher is concerned with examining urban and regional development under forms of colonization.

Those scholars who list "identity" as a research interest generally do so by aligning it with the paradigm of urban social movements; however, a small number of writers refer to such things as the "ethnic crisis," "inter-ethnic relations," "ethnic conflict," "ethnic communities in the inner city," "urban ethnicity," or "women's research" and "feminism and the built environment." Of the nearly 280 active members listed, only four described their research as taking buildings, architecture, design or urban imagery and symbols as their principal object of analysis; two used "meaning" or "semiotics" to describe their research.

99 John Walton, "Urban Sociology: The Contributions and Limits of Political Economy," *Annual Review of Sociology* 19 (1993): 301–320.

100 John Logan, "A Note from the President," *International Sociological Association on the Sociology of Urban and Regional Development Newsletter* (November 1994): 3.

101 Michael Harloe, Enzo Mingione, Chris Pickvance and Edward Preteceille, "IJURR: Looking Back Twenty-One Years Later," *IJURR* 22, no. 3 (March 1998): ii.

102 Special Issue: Urban Rituals and Symbols, *IJURR* 22, no. 4 (December 1998).

103 Patrick Le Galès, Susan Fainstein and Linda McDowell, "Policy Statement," *IJURR* 22, no. 1 (March 1998): vi.

104 Ibid., vii.

105 Ibid., vii.

Cover of "Environment and Planning D. Society and Space," vol. 18, no. 1 (February 2000), courtesy of Pion Limited.

Chapter 6: Bodies of Theory

"Environment and Planning D. Society and Space"

In the previous chapter I suggested that the last two journals to be considered in this study operate at different scales of analyses from the others I have discussed. In moving from the scale of the urban region to the world, the *International Journal* operates at a level of generalization and abstraction that is very different from what predominates in the architectural discourses of the first three chapters. This scale of analysis permits the interdependence between places to be represented and analyzed in a way that rarely occurs in architectural writing, and reveals how the idea of the "city" as a bounded and self-enclosed domain may be obsolete. The writing in the *International Journal* also underscores the problems produced by the conflation of disciplines with particular scales of analysis. Though *IJURR* rarely discusses individual buildings its extensive consideration of how entire categories of buildings (particularly housing) are linked to the political economies of cities and state policies, suggests that the processes that affect the production of built form occur at multiple scales simultaneously.

While redefining urban research in a way that emphasizes the interconnections between cities, the *IJURR*'s emphasis on base/superstructure models of analyses has meant that built form has been treated as a reflection of the processes that constitute it as such. Until the recent attempts to discuss "cultural economy," consideration of the roles of signification and meaning inherent in built form have been almost completely absent from the journal. And as suggested in the previous chapter, in the absence of other models to draw upon, the journal seems to be reverting to the model of urban ecology as a way to understand the role of memory, history, ritual in urban contexts, or further developing neo-Marxist explanations that ultimately link changes in cultural forms to transformations in the mode of production. Thus the discourse on the cultural meaning of built forms is restricted to opposing sides of a dichotomy, either reduced to sophisticated reflections of capitalism, or separated from it, and understood through biological metaphors of "symbolic ecology."

Overcoming the opposition between social structure and human agency inherent in this dichotomy is the central concern of the last journal in this study.

The insights offered by *Environment and Planning D. Society and Space* are relevant not only to the critical issues raised in my discussion of the *International Journal*, but to the larger field of built environment discourses constituted by all the journals in this study. As I have suggested, it is not only an inflexible concept of scale that arbitrarily separates the discourses I have considered so far; the opposition between built form and social processes cuts across and divides the field as a whole. This is perhaps most dramatically illustrated by the silence on issues of political economy, particularly in the *JSAH* and *Assemblage*, and the extensive consideration it receives in *Society and Space* and the *International Journal*, both based in the social sciences. It is precisely this impasse that *Society and Space* sought to overcome.

As the title suggests, from its inception *Society and Space* sought to explore the relationship between two broad categories of investigation that have been either treated independently from each other, or arranged in a dominant/subordinate relationship, where (embodied, domestic, architectural vernacular, urban, regional, national or global) space is a reflection of society (as it is constituted through the social processes and practices of economies, politics, and culture).[1]

The central concern of this chapter will be to track the journal's discourses of "space" and consider how differing conceptions of "society" are related to them. Because the journal is not confined to a single object of analysis (as in "urban" or "architectural" space) or interpretive system, the meanings attached to both terms are diverse, and have multiplied over the journal's history. As a result, *Society and Space* is more difficult to summarize than the other journals in this study, and it is certainly not possible for this chapter to examine all the debates that have developed around these terms over the journal's history.[2]

As with all the journals in the study, at any given moment there are several different conversations occurring at once within the journal, although some are inevitably "louder" than others. The journal began by seeking to develop an analytic framework capable of combining discourses of political economy with those concerned with the experiential and cultural meanings of cities and constructed landscapes, without reducing one to the other. At the level of grand theory-building, this effort is similar to the "world cities" paradigm I discussed in the last chapter, because the goal was to develop a theoretical meta-system that would dismantle the opposition between the social and the spatial, and provide a single, flexibly defined analytical system that could be applied to all scales of space.

The first part of the chapter examines several important discourses that played a role in elaborating the terms of this debate. I begin by discussing "interactionism" and the "socio-spatial dialectic," both of which constitute attempts to define a synthesis between the antinomies of *Society and Space* in a single explanatory system. I then contrast these paradigms with "locality studies," which attempted to make spatial analysis "contingent" upon particular social and historical conditions. Although "locality studies" employs a different theoretical language, and considers different contexts, it also stresses "reciprocal determination" and interaction between "social processes and spatial relations." All three debates provide an opportunity to examine the limits and potential of integrative theories that attempt to analyze "the structure and evolution of society and space over space and time."[3]

The search for a meta-theory of space was, for some critics in the journal, a paradigmatically modernist project, defined by the "unlocated" and omnipotent position of the writer. By the early 1990s, debates in *Society and Space* about the "politics of representation" and theories of cultural difference helped to challenge and redefine the journal's initial mission of developing a "fusion" of human and social geography. In this respect, *Society and Space* shares some concerns with *Assemblage*, which attempted to engage in "criticism through representations." Yet in *Society and Space*, critical reflection on how practices of representation shape the object represented goes beyond the discussion of conventional geographic writing as a "disciplinary apparatus," though this certainly becomes part of the question. In general, there has been a shift away from examining space as an objective, physical setting, and towards analysis of the conceptual, theoretical, and institutional practices that enable representation. This has opened up a range of investigations into the genealogy, practices and techniques of scholarly writing, and the history of geography as a discipline. In recent years, discussion of "identity" has also become commonplace in the journal, as writers begin to consider how embodied experience within larger social groups shape, and are shaped by, various scales of physical space.

The journal's discourses on representation have also raised larger questions about self-representation, and the limits of critical reflexivity in scholarly writing. The intellectual network defined by *Society and Space* is primarily based in the United Kingdom, the former settler colonies of the British empire (Australia, Canada, New Zealand, South Africa, Canada) and the United States. How do academics, who, for the most part, write from universities in this largely post-imperial and anglophone context, acknowledge and represent their own positions? To what degree have debates about identity and position led to critical consideration of the identity they share, as members of a privileged professoriate located in the higher echelons of an international hierarchy of knowledge and power? And to what extent does the turn to critical reflexivity in geographic writing acknowledge the historical role of the discipline in global processes of domination, such as colonization and imperialism? This latter question is of relevance not only to *Society and Space* but to all the English language journals in this study. It suggests that any consideration of the role of "space" in social or critical theory must be accompanied by an understanding of the ("post-imperial," global) history that makes such theories possible. Finally, the more recent discourses of critical reflexivity also seem to exclude or marginalize what is sometimes constructed as their reverse: the modernist position of objective exteriority they claim to leave behind. Is there any "space" for objectivity in these carefully qualified and self-positioned representations?

BRIDGING BETWEEN SPECIALIZATIONS

Plans for *Society and Space*, which began publication in 1983, grew out of discussions and meetings held between five geographers from the United Kingdom and Australia in 1981. According to Michael Dear (the journal's first editor) and Nigel Thrift (one of its founders), the pivotal moment in establishing the journal was an informal meeting held at a tea-house in Australia in 1981, where Dear, Thrift, and the other three founders (all UK-educated) were either employed or on academic leave.[4]

With its post-imperial setting, and its UK-educated participants (all of whom held a critical relationship to existing scholarship in the field), the meeting underscores the Anglo-American geography that has characterized the journal since its inception. Almost 50 percent of the contributors to *Society and Space* are based in the sub-discipline of human geography, and the majority are located in large metropolitan centers of the United Kingdom and the formerly "white" nation-states or "settler colonies" of the British Commonwealth or the United States.[5] Many have migrated from the United Kingdom to departments of geography in Canada, Australia, New Zealand, and large cities in the United States including former editor Michael Dear (based at the University of California, Los Angeles).

Dear and Thrift have referred to the founding meeting as the "Berrima Summit" after the small Australian town where it took place.[6] Though conveyed with self-deprecating irony, the metaphor of a "summit" between scholars who represented distinct political positions and disciplinary specializations within Anglo-American geography encapsulates the founding mission of the journal. All five of the founders (Michael Dear, Nigel Thrift, Dean Forbes, Gordon Clark, and Peter Williams) were critical of the fragmentation of human geography into two opposed sub-disciplines. The first specialization, represented by Michael Dear, constituted human geography according to theoretical viewpoints derived from existential philosophy, phenomenology and anthropology, and stressed the role of human agency in shaping the physical landscape. The other four founders were more closely affiliated with various aspects of Marxist-oriented research. Collectively the founders hoped that *Society and Space* would help to bring the discourses of Marxist and "humanistic" geography, structure and agency (and hence society and space), together in a common research endeavor.[7]

Until the early 1980s, each of these approaches was mutually exclusive. For those geographers in the "humanistic" camp, the emphasis on social processes seemed to reduce human behavior to "effects" of structures, denying them agency and dehumanizing the study of geography. It also made the study of the physical environment unnecessary, since its real cause was presumed to reside in "social processes." The humanistic approach challenged these presuppositions by stressing the impact of subjectivity on understanding the social meaning of the built environment. In their introduction to the influential 1981 book *Humanistic Geography, Prospects and Problems*, David Ley and Marwyn S. Samuels (both of whom have been members of the editorial board of *Society and Space*) state that the primary characteristic of human geography is anthropocentrism, where

> The abstract notion of spatiality is transformed into dimensions of meaning, and distance becomes the language alternatively of human relations and human alienation. No object is free of a subject; whether in thought or action each object is part of a field of human concern. The intent of an author is present in all actions and all facts, including . . . the subjectivity behind the apparent objectivity of scientific concepts.[8]

For the Marxists, "humanistic" discourses carried the threat of "spatial fetishism" and all the implications of false consciousness that accompanied the analysis of space as a source of causality. For politically engaged British geographers, particularly those living in areas of industrial decline in the North, the reduction of geographic explanation to "man's interaction with place" was both intellectually and morally inconceivable.

Attempts to reconcile humanistic and Marxist positions began to emerge in the late 1970s and early 1980s. These were outlined in a series of key papers published in the 1980s and consolidated in a collection of essays published in 1985, edited by University of British Columbia geographer Derek Gregory and Lancaster University sociologist John Urry, entitled *Social Relations and Spatial Structures*.[9] The contributors (some of whom, including Derek Gregory, Doreen Massey, and John Urry, continue to be involved with *Society and Space* as authors or board members) argue that space is an essential feature of all social relations. Considering "spatial structure" as a "medium" through which social life is produced and reproduced challenges the opposition between space and social processes. Geographers who had placed considerable emphasis on incorporating Marxist-based social theory into their research suggested that such frameworks tended to eliminate physical space as an object of analysis. As Doreen Massey writes in her contribution to the volume entitled "New Directions in Space,"

> geography had discovered that the root causes of what it wanted to explain lay outside the discipline. Geographers had to either go off and learn another social science, or take up a position at the end of the intellectual transmission belt of the social sciences, dutifully mapping the outcomes of social processes it was the role of others to study.[10]

Challenges to the opposition between structure and agency in the early 1980s initiated a broader debate about the role of space in Marxist social theory. Prominent scholars in urban studies, argued that although the incorporation of Marxism into urban studies had contributed substantial insights into the development of urban processes under capitalism, the emphasis on understanding urban form in terms of changes in the mode of production also reinforced a pervasive emphasis of time over space in the social sciences. By the end of the decade, Edward Soja (whose research I will return to in a subsequent section of this chapter) would predict that the growing understanding of the centrality of space to social life would ultimately place geography at the heart of contemporary social theory:

> Geography may not yet have displaced history at the heart of contemporary theory and criticism, but there is a new animating polemic on the theoretical and political agenda, one which rings with significantly different ways of seeing time and space together, the interplay of history and geography. The "vertical and horizontal" dimension of being in the world freed from the imposition of categorical privilege.[11]

Soja's comments express the sense of optimism and purpose that inspired not only the founding of *Society and Space*, but much of the writing it has published since then. Indeed, from its inception the editors and contributors have argued that the "spatialization of social theory" would not only transform the underlying conceptual structure of social theory, but the very organization of social sciences themselves. The opening editorial of *Society and Space* (1983) outlined this agenda:

> The need for "Society and Space" is born of extraordinary importance of the rich and fertile debate which it seeks to encompass. At the core of our concern is the structure and evolution of society over time and space. "Society and Space" is created in a spirit of optimism which holds that it is possible to mould a social theory that will directly help to unravel some of the key problems in contemporary society. The fusion of such a theory requires that we boldly confront the issues facing society and the contradictions between competing philosophies in the social sciences.[12]

SPATIAL DIALECTICS

The journal's interest in fusing together competing forms of theory is initially signaled by the attention devoted to the research of British sociologist Anthony Giddens[13] in the journal's first few years of publication. In the early 1980s when *Society and Space* was becoming established, Giddens' research was centered on "structuration theory."[14] This argued that social structures are reproduced through human actions in everyday contexts. Though invariably discussed in highly abstract terms in the pages of *Society and Space*, Giddens' thesis was nevertheless grounded in the routine experiences of everyday life where people built up a knowledge of how society worked through their respective interactions with its institutions. As Gillian Rose has noted,

> It was argued that this perspective would resolve a central problematic of modern social theory, that of agency and structure. The grand debate in social theory, between those stressing the causal power of human subjectivity and meaning – represented in geography by humanists – and those who emphasized structure – Marxists in geography – would be ended by the recognition that individual human agents knowledgeably undertaking everyday routine tasks through time and space produced and reproduced the structures of society, the economy, the polity and culture.[15]

The attempt to adapt Giddens' ideas to geographic research in *Society and Space* resulted in complex arguments that approach the same level of technical complexity as discussions of state intervention in the *International Journal*, or deconstruction in *Assemblage*. The linguistic density stems not only from the range of theoretical systems being joined together (ranging from Marxism to deconstruction), but from the difficulties inherent in "spatializing" the resulting meta-theory.[16] Giddens did not address the city or urban space directly, and geographers turned to the "time-geography" of Torsten Haggerstrand to provide the framework to do so. Haggerstrand's work described individuals undertaking their everyday tasks according to specific "temporal–spatial" paths, each defined by a range of differentially applied social constraints.[17]

Time-geography linked space and time in a dynamic relationship, and opened up everyday life to geographers in a new way. There was, as Rose notes, a groundswell of feminist research into women's "time–space" that analyzed the "time–space zoning" of women in their homes and neighborhoods.[18] Yet in their quest for a manageable yet total system, the theorists of time–space interactionism reduced all social groups to the status of a path. Space was equated with the time taken to move through it. The role of the body in mediating experience was displaced to the analysis of paths and their routes. Although the influence of interactionism has waned, it has nevertheless served to underscore the "recursiveness" of social life, or the capacity of space to "act back" on social relations and vice versa. This idea has gained broad acceptance in urban studies and geographic research and continues to be an important part of debates in *Society and Space* up to the present.

Arguments about recursiveness and reciprocal determination have also been explored in *Society and Space* through the spatialized theory of capitalism developed by the French Marxist and philosopher Henri Lefebvre.[19] His writings on space share with Giddens' structurationism a desire to consider multiple forms of social interaction at a single point, outside the constraints of disciplinary categories of analysis. Yet the argument is theorized from the beginning in spatial terms at scales extending from the domestic interior to the national territory, and historically from Ancient Greece through the Venetian city-state to the era of post-Second World War capitalism. In his definitive text *The Production of Space*, Lefebvre argued that space (whether defined as a room or city) was not simply a container for social processes, but a complex process in itself, whose production, control and manipulation was central to the historical development of capitalism. As the Canadian social theorist and cultural geographer Rob Shields has argued, Lefebvre's thesis is important because

> Lefebvre goes beyond previous philosophical debates on the nature of space, and beyond human geography, planning and architecture, which considered people and things merely "in" space, to present a coherent theory of the development of different systems of spatiality in different historical periods. These "spatializations" are not just physical arrangements of things but also spatial patterns of social action and routine as well as historical conceptions of space and the world.[20]

Lefebvre's arguments have informed studies of "uneven development," regional restructuring, and the discourses of the post-Fordist city.[21] Though often fixed at one scale of analysis, this writing shares with Lefebvre's an attempt to show how the reorganization of (regional) space is central to the "restructuring" of capitalism. For example, "post-Fordism," which is based on the fragmented distribution of production across national boundaries, is interpreted as a fundamentally "spatial" process, and not simply a post facto reflection of economic change. Once an urban area is reorganized to accommodate the break-up of a formerly centralized industry the resulting spaces "act back" on the social life of the city, potentially leading to another round of spatial restructuring.

Edward Soja is one of the most influential figures in these debates. He adapted Lefebvre's ideas to urban studies over the 1980s, and published some of the key essays in his 1989 book *Postmodern Geographies. The Reassertion of Space in Social Theory*. The book attempts to "trace a reconfigurative path" towards the contemporary reassertion of space. He argues that Marxist research has typically represented space as fixed and undialectical, and understood the world in terms of being and becoming within the interpretive context of time. His alternative attempts to "appreciate the essentially dialectical character of social and spatial relationships, as well as that of other structurally linked spheres like production and consumption . . . (space) represents a dialectically defined component of the general relations of production, relations which are simultaneously social and spatial."[22]

Much of Soja's research on regional restructuring has been based in Los Angeles, where he teaches at UCLA. He and a group of other US-based scholars have argued that Los Angeles constitutes a paradigmatic example of regional restructuring with global consequences. Their arguments are presented in a special issue of *Society and Space* published in 1986. Lefebvre's concern for the history of different spatializations of capital is developed in relation to the changing processes of centralization and dispersion in Los Angeles.[23] Contributors examine the "vertical disorganization" and redistribution of production in "agglomerations" scattered across the "regional space" of Los Angeles.[24] Investments in transit are studied as "strategic weapons in creating location advantages,"[25] and the history of the city's auto industry is used to explore the changing spatial organization of production as the city shifts from a "Fordist" to a "post-Fordist" economy.[26] In the process, the authors reveal how severe inequalities result in terms of access to urban resources, such as jobs, schools, and homes. Regions are defined by "labor patterns" and the relations of "spatial differentiation and equalization" between them.

Soja's contribution is the most explicit attempt to develop a Lefebvrian model of urban analysis. He begins by describing Los Angeles as a "restless geographical landscape" composed of the ever-shifting patterns enclosed by a "Herculean wall" that defines the outer edge of the greater Los Angeles region:

> ... the Sixty-Mile circle today encloses a shattered metro-sea of fragmented yet homogenized communities, cultures, and economies confusingly arranged into a contingently ordered spatial division of labor and power.[27]

As other commentators have noted, Soja's creative use of language marked a significant break with the dryly empirical, technical writing typically associated with urban political economy.[28] But the claim that the methodology embodied by the article somehow defines a more reciprocal, less economistic model of urban studies is more difficult to sustain. Although the intent is dialectical, Los Angeles is represented as a flattened globe, whose edge is delineated by a circular perimeter boundary, and whose interior contains differently scaled center/periphery relationships, each juxtaposed with the next in a kaleidoscopic pattern: "The specifying centrifuge is always spinning, but the centripetal force of nodality never disappears."[29] The space that is made central to Marxist social theory is the space of the two-dimensional pattern observed by an omnipotent observer who first looks down on the city-as-pattern from the top of the city hall, and then takes the reader on an imaginative "cruise" along and within its circumference.[30] The multiplication of dominant centers and subordinate peripheries within a circular boundary transforms Los Angeles into a representation of the world in miniature. Los Angeles thus becomes an "ideal type" at once symbolizing the world and acting as a paradigm of the "world city" which, according to Soja, all cities will ultimately come to resemble:

> ... we feel justified in advancing the claim that ... [Los Angeles] has now become the very capital of the late 20th century, the paradigmatic industrial metropolis of the modern world. We feel confident in predicting that over the next few decades the scholarly literature on Los Angeles will rapidly come to match the existing corpus of work on Chicago and other paradigmatic cities of earlier regimes of accumulation ... [31]

The connection posed by Soja between the "new" urban ecology of the Los Angeles School and the "old" urban ecology of the Chicago School recalls the recent turn to "symbolic ecology" in the *International Journal*. While the underlying forces that shape the "ecology" of the city are different (urban culture in the former and urban political economy in the latter) both discourses result in the image of a bounded "ideal type" based on Euro-American experiences of capitalist development.

Here, as in the other texts published in *Society and Space* that are concerned with "regional restructuring," the use of Lefebvre's ideas of "spatial trialectics" (or the interrelationship between perceived, conceived and lived space) actually seem closer to Marxist base/superstucture analyses.[32] The results recall some of the more frankly economistic accounts in the *International Journal*, where changes in the organization of urban space are understood as a reflection of changes in the mode of production. These studies also rely, if only indirectly, on Lefebvre's monolithic and weakly theorized conception of historical time, which plots a Eurocentric history that begins in sacred and mystical space, and culminates in the "abstract space" of technical–rational domination and its resistances.

Yet there is another strand of analysis in *Society and Space* that places less emphasis on Lefebvre's historical periodization and is more attentive to his "trialectics" of space. This considers the production of space through its representation and use, while also taking on the idea of recursiveness, or the capacity of spatial representations and practices to shape subsequent action. Because the analytic framework is three-fold, it is not reducible to the interaction between given terms in a dichotomy. One of the most interesting examples is Rob Shields' article on the West Edmonton Mall in Canada, which he investigates as a site of "social spatialization."[33]

This article is a methodological departure in *Society and Space*, because it shifts attention towards an alternate, less economistic reading of Lefebvre. It also analyses a building, which is relatively rare in *Society and Space*. The building in question, the West Edmonton Mall in Canada, is by virtue of its massive size, almost regional in scale and its status as building and consumption "region" is part of what makes it appropriate for a Lefebvrian analysis. Shields considers the shopping mall through the category of "lived space" or, as Lefebvre also called it, the "space of representation."[34] This is more than a space where the routines of daily life take place. It is where "surrealist eruptions" of alternative futures occur, through spontaneous appropriations of everyday space. Everything from skateboarders doing turns on an exterior wall to a loud argument in the food court about pro-choice politics would be examples of such events.

Thus Shields focuses on how shoppers appropriate what is sometimes interpreted as a space of absolute social control for purposes that may contest that control, or simply ignore it altogether. His argument suggests that shoppers bring with them cultural attitudes, histories, and shared ideas that may not align with the intended narratives of consumption (or representation of space) promoted by the mall owners. What results is a social "dialogue" in which the "space of representation" produced by the visitor influences (and is transformed by) the conceived space of the mall. The figure that links the two is that of "spatial practice" or the "perceived space" of everyday life, through which the intended narrative and its lived alternatives undergo unpredictable change. Because many groups of visitors enact different representations of space at the same time, these spatial practices are not reducible to a single point of origin, and have different, but overlapping time spans.

LOCALITY STUDIES

The idea that a universally valid "ideal type" can be derived from research into a single (world) city is one of the grander conclusions of the debates on regional restructuring and the socio-spatial dialectic. It is also one of the central ideas that separates such debates from locality studies. While Soja and the other members of the "Los Angeles School" constituted Los Angeles as an internationally applicable paradigm, the discourse on localities in *Society and Space* refuses such generalizations. And while the conceptual optics of the socio-spatial dialectic represent the kaleidoscopic restructuring of late capitalism from above, the optics of locality studies are socially situated and view the world from "the ground up." In locality studies there is no general set of "patterns" that recur from place to place – only locally specific relationships between spaces that are shaped by objective "causal mechanisms."[35] Though not limited to a particular locality, these causal mechanisms can only be understood through their effects in particular instances. This argument is concisely summarized by John Urry. He states that localities are the

> prime sites in which social practices are made and sustained, social practices which constitute social systems . . . The significance of spatial relationships depends upon the particular character of the social objects in question. So the spatial relationships cannot be limited to some general effect – they only have effects because the social objects in question possess particular characteristics, namely different causal powers.[36]

Locality studies seek to devolve research from large-scale generalizing meta-systems to those that are more sensitive to the emergence of fragmented and competing local economies which operate within a "disorganized" but international capitalist framework.[37] In as much as locality studies take the fragmentation of national economic space under particular, market-oriented political regimes and the emergence of "local" political consciousness as the object of analysis, they are indirectly connected to the discourses of urban social movements. These also sought to study acts of political resistance to state policies. In this case, however, resistance is directed towards the privatization and "restructuring" of state-owned industries (such as the coal or steel industry in the United Kingdom) rather than the increasing penetration of the state into everyday life. In their emphasis on communities and "local cultures," these articles reflect an earlier genre of "community studies" that dominated social research in the 1950s. They also draw upon discourses of cultural anthropology and the study of "folk models" of social organization, including more recent research by writers such as Clifford Geertz.[38] As Nigel Thrift writes in 1983, the geographer should now seek to become "contextually sensitive" by practicing a "near model of social theory" that could "burrow into the hearts of people practicing in place."[39] He states that

> Contextually sensitive social theory tends to be more interested in difference and variation for its own sake. This is in recognition of the fact that society is made up of locales and regions, which contain not only general but also specific features, and because such specific features can act as generators or conductors of different kinds of organizations of social action that are differentially effective.[40]

Locality studies in *Society and Space* are written almost exclusively by scholars based in United Kingdom institutions who study the declining industrial base of the north of England.[41] For Doreen Massey and other British Marxists, the turn to locality studies emerged in part as a means to understand how corporate as well as government economic restructuring was changing the basis of national politics. Massey explains that

> Something that might be called "restructuring" was clearly going on, but its implications, both for everyday life and for the mode and potential of political organizing, were clearly highly differentiated and we needed to know how. It was in this context that the localities projects in the United Kingdom were first imagined and proposed. It was research with an immediate, even urgent relevance beyond academe.[42]

She argues in her 1984 book *Spatial Divisions of Labour: Social Structures and the Geography of Production*,[43] that the distinctive political characteristics of a locality can be traced to the effects of successive rounds of accumulation and their impact on the working class; local political cultures emerge from the "shared knowledge" of the "layers" of past practices of oppression and resistance.

In the late 1980s, *Society and Space* became an important forum for locality studies dealing with the impact of Thatcherite economic restructuring on the coal industry in South Wales,[44] as well as case studies of "local towns in Northwest England" and "those mechanisms which underlie local political practices: The factory regime, local labor markets and the mode of provision of services."[45] The journal has also published historical analyses of the working class in urban contexts such as London's East End. Whether examining the "coal field culture" of mining communities,[46] or the history of the labor movement in London,[47] these articles suggest that the "moral ideology,"[48] "shared sense of community," and "ethical strength"[49] they uncover might provide models for contemporary political organization.

One of the consequences of locality studies is to "spatialize" forms of consciousness: to suggest, for example, that a particular form of "moral identity" or "social practice" can be mapped out in relation to physical territory. As P. R. Hall *et al.* suggest, locality studies seek "to identify objective patterns based upon boundaries and upon local organization, property ownership and kinship connections."[50] To the extent that locality studies represent space as a zone within which certain social practices occur, they recall the regional political economy of the Los Angeles School. However, the way in which the contents of that zone are defined is different. In regional political economy "regions" are composed of labor patterns, while localities are often defined by shared social or community consciousness, and local political practices. While the socio-spatial dialectic describes capitalism as a dynamic force producing new forms of "post-Fordist" industrial organization, locality studies examine capitalism primarily through examples of industrial decline and collapse. The differences may be traced back to the contrasting experiences of post-industrial capitalism in Los Angeles and the north of England. During the mid-1980s, Los Angeles entered a period of rapid growth and restructuring, while an extended period of industrial decline affecting the industrial north of England was exacerbated by the initiatives of the Thatcher regime and its privatization of nationalized industries.

Locality studies show how economic forces are mediated and transformed by "local" institutions, social practices and the unique histories of particular cultures. Yet these "near models" of social analysis are in many ways as problematic as their more "distant" and elevated counterparts. Indeed, locality studies, which often explore the impact of global restructuring on working class communities, can, in some ways, be thought of as the post-industrial equivalents of the "ethnographic pastoral" discussed in relation to the *TDSR*. Here it is not a bounded, Eden-like pre-industrial culture that is about to be lost to the forces of global modernization. Rather, it is the communities of working class industrial culture that are about to be lost to the forces of post-industrial, post-Fordist social and spatial restructuring. Just as the ethnographic pastoral constitutes indigenous cultures as homogeneous social groups that are unified around "shared values" passed down from generation to generation, so too are industrial cultures examined here defined by shared elements of, for example, "coalfield culture."[51]

In both cases the communities examined (whether they are "pre-industrial" becoming industrial, or industrial becoming post-industrial) are presumed to have a common, shared consciousness, which is distilled in the material artifacts and social practices of their collective cultures. Thus we have two narratives of loss, the first pre-industrial and the second industrial, both positioned in opposition to the forces of global capitalism. What links these two very different contexts is a shared conception of the local, which is positioned as something outside, rather than within, the global.

SPACES OF EMBODIED IDENTITY: GENDER AND SEXUALITY

While research based on political economy continues to be influential in *Society and Space* up to the present, there has been a deliberate effort on the part of the editors and contributors to expose this form of analysis to criticism. The attempt to relate political economy to space in a non-foundational manner that begins with the consideration of Giddens and Lefebvre continues in the 1990s when Chantal Mouffe's and Ernesto Laclau's post-structuralist synthesis of Marxism and post-structuralism enters the journal through a special issue that explores the spatial implications of their work, with the first article written by Mouffe.[52] Her 1985 book *Capitalist Hegemony and Socialist Strategy*, co-written with Ernesto Laclau, attempted to redefine class-based politics based through a model of collective action that is subject to constant negotiation, as conditions change on the ground. They do not assign a foundational role to class in the formation of political identity, but rather foresee a "disaggregated" society in which collective action occurs through dialogue and temporary alignments between disparate social groups.[53]

If there is a definitive moment in the journal when the predominance of urban political economy comes to an end in *Society and Space*, it is probably when two article-length reviews of recent books by David Harvey and Edward Soja were published side by side in the same issue of the journal in 1990. Until their seminal critiques appear in *Society and Space*, writing on the relationship between gender and space focused primarily on domestic space and its immediate environs, either at the scale of neighborhood or community, and was primarily located in the United Kingdom. Indeed the first two articles to be published on the subject are from the perspective of the white, middle class

British suburban woman.[54] This and subsequent writing draws upon paradigms of political economy, and recalls similar texts in the *International Journal*, where various forms of identity, including gender, are understood as supplements to the primacy of class position.[55]

Deutsche's and Massey's articles mark the beginning of a shift away from these Marxist-based analyses.[56] They argue that both Harvey's *The Condition of Postmodernity*[57] and Soja's *Postmodern Geographies*, represent identity politics and feminist practice as cultural symptoms of changes in the capitalist mode of production. Massey suggests that Harvey dissolves feminism into a larger, reactionary "postmodernism" that is merely a reflection of the "space–time compression" associated with post-Fordist economic restructuring.[58] She also interprets the refusal of both authors to acknowledge the salience of feminist analysis as an unstated strategy to retain their positions of authority in the face of the rising influence of women and minorities in the academy. For Massey, both authors appropriate postmodern practices only to recenter them within Marxist debate:

> These issues arise most acutely for those who are already established and, within these, for those who are members of the already dominant group of white males. For them, if ventures into postmodernism are not to represent simply an attempt at the restoration of their shaky authority as purveyors of truth (even if the whole concept is a lot more complicated than it was previously thought to be) and if it is to be more than another play for status within academe among those who already hold, as a group, most of the positions of power, then there has to be a fundamental questioning of the way they go about their craft.[59]

Deutsche and Massey claim that both authors engage in "masculine modernism," by writing from an ethereal, god-like distance.[60] In a telling section on Harvey's urban writing, Rosalyn Deutsche returns to an earlier text to illustrate what she regards as his characteristic position as an urban voyeur. Harvey begins his 1988 book by describing the thrill he experiences in ascending to the highest point in a city and looking down on what he believes to be the city as whole:

> Citing Michel de Certeau's "The Practice of Everyday Life," Harvey calls this elevated vantage point the perspective of the voyeur and contrasts it, as does de Certeau, with the condition of being immersed in the city's streets. Both perspectives, Harvey asserts, are "real enough" although unequal: the voyeur's perspective offers a superior – because total – view of social reality.[61]

Deutsche suggests that Harvey's writing conflates the voyeur's viewpoint with the "real." What he sees, she argues, is "more like an optical illusion."[62]

She suggests, following Michel de Certeau, that the coherence of such viewpoints is obtained not so much by the clarity of what they show, but by the contradictions they exclude. They are governed by "leveling rationalities" that are a source of pleasure to the masterful eye but have serious consequences for those who are pushed out of the picture.

Voyeurism is an act in which sexual gratification is obtained by looking without being seen. When displaced onto the city, the "imaginary ascent to the top of the city expresses a desire for exteriority, and the image that they produce is not a reproduction but a self-image."[63] Although Harvey claims to write about the city as an objective condition, Deutsche argues that he is actually writing about his own imaginary, sexually charged relation to it. Massey finds a similar tendency to flatten the city into a singular viewpoint in Harvey's writing and refers to his work as "exclusively masculine modernism." She also shows how Edward Soja's "long-distance" history of spatial theory narcissistically culminates in his own research.

SUBJECTS OF REPRESENTATION

Massey and Deutsche not only criticize the subordination of feminist thought to Marxist theory in Soja's and Harvey's books, they also argue that the relationship these texts construct between the reader and the space examined reproduces gendered relations of power. Readers of Harvey's and Soja's texts encounter the city from the position of an elevated voyeur, where the exclusion of women is represented as a "real," rather than constructed phenomenon. By examining not only what these books represent, but how they do so, Deutsche and Massey mark the beginning of a wide range of experiments in the journal that operate at the level of the text. The resulting writing recalls the textual "strategies of disturbance" that contributors to *Assemblage* employed to "loosen" up architectural writing as an institutions. The crucial difference here is that writers challenge the institution of patriarchy *through* geographic writing, rather than geography as a "disciplinary" institution.

An early example of this strategy is illustrated by Gillian Rose's 1990 article "The Struggle for Political Democracy: Emancipation, Gender and Geography," in which she examines the history of early twentieth century British feminists Sylvia Pankhurst and Doris Lester.[64] On the one hand, Rose recovers a marginalized history of feminist practice in nineteenth century London. She also attempts to show how the "imaginative geographies" of writing "are the conceptual frame-works through which places are understood." Beginning from the position that "any imaginative geography legitimates some practices and hinders others" she argues that emancipation from patriarchy is only possible for feminist geographers who

> boldly go where no man has gone before, searching among the silenced for new languages of resistance, naming the unnamed, renaming the misnamed, and above all challenging the structures of signification which disable certain forms of action.
>
> Unfixity must become the condition of every social identity and theory if the struggle for emancipation is to go on.[65]

She suggests that locations become significant through attempts to control them: "the representation of places is constitutive of political struggle."[66] Rose recuperates a previously marginalized representation of a "revolutionary movement which has centered around a certain spatial imaginary: nineteenth-century feminism."[67] Here, the city is not simply gendered because it is differentially occupied by men and women. The way we access the city through representation is defined by gendered relations of power and reimagining such representations from a feminist point of view allows a different understanding of the city to emerge.

While Rose's attention to representation brings an important and marginalized history to the fore, the larger spatial dynamic of that history remains curiously fixed in the temporal and geographical space of Euro-American modernity. This is particularly ironic because Pankhurst and Lester were active in the docklands of East London at the height of the British imperial power. Placing the "space of feminist practice" in a larger imperial context would have raised questions about the global inclusions and exclusions specific to their working class "British" feminism.

The global dynamics of such (imperial) feminism become more explicit in an article by Maureen Hays-Mitchell in the same issue. In "Voices and Visions from the Street: Gender Interest and Political Participation among Women Informal Traders in Latin America,"[68] Hays-Mitchell documents the emergence of "women's agency in social movements" in order to test Molyneux's "gender interest model."[69] The urban space of the Latin American traders becomes visible through theoretical systems defined in advance by the "first world" academic, and the "third world woman" is rendered as an effect of first world theory. In this case, a feminist narrative that challenges the modernist invisibility of women's political agency in the city reactivates Orientalist techniques to do so.

The writing on gender I have discussed above expands the critical terrain for spatial theory in *Society and Space*. The operations of theory no longer center on how to examine the relationship between social processes and spaces that are presumed to be exterior to the consciousness of the writer. Although this writing began by representing gender as a supplement to class, the articles I have discussed here move beyond economic determination, to consider gender through the historical struggles of feminists and questions of "gender interest."

Yet the representations of the city that result are not somehow more complete, or more "accurate" than the disembodied modernism they challenge.

While they open up questions of, for example, patriarchy and its relationship to the spaces of the city, they also constitute their own global exclusions. In this respect, Hays Mitchell's article is perhaps most significant for the absence that it signals of scholarship on gender outside the United Kingdom. It is one of five articles published in the journal up to 2000 that deal with gender issues outside the United Kingdom or North America.[70]

THE BODY AS TEXT

It is precisely the status of gender or "woman" as an independent category that subsequent writing in the journal begins to question. The dissolution of stable categories of identity into ones that are relational and historically determined is a further elaboration of the politics of position I have already discussed. In this case, the body is defined by an array of culturally constructed categories, codes and experiences. Identity formations that not only cross the lines of the nation-state, but also those of gender and sexuality (such as "lesbian man"[71]) become possible. Here the body, as an almost infinite spectrum of physical characteristics, becomes a site of contest over the way categories of identity are inscribed and performed in everyday life.[72]

The latter approach also represents sense experience as culturally mediated experience, so that even feelings of physical pain or anger can be understood as cultural artifacts and their social meaning traced historically.[73] The "body" is understood as a social construction, and depending on one's epistemological standpoint, even our pulsating flesh becomes inauthentic and "unreal." The opposite formulation also emerges in the journal, where the body is defined as essential and given with predetermined qualities: the final category that can't be deconstructed. In this interpretation it becomes the "real" starting point for a range of inscriptions and constructions, much as biological distinctions were asserted (and later dismantled) as the basis for cultural constructions of gender three decades ago.[74] In reflecting on the recent interest in the body as an essential category of analysis, David Harvey argues that it offers a comforting point of stability in an otherwise de-essentialized world of shifting perceptions and values associated with academic postmodernism.[75] The full complexity of the argument has only started to emerge in *Society and Space* (2002).[76] This clearly raises many important questions for the analysis of buildings and urban spaces, most notably in the realm of "aesthetic experience," which is fundamentally tied to embodied sense perception.

Extending the politics of position to include the space of the writer's body and its cultural coding becomes integral to writing on sexuality and space in the journal, and in particular, in writing on queer space. For example, T. Geltmaker's 1992 article entitled "The Queer Nation Acts Up: Health Care, Politics, and Sexual Diversity in the County of Angels"[77] begins with the following statement:

> I would like to ask readers to imagine me speaking these words while stickering myself with the slogans and logos which have made AIDS activism as much a fashion statement as a political vision. I do this not only to remind everyone that "AIDS is Not Over," that "Women Die Faster," that "I am a fag" and that "Silence Equals Death" but also to appropriate my body itself as a politically trespassed public space.[78]

But as this article suggests, the author not only appears in the text through the vivid image of the stickered self; s/he also assumes a tangible form and specificity through the emotion the writing exudes. The conventions of academic writing require the repression of emotion in order to be accepted as "rational." Disrupting this repression becomes another strategy through which to represent the embodied identity of the writer. For example, in 1992 M. Keith writes that "anger routinely disqualifies writing from academic status ... the smugness of the academy sits comfortably beside ostentatious angst over academic method."[79] He praises the virtues of "angry writing,"[80] and challenges the emotionless objectivity of social scientific texts.

David Bell's 1995 editorial entitled "(screw)ING GEOGRAPHY (censor's version)"[81] argues that a pervasive "squeamishness" characterizes discussions about sexual issues among geographers. His paper was originally entitled "Fucking Geography" when presented at the 1994 annual meeting of the Association of American Geographers in San Francisco. The editors of the conference handbook argued "that there are times and places when obscenities are appropriate," and required the author to change the title for publication. Bell interprets the demand for censorship as symptomatic of a larger conservatism built around lack of personal reference in writing:

> My first point then is about the academy. . . . Maybe we can dismiss this as a fairly trivial point – my use of "fucking" was in part a shock tactic (though of course I also intended it as a word game around different uses of the word). But when it is added to the growing list of censoring and discriminatory practices within our discipline – having our articles pulled from library collections, gaining negative reviews when we get public money to do our work . . . we begin to uncover many more of the limits of working within geography on issues of sex and sexuality . . . I shall continue free from the censor's hand at last, to talk about this thing, this fucking geography . . .[82]

Bell suggests a stark opposition exists between a censoring modernist mainstream and a suppressed group of postmodern others. However, a number of contributors during the same period question this characterization. In "All or Nothing? Politics and Critique in the Modernism–Postmodernism Debate,"[83] S. Pile and G. Rose claim that the special issue in which their article is included attempts to "consolidate postmodernism's place on the map of geographical knowledge." They argue that the rush to legitimate "postmodernism" is based on a rejection of "modernism," a position that they refuse to adopt:

> We are being offered a clear choice in the writings by geographers on post-modernism. Their discussions characterize contemporary social theory as a set of struggles between modernists and postmodernists. . . . We are being shown modernism and postmodernism in a tug-of-war, pulling in opposite directions, and we are told that in order to win the war we need only select the best players from each side.[84]

While these and other writers reject the dichotomized struggle for authority that the debate on modernism and postmodernism signifies, little attention is paid to the closed geographic space in which this debate is conducted and the relatively limited selection of white male Euro-American academics it features. For example, Pile and Rose associate a cadre of intellectual luminaries with each of the two positions: modernism is linked to figures such as Frederic Jameson, David Harvey, Edward Soja, Mike Davis, Raymond Williams, Henri Lefebvre; post-modernism is associated with Michel Foucault, Jacques Derrida, Mikhail Bakhtin, Michel de Certeau, and J. F. Lyotard. While questioning the oppositions constituted by the relationship between these authors, the larger (white male) ethnocentrism of the debate is left unexamined.[85]

FROM CATEGORIES OF RACE TO RACIALIZED CATEGORIES

In the arguments above, I have traced a path in the debates in *Society and Space* from gender as a given category to the body as a social construction. Yet for all the complexity of this debate (which I have only been able to suggest in the most general of forms here), I would maintain that it is ultimately a tempest in a (white) Anglo-American teapot. Although there are several important exceptions, for the most part the journal constitutes what might be called divided "geo-bodies." Studies of gendered and sexed bodies are located in the post-imperial, post-industrial West, while those of racial and ethnic others are examined most frequently – if not always – in the former colonial territories of the British empire, as well as Central and South America. And perhaps most notably (with one important exception) white, Anglo-American communities have remained almost invisible in the journal's discussion of race and ethnicity. Whiteness is apparently not an "ethnicity."[86]

Writing on gender and sexuality becomes the staging ground for elaborate experiments in reflexivity and discourses of the culturally constructed body. The writing on race and ethnicity gradually shifts from operating within given (social scientific) categories, towards exploring of the construction of racialized categories. In what follows, I suggest that despite this conceptual shift, the larger geographical divisions separating race and ethnicity from gender and sexuality remain in place, and are in fact reinforced by a growing post-imperial interest in post-colonial contexts.

Perhaps the most pointed examples of texts that reproduce given categories of race are two articles published in the same issues of *Society and Space* in 1990. Both are written by academics based in the United Kingdom, and both introduce a focus on colonial regimes of power. J. D. Overton's study of "social control and spatial engineering" examines the African "reserves" in Kenya between 1895 and 1920.[87] The analysis occurs at the level of large-scale mapping of the "size and pattern of reserves," while J. Robinson examines "native locations" in South Africa in relation to "power and the state apparatus."[88] In both cases the racial identity of the subordinated groups is taken as given and located in space as a subject "population." Though both articles are deeply critical of how the state marginalizes and controls such groups, the way the categories are created, and the ongoing rule of the state in producing and maintaining them (and of subordinated groups in contesting them) over time is not examined.

It is interesting to contrast these arguments with those outlined in Kay Anderson's research on cultural hegemony in Vancouver's Chinatown, the first article published in the journal to deal explicitly with the social construction of racialized categories.[89] She explores the historically evolving relationship between racial discourse, place and government policy, revealing how an area once regarded as a ghetto for stigmatized Chinese immigrants becomes, by 1980, a municipal heritage site. The emergence of Chinatown as a site of cultural heritage is understood here in terms that are similar to those of Kathryne Mitchell in the *TDSR*: Chinatown as a heritage site is less a sign of "tolerance" than an attempt to fix the identity of the "Chinese community" from without. The investigation of the process of race definition, which in this case involves a struggle over government planning policy, underscores the history of the "Chinese" as a category and discourse.[90]

Yet even this careful attempt to explore the production of racial categories becomes coherent through a series of dichotomies that oppose the British colonial self to the Chinese other. In an essay published almost a decade after this article (and the book it was based on) first appeared, Anderson returned to her research, through an "auto-critique" that explores her exclusions of gender and sexuality. She situates her earlier writing within "epistemology of separation" implicit in much of race research, and writes that the

> fictionalized collectivities of "Black", "White", "European", "Asian", and so on . . . are often corollaries of a dichotomized us/them framework that unwittingly obscures the subjectivities of identities internal to those categories.[91]

Her article is a powerful critique of her own work, as well as much categorically divided research on embodied identities. Her response is to foreground the "gendered meanings and practices that at times reinforced and at other times disrupted" normative race categorizations and relations.[92] The oppositions that gave coherence to the former analysis are abandoned, and are now cut across by structures of desire that join them together.

At a larger conceptual level, the shift effected in Anderson's work – from studying objects within a given category to studying the terms and conditions that define the category itself – acknowledges the inextricable relationship between an object of investigation and the practices of representation that constitute it as such. The shift opens up a potentially vast range of cultural artifacts as "constitutive" elements of discourses on race. The rich potential of this expanded field has quickly become apparent in the journal with topics ranging from studies of the "ersatz Edens" of aristocratic nature preservationists in colonial Africa, to the discourses of race and gender in geography school texts during the height of the British empire.[93] Yet, as I discuss in further detail below, contributors to the journal have argued that the fascination with textual analysis can also serve to efface analysis of the human experiences and consequences of colonization.

BEYOND THE CRITICALLY REFLEXIVE SELF

For some critics, the emphasis on representation seemed to mark an evaporation of social science into the world of textual analysis, where the experiences and struggles of subordinated social groups are replaced by discussions of what are regarded by some as their textual surrogates. The apparent displacement of all social analysis into the space of the text appears to be buttressed by the claims that there is no reality outside representation. Thus, it is no longer possible to study geography *per se*; one studies representations of geography, how it is constituted as a category, how the subject position of the geographer has been socially produced over time. The idea of a "world out there" that can be modeled, studied, and acted upon seems to vanish, and with it the different categories of "subject-populations" that inhabit it. The situation recalls the "abolition" of the "real world" in *Assemblage*, and with it the "subject/object" dichotomy that permits "architecture" to exist as a stable category. Just as architecture becomes the result of the critical systems and taxonomies that constitute it as such, so too do urban communities, distributions of labor, and seemingly natural categories of gender, race and sexuality become constructions whose basis in representation can be tracked historically.

Does this mean that all research is consigned to a dichotomy that opposes the real to the represented, the modern to the postmodern, and the scientifically objective to the self-reflexive politics of location? The answer that emerges in

Society and Space is one that accepts the value of "objectivity" and traditional social scientific research as one mode of representation among many. The question is therefore not whether some ways of knowing are universally good or bad in relation to others, but rather, once the inherent limitations of different systems of representation are understood, how can they be used strategically to achieve particular objectives? This point of view moves beyond thinking, for example, of binarized racial categories as necessarily a "bad" thing. In 1996, Jane M. Jacobs and Peter Jackson argued that while "objectivist" models are often based upon fixed, even reductive conceptions of identity, they can nevertheless operate as powerful (if temporary) political tools that are capable of consolidating disparate groups into action:

> The binaries which helped drive an anti-racist politics have been unsettled. This does not mean that we should abandon an anti-racist politics. For all our understanding of the fractured nature of contemporary identity politics, we must recognize that in specific political mobilizations there will always be a need to "fix" identities.[94]

Indeed, they suggest that critics who study the constitutive sites of racist discourse can unwittingly "revel in the effects of colonial desire" and hence reactivate their "racist potency." They recount a revealing incident that occurred at the annual meeting of the Association of American Geographers. They claim that the audience seemed much more comfortable debating the epistemological questions surrounding different forms of post-colonial theory than with discussions centered on the politics of race in the present:

> The parallel sessions at the AAG meetings generated quite different responses in their respective audiences. In one, a sophisticated discussion of postcolonial theory rarely discomforted the participants. In fact these critical reflections seemed to act as some form of cathartic absolution. In the other the audience was directly confronted with a very active politics of race, made to feel uncomfortable, and reminded of the persistent imperative of a racialized present.[95]

These remarks underscore how debates over the politics of representation can sometimes serve as a proxy for involvement in political struggles between differently empowered social groups, both within and beyond the academy. Indeed as Jacobs and Jackson suggest, critical refection on scholarly practice sometimes acts as a form of moral "absolution" that is constructed by backing away from objectivity and other modernist forms of generalization. In this way, the turn towards carefully positioned and "located" accounts can displace modes of analysis that in their very generality may illuminate conditions and raise issues that would not be otherwise visible. Such arguments are clearly polarizing and what has transpired in *Society and Space* (perhaps quite predictably, given the terms of the debate) is critical reflexivity about the practices of critical reflexivity. In an editorial entitled "More Critically Reflexive than Thou,"[96] for a special issue on the politics of position, George Marcus suggests that the emergence of "located" writing has become

> The mode of rather puritanical, competitive self-assessment among scholars of the relative virtue of each other's practices of self-identification and self-presentation. What is at stake in the politics of identity is the construction of a space of critical authority from which analyse, interpretation, in short, academic social scientific work, might once again be generated amid the ruins of so-called meta-narratives like Marxism, systems theory, etc. Some sort of reflexive identification of the academic with the "other" interpreted, analyzed, or written about, is so important in re-establishing critical authority in the rubble of paradigms precisely because the most powerful and paralyzing aspect of the critique of representation has been its ethical implications for the very mode of communication – discursive impersonal writing – so basic to academic work.[97]

Marcus argues that a "non-innocent" version of reflexive practice is required that does not require the scholar to make moral choices between "located writing" and "objectivism" but rather to understand the limits of each and use them strategically. Beyond this, he cites two other important forms of reflexive knowledge that are of relevance to both *Society and Space* and the other journals in this study. The first, based in Foucaultian post-structuralism, provides situated accounts of the micro-practices of academia in order to ground and critically assess the grander claims of geographic writing, while the second, based in the writing on cultural capital by Pierre Bourdieu and other Marxist sociologists, examines how these practices are shaped by "objective" social structures.[98]

The larger questions raised by Marcus concern the intellectual's site of political action. Since its founding, *Society and Space* has sought to develop a "social theory" that could "unravel some of the key issues facing contemporary society."[99] Contributions to the journal from the mid-1990s have begun to question exactly how such critical analysis of key social issues might be linked to real political struggles within or beyond the academy, and as such, they directly address how academics perceive themselves as political subjects. A 1995 editorial entitled "Activism and the Academy" describes how, from the 1990s, recent conferences of the Association of American Geographers have been

> thick with calls for challenging power and contesting hierarchy . . . these battle cries, all too frequently, were made in language that made sense only to the cogniscenti.

> There was little if any talk of the political purchase of critical ideas beyond the walls of the classroom or the spaces of academic journals.[100]

The author identifies a range of political positions – extending from the "specific intellectual" who chooses the institutional setting in which s/he works as the context for political action, to attempts to form links with community groups and political organizations with no direct links to the academy. While raising important questions about who benefits from the political positions of the Anglo-American academic community, the debate over activism launched by Keith has tended to assume that the larger "space" in which the debate is constituted is limited to the Anglo-American geography of the journal. There have been no attempts as yet to consider, for example, how political alliances might be formed internationally in a way that would bring the competing experiences of "first" and "third" world scholars together in a common frame.

CONCLUSION

Other journals in this study have tended either to promote one theoretical perspective (deconstructive literary theory in *Assemblage*, for example) or to move from one position to the next within a larger theoretical field (such as the progressive internationalization of political economy in the *International Journal*). *Society and Space*, however, has tended to add new, and sometimes contradictory, approaches to the analysis of space (broadly defined) without eliminating prior positions. Recent issues of the journal contain a wide range of subject matter, including, among others, articles on locality studies, the socio-spatial dialectic, research drawing upon the writing of the "regulation school" of Marxists, questions about globalization, a wide range of approaches organized around the politics of cultural identity, and continuing discussion about the potential and limitations of critical reflexivity.

Although *Society and Space* represents an increasingly broad range of positions, it has managed to avoid representing them as non-communicating sub-specializations that are merely juxtaposed in a pluralist relationship with each other. What makes the journal unique, not only from the others in this study, but in the realm of academic production *per se*, is the consistent attention that is given to how and why theoretical debates change.

The journal's open-ended editorial policy and its capacity to encourage and reflect on the merits of competing positions are partly due to the role of the editors and guest editors, who write editorials that make provocative connections between research published in the journal and wider changes, not only in the academy, but the world at large. The editorials, which sometimes are less concerned with introducing articles than with raising important issues for future discussion and debate, extend from the consideration of different styles of scholarly citation as a form of academic self-representation, and the issues surrounding geographic writing as a form of representation, to the question of how "cultural boundaries limit intellectual horizons."

Perhaps the most valuable contribution of the editors is the attention they pay to the politics of knowledge and intellectual identity. As the case study has suggested, this has become a major theme in the research published in *Society and Space*. The journal has opened up the investigation of "located scholarship," and considered the embodied identity and socio-historical position of the writer in relation to the spaces represented. When these situated accounts first emerged in the journal, they were sometimes defined through opposition to "modernist" positions of objective exteriority that sought a grand synthesis of "society and space." Yet even the terms of this dichotomy, which tends to oppose the modern to the postmodern, and the objective to the self-reflexive, have been examined critically. It is now possible to read the journal and find analyses based on Marxist urban political economy presented alongside research concerned with "making sense of men's lifestyle magazines"[101]; just as it is possible to find debates about the global command economy appearing together with articles on "place and metaphor."[102] The editorial commentaries provide the critical thread that connects these together and for the most part mitigates the impression that the journal is dissolving into a patchwork of equivalent but different positions.

In a way that certainly could not have been predicted when the journal began, *Society and Space* has managed to construct a forum in which competing positions are represented and their interconnections traced, without imposing a fixed hierarchy upon them as part of a strategy to "organize" and assimilate them within a larger theoretical frame. It has not done so by subordinating all positions to the mechanics of unifying meta-theory: the cumbersome inflexibility and ethnocentrism of such systems was recognized early on. Instead, the editors and contributors have fashioned a contradictory space, in which divergent interpretations of the relation between "society and space" (and how the two terms are constituted) appear in one place. In its most memorable moments the journal has revealed how these positions, which initially seem incommensurable with each other, are ultimately defined in a manner that is interdependent – both at the level of their epistemological development, and in terms of the institutional struggles of which they are a part. The journal has also explored connections between arguments about theory and what is happening in cities and built environments outside the academy, particularly in relation to political struggles around urban change. Such efforts are more prominent here than in other journals in this study.

Despite its success in constructing bridges between competing specializations, and in linking the ongoing agenda of the journal to changes in various metropolitan contexts, *Society and Space* remains primarily "Anglo-North

American" in its outlook and priorities. This has also been addressed in the journal, most directly when Michael Dear stepped down as editor in 1992. Since that time, the journal has included more discussion about the entanglements of geography as a discipline with world historical forces such as colonialism and imperialism. So far at least, this has been undertaken almost completely from a "British" perspective, tending to reinforce the problematic conflation of post-colonial studies with British colonialism, rather than addressing issues in regard to other colonial empires, such as the French, Dutch, or Portuguese. This is arguably less the result of any deliberate intention on the part of the editors, than an indication of how post-colonial studies have emerged and been institutionalized in the academic systems of Europe and North America.

Society and Space is not only the most open-ended and mutable in terms of the theoretical positions it represents: it has also, perhaps more than any other journal in this study, published research at a wide range of scales. Indeed, over the last decade the "scale politics" of spatiality itself has been addressed in the journal in a manner that is of direct relevance to this study. David Livingstone's 1995 essay on "The Spaces of Knowledge"[103] considers the emergence of a critical understanding of the spatiality of knowledge in the "science community" and then extends the argument to geography:

> It is noteworthy that historians of science have begun to take account of the spatial . . . it is ironic that historians of geography have taken so little account of the spatial in the histories they have produced . . . geography's historians have too frequently been content to operate at the level of what Clifford Geertz in another context referred to as the "wall-sized culturescapes of the nation, the epoch, the continent or the colonizer." Geographers, of all people, should surely be aware of the significance of scale in matters spatial.[104]

As this chapter has suggested, initially the journal's research was primarily concerned with regions and localities, and in some respects reproduced the subnational "culturescapes" Livingstone refers to. Writing in *Society and Space* now extends from the transnational territory to the socio-historical space of the embodied subject. There is, however, comparatively little discussion at the scale "in between," where buildings become understandable as distinct forms of social production, organization, and aesthetic experience. The journal has developed powerful techniques for analyzing how urban space is represented in an increasingly wide array of cultural productions, yet the status of buildings as signifying systems that are bound up in the spatial politics of the contemporary metropolis remains largely unexamined. Yet the journal's investigations into the scale politics of geographic research and the openness of its editorial program to critical revision suggests that this may soon change.[105]

NOTES

1. This basic premise has helped to shape the journal's editorial structure, which has always been considerably more open-ended than in the other journals in this study. Each issue contains an editorial or "commentary" that is often written by a member of the advisory board or an invited outsider, rather than the editor. These brief opinion pieces are sometimes used to introduce a cluster of thematically related articles; in other cases they operate as polemical statements that link theoretical developments in the humanities and social sciences with current issues in geographic research.

   In addition to these commentaries, a second feature, referred to as "knowledge surveys" has played an important role in introducing significant theoretical developments in other fields to the journal's readership. These surveys, which often discuss as many as twenty books in a single extended essay, examine the development of new critical paradigms in geography and urban studies. A total of sixteen of these surveys was published in the journal until they were replaced with article-length book reviews in 1990. While these do not attempt to provide the same breadth of coverage of developments within and between fields of knowledge they have also played an important role in challenging existing research paradigms and making a strong argument for new directions in research.

2. Some of the debates in *Society and Space* overlap with the *International Journal*. In the early years of publication *Society and Space* published research into urban social movements and theories of the state. There is also extensive discussion of various aspects of post-Fordism and urban restructuring. While these receive substantial attention in the journal, I do not discuss them here because I have dealt with the issues they raise in the previous chapter.

3. Michael Dear, "Editorial" *Society and Space* 1, no. 1 (March 1993): 1.

4. M. Dear and N. J. Thrift, "Unfinished Business: Ten Years of *Society and Space*, 1983–1992," *Society and Space* 10, no. 6 (December 1992): 715–720.

   This article was published in *Society and Space* in 1992 to mark the transfer of Dear's editorship to Geraldine Pratt. A photograph included with the article shows the five founding members seated together outside a tea-house in the town of Berrima, halfway between Sydney and the Australian National University in Canberra.

5. Based on my analysis of 256 articles published between 1983 and 1992 inclusive. Of these articles, 47 percent were written by scholars based in the discipline of geography; 15 percent from sociology; 11 percent from urban planning; 7 percent from architecture; 8 percent from independent scholars and scholars based in research centers; 3 percent each from economics,

psychology, anthropology, and political science. 42 percent of the articles were written by scholars located in the United Kingdom, 25 percent by scholars located in the United States; 10 percent are by authors located in Australia and Canada respectively; 2 percent from France; and 1 percent or less from each of the following: Brazil, Denmark, Germany, Greece, Hong Kong, Nicaragua, New Zealand, Switzerland.

In their account of *Society and Space*'s history, Dear and Thrift describe the journal's limited social geography of contributors, and its reliance on scholars based in human geography to be two of the journal's disappointing features. Dear and Thrift, "Unfinished Business": 715.

6   Ibid.
7   Ibid.
8   David Ley and Marwyn S. Samuels, "Introduction" in David Ley and Marwyn S. Samuels (eds.), *Humanistic Geography. Prospects and Problems* (Chicago: Maaroufa Press, 1978), 11.
9   John Urry and Derek Gregory (eds), *Social Relations and Spatial Structures* (Basingstoke: Macmillan, 1985). Published in the "Critical Human Geography" series by Macmillan (1985), the collection contained fourteen essays by prominent geographers (nine) and sociologists (five), at British (ten) and American (four) universities.
10 Doreen Massey, "New Directions in Space" in John Urry and Derek Gregory (eds), *Social Relations and Spatial Structures* (Basingstoke: Macmillan, 1985), 12.
11 Edward Soja, *Postmodern Geographies. The Reassertion of Space in Critical Theory* (London: Verso, 1989), 11.
12 Dear, "*Society and Space*: An Introduction," *Society and Space* 1, no. 1 (March 1983): 1.
13 See, for example, Anthony Giddens, *Central Problems in Social Theory: Action Structure and Contradiction in Social Analysis* (London: Macmillan, 1979).
14 See, for example, Anthony Giddens, *The Constitution of Society: Outline of a Theory of Structuration* (Cambridge: Polity Press, 1984).
15 Gillian Rose, *Feminism and Geography. The Limits of Geographical Knowledge* (Cambridge: Polity Press, 1993), 20.
16 See, for example, Nigel Thrift "On the Determination of Social Action in Space and Time," *Society and Space* 1, no. 1 (March 1983) 23–57; Derek Gregory, "Space, Time and Politics in Social Theory: An Interview with Anthony Giddens," *Society and Space* 2, no. 2 (June 1984): 123–132; A. Pred, "Structuration, Biography Formation and Knowledge: Observations in Port Growth during the Last Mercantile Period," *Society and Space* 2, no. 3 (September, 1984): 251–276.

17 See, for example, Torsten Haggerstrand, "Survival and Arena: On the Life History of Individuals in Relation to their Geographical Environments" in T. Carlstein, D. Parkes, and N. Thrift (eds), *Human Activity and Time Geography* no. 2. (London: Routledge and Kegan Paul, 1975).
18 Rose, op. cit. Rose cites as a paradigmatic example R. Miller, "Household Activity Patterns in Nineteenth Century Suburbs: A Time-geographic Exploration," *Annals of the Association of American Geographers*, 72 (1980): 291–299.
19 For an interesting overview of Lefebvre's urban research see Eleonore Kofman and Elizabeth Lebas, "Lost in Transposition: Time Space and the City" in Eleonore Kofman and Elizabeth Lebas (eds), *Henri Lefebvre, Writings on Cities* (Oxford: Blackwell, 1996), 3–62; Rob Shields, "The Production of Space" in *Lefebvre, Love and Struggle* (London and New York: Routledge, 1999), 141–185.
20 Shields, op. cit., 146
21 See, for example A. J. Scott, "Territorial Reproduction and Transformation in a Local Labor Market: The Animated Film Workers of Los Angeles," *Society and Space* 2, no. 3 (1984): 277–307; E. Schoenberger, "From Fordism to Flexible Accumulation: Technology, Competitive Strategies, and International Location," *Society and Space*, 6, no. 3 (1988): 245–262; A. Amin and K. Robbins, "The Re-Emergence of Regional Economies? The Mythical Geography of Flexible Accumulation," *Society and Space*, 8, no. 1 (1990): 7–34; S. Watson, "Gilding the Smokestacks: The New Symbolic Representations of Deindustrialized Regions," *Society and Space* 9, no. 1 (1991): 59–70; J. Graham, "Postfordism as Politics: The Political Consequences of Narratives on the Left," *Society and Space* 10, no. 4 (1992): 393–410; M. Goodwin, S. Duncan and S. Halford, "Regulation Theory, the Local State, and the Transitions of Urban Politics," *Society and Space* 11, no. 1 (1993): 67–88; Roger Keil, "Global Sprawl, Urban Form after Fordism," *Society and Space* 12, no. 2 (1994): 131–136.
22 Soja, *Postmodern Geographies*, 78.
23 *Society and Space*, 4 (September 1986): 249–392.
24 S. Christopherson and M. Storper, "The City as Studio; The World as Backlot: The Impact of Vertical Disintegration on the Location of the Motion Picture Industry," *Society and Space* 14, no. 3 (September 1986): 305–320.
25 J. Addler, "The Dynamics of Transit Innovation in Los Angeles," *Society and Space* 4, no. 3 (September 1986): 321–336.
26 R. Morales, "The Los Angeles Automobile Industry in Historical Perspective," *Society and Space* 4, no. 3 (September 1986): 289–304.
27 E. W. Soja, "Taking Los Angeles Apart," *Society and Space*, 4, no. 3 (September 1986): 268.

28 See, for example, "The Premature Death of Postmodern Urbanism" in Michael J. Dear, *The Postmodern Urban Condition* (Oxford: Blackwell: 2000), 70–90.
29 Soja, "Taking Los Angeles Apart," 263.
30 Ibid.
31 A. J. Scott and E. W. Soja, "Los Angeles: Capital of the Late Twentieth Century," *Society and Space* 4, no. 3 (September 1986): 249. See also Edward Soja and Allen J. Scott (eds), *The City. Los Angeles and Urban Theory at the End of the Twentieth Century* (Berkeley, Los Angeles and London: University of California Press, 1996).
32 Michael Crang, "Globalization as Conceived, Perceived and Lived Spaces," *Theory, Culture and Society* (1999) 16, no. 1: 167–177.
33 Rob Shields, "Social Spatialization and the Built Environment: The Case of the West Edmonton Mall," *Society and Space* 7, no. 2 (1989): 147–164.
34 Shields, 162.
35 This approach to the analysis of localities is sometimes associated with "realist" philosophies of scientific investigation, in which interrelationships between social spaces are emphasized. See, for example, J. Allen, "Property Relations and Landlordism – A Realist Approach," *Society and Space* 1, no. 2 (June 1983): 191–203; John Urry, "Survey 12: Society, Space and Locality," *Society and Space* 5, no. 4 (December 1987): 435–444.
36 John Urry, "Localities, Regions and Social Class," *IJURR* 5, no. 4 (December 1981): 458.
37 Scott Lash and John Urry, *The End of Organized Capitalism* (Cambridge, United Kingdom: Polity Press, 1987).
38 For example, Thrift cites R. Jenkins' article entitled "Thinking and Doing: Towards a Model of Cognitive Practice" in Ladislav Holy and Milan Stuchlik (eds), *The Structure of Folk Models* (New York: Academic Press, 1981).
39 Nigel Thrift, "The Politics of Context," *Society and Space* 1 (December 1983): 375.
40 Ibid., 371.
41 In the early 1980s, Massey was also involved in establishing the program in locality studies called the "Changing Urban and Regional System" at the Open University. Doreen Massey, *Space, Place and Gender* (Minneapolis: University of Minnesota Press, 1994), 125.
42 Ibid., 128.
43 Doreen Massey, *Spatial Variations of Labour: Social Structures and the Geography of Production* (New York: Methuen, 1984).
44 P. Cooke, "Regional Restructuring: Class, Politics, and Popular Protest in South Wales," *Society and Space* 1, no. 3 (August 1983): 265–280.
45 Alan Warde, "Industrial Restructuring, Local Politics and the Reproduction of Labor Power: Some Theoretical Considerations," *Society and Space* 6, no. 1 (1988): 75–95.

46 G. Rees, "Regional Restructuring, Class Change and Political Action: Preliminary Comments on the 1984–85 Miners' Strike in South Wales," *Society and Space* 3, no. 4 (December 1985): 389–406; R. Hudson, "National Industrial Policies and Regional Politics: The Role of the State in Capitalist Societies in the Deindustrialization and Reindustrialization of Regions," *Society and Space* 4, no. 1 (March 1986): 7–26: P. Sunley, "Regional Restructuring, Class Change and Political Action: A Comment," *Society and Space* 4, no. 4 (1986): 465–468.

47 Clifford Geertz, *Local Knowledge. Further Essays in Interpretive Anthropology* (New York: Basic Books, 1983). Rose states that Geertz's "notion of culture best describes what studies of the local state and local politics have so far omitted: Local ideas and attitudes." See Gillian Rose, "Locality, Politics and Culture: Poplar in the 1920s," *Society and Space* 6, no. 2 (June 1988): 153.

48 J. Eyles and M. Evans, "Popular Consciousness, Moral Ideology and Locality," *Society and Space* 5, no. 1 (March 1987): 39–71.

49 Gillian Rose argues that the form of "community life uniquely based in the structure of both a large family and a small village" in the 1920s East End community of Poplar is relevant to the geographically fragmented political context of the United Kingdom in the 1980s. Rose, "Locality, Politics and Culture": 157.

50 P. R. Hall, D. C. Thorns, and W. E. Willmott, "Community, Class and Kinship – Bases for Collective Action within Localities," *Society and Space* 2, no. 2 (1984): 201–215.

51 See, for example, P. Sunley, "Regional Restructuring, Class Change and Political Action: A Comment," *Society and Space* 4, no. 4 (1986): 465–468; G. Rees, 'Coalfield Culture' and the 1984–1985 Miners' Strike: A Reply to Sunley," *Society and Space* 4, no. 4 (1985): 75–102; J. L. Morris, "The State and Industrial Restructuring: Government Policies in Industrial Wales," *Society and Space* 5, no. 2 (1987): 195–213; Alan Warde, "Industrial Restructuring, Local Politics and the Reproduction of Labor Power: Some Theoretical Considerations," *Society and Space* 6, no. 1 (1988): 75–95.

52 Chantal Mouffe, "Post-Marxism, Democracy and Identity": 259–265; other articles in the same issue include Wolfgang Natter, "Radical Democracy, Hegemony, Reason, Time and Space": 267–274; J. K. Gibson-Graham, "Identity and Economic Plurality: Rethinking Capitalism and 'Capitalist Hegemony'": 275–282; and Doreen Massey, "Thinking Radical Democracy Spatially": 283–288. All articles in *Society and Space*, 13, no. 3, 1995.

53 Ernesto Laclau and Chantal Mouffe, *Capitalist Hegemony and Socialist Strategy: Towards a Radical Democratic Politics* (London: Verso, 1985).

54 In "The Hoover in the Garden: Middle-Class Women and Suburbanization, 1850–1920," *Society and Space* 1, no. 4 (September 1983): 73–87, R. Miller employs a "structurationist perspective" to examine the emergence of

"domestic work" in relation to the growth of suburbs, social mobility and domestic consumption. This is followed by S. R. Bowlby's 1984 article entitled "Planning for Women to Shop in Postwar Britain," *Society and Space* 2, no. 2 (June 1984): 179–200, in which she considers how changing ideologies of women's domestic roles were related to "retail planning" in postwar Britain.

55 G. Pratt and S. Hanson, "Gender, Class and Space," *Society and Space* 6 (March 1988): 15–36; see also S. Walby and P. Baggualey, "Gender Restructuring: Five Labour Markets Compared," *Society and Space* 7, no. 3 (September, 1989): 277–292.

56 Rosalyn Deutsche, "Boystown," *Society and Space* 9, no. 1 (March 1991): 5–30; Doreen Massey, "Flexible Sexism," *Society and Space* 9, no. 1 (March 1991): 31–57.

57 D. Harvey, *The Condition of Postmodernity* (Oxford: Blackwell Press, 1989).

58 She claims that while Harvey attempts to redefine "Marxism in order to treat more satisfactorily the questions of difference and otherness . . . (in) his own analysis of modernism and postmodernism, one of the most significant those differences – that which revolves around gender, is absent." Massey, "Flexible Sexism": 51.

59 Ibid., 34

60 Rosalyn Deutsche, "Boystown," in R. Deutsche, *Evictions. Art and Spatial Politics* (Cambridge, MA: MIT Press, 1996), 209.

Massey situates Harvey's writing within a modernism "both privileged vision over the other senses and established a way of seeing from the point of view of an authoritative, privileged, male position . . ." Massey, op. cit., 232.

61 Deustche, op. cit., 209.

62 Ibid., 210.

63 Ibid., 213.

64 Gillian Rose, "The Struggle for Political Democracy: Emancipation, Gender and Geography," *Society and Space* 8, no. 4 (December 1990): 395–408.

65 Ibid., 406.

66 Ibid.

67 Ibid.

68 Maureen Hays-Mitchell, "Voices and Visions from the Streets: Gender Interests and Political Participation Among Women Informal Traders in Latin America," *Society and Space* 13, no. 4 (August 1995): 445–469.

69 Ibid., 495.

70 The articles published in *Society and Space* from its inception that deal with gender issues outside Europe and North America are: L. Bondi and M. Domash, "Other Figures in Other Places," *Society and Space* 10, no. 2 (1992): 199–213; Lawrence D. Berg and Robin A. Kearns, "Naming as Norming:

'Race', Gender and the Identity Politics of Naming Place in Aotearoea, New Zealand," *Society and Space* 14, no. 1 (1996): 99–122; J. A. Peck, " 'Invisible Threads': Homeworking, Labour Market Relations, and Industrial Restructuring in the Australian Clothing Trade," *Society and Space* 6 (1988); and Barbara M. Cooper, "Gender, Movement and History: Social and Spatial Transformations in 20th Century Maradi, Niger," *Society and Space*, 15, no. 2 (1997): 195–221.

71 For a concise discussion of this point, see Tamsin Spargo's interesting essay published as *Foucault and Queer Theory* (Cambridge: Icon Books, 1999).

72 Judith Butler, "Subjects of Sex/Gender /Desire" in *Gender Trouble* (London and New York: Routledge, 1990), 1–34; see also "Against Proper Objects" reprinted in E. Weed and N. Schor (eds), *Feminism Meets Queer Theory* (Bloomington, IN: Indiana University Press, 1997) 1–30; and "Gender is Burning: Questions of Appropriation and Subversion" in J. Butler, *Bodies that Matter* (New York and London: Routledge, 1993), 121–142. For an introduction to Butler's idea of performance see Annamarie Jagose, *Queer Theory. An Introduction* (New York: NYU Press, 1996).

73 Arjun Appadurai, "Dead Certain: Ethnic Violence in the Era of Globalization," *Public Culture*. 10, no. 2 (Winter 1998): 225–248.

74 Liz Bondi provides a clear introduction to the sex/gender system in "Sexing the City," in Ruth Fincher and Jane M. Jacobs (eds), *Cities of Difference* (London and New York: The Guildford Press, 1998), 177–200; see Naomi Schor, "Introduction" in E. Weed and N. Schor (eds), *Feminism Meets Queer Theory* (Bloomington, IN: Indiana University Press, 1997), vii–xix.

75 David Harvey, "The Body as an Accumulation Strategy," *Society and Space* 16, no. 4 (1998): 401–421.

76 The body in post-structuralist theory is summarized in Felicity J. Callard's article "The Body in Theory," in *Society and Space* 16, no. 3 (1998): 387–400. A consideration of the body in relation to the social norms and public policy appears in a special issue on "Geographies of Disability," edited by Vera Chouinard and Liisa Cormode, *Society and Space*. 15, no. 4 (1997).

77 This is also the first article in *Society and Space* in which the author explicitly identifies his or her sexuality. T. Geltmaker, "The Queer Nation Acts Up: Health Care, Politics and Sexual Diversity in the County of Angels," *Society and Space* 10, no. 6 (December 1992): 609.

78 Ibid., 609.

79 M. Keith, "Angry Writing: Representing the Unethical World of the Ethnographer," *Society and Space* 10, no. 5 (October 1992): 551.

80 Ibid., 551.

81 David J. Bell, "(screw)ING GEOGRAPHY (censor's version)," *Society and Space* 13, no. 2 (April 1995): 127.

82 Ibid., 127.
83 S. Pile and G. Rose, "All or Nothing? Politics and Critique in the Modernism-Postmodernism Debate," *Society and Space* 10, no. 2 (April, 1992): 123–136.
84 Ibid., 123.
85 The authors state that "certain phrases and procedures have become set, through which the debate between postmodernists and modernists takes place even to the extent of always citing key writers and texts: Baudrillard Lyotard, Derrida, Lyotard against Habermas, Jameson, Habermas against Foucault, Foucault, Deleuze and Guattari . . ."
    Pile and Rose, "All or Nothing": 124.
86 See Susanne Schech and Jane Haggis, "Postcolonialism, Identity, and Location: Being White Australian in Asia," *Society and Space* 16, no. 5 (1999): 615–629.
87 J. D. Overton, "Social Control and Social Engineering: African Reserves in Kenya 1895–1920)," *Society and Space* 8, no. 2 (June 1990): 163–174.
88 J. Robinson, "A Perfect System of Control? State Power and 'Native Locations' in South Africa," *Society and Space* 8, no. 2 (June 1990): 135.
89 K. J. Anderson, "Cultural Hegemony and Race Definition Processes in Chinatown, Vancouver, 1880–1980," *Society and Space* 6, no. 2 (June 1988): 127–149.
90 Ibid., 127
91 Kay Anderson, "Engendering Race Research: Unsettling the Self/Other Dichotomy," in Nancy Duncan (ed.), *Bodyspace* (New York and London: Routledge, 1996), 197.
92 Ibid.
93 See Roderick P. Neumann, "Dukes, Earls and Ersatz Edens: Aristocratic Nature Preservationists in Colonial Africa," *Society and Space*, 14, no. 1 (1996): 79–98 and Avril M. C. Maddrell, "Discourses of Race and Gender and the Comparative Method in Geography School Texts, 1830–1918," *Society and Space* 16, no. 1 (1998): 81–103.
94 Jane M. Jacobs and Peter Jackson, "Editorial," *Society and Space*, 14, no. 1 (1996): 3.
95 Ibid., 3.
96 George Marcus, "More Critically Reflexive than Thou," *Society and Space* 10, no. 5 (October 1992): 489–494.
97 Ibid., 489–490.
98 Ibid., 490–491.
99 M. Dear, "*Society and Space*: An Introduction": 1.
100 N. K. Bromley, "Activism and the Academy," *Society and Space* 12, no. 4 (August 1994): 383–386.

101 Peter Jackson, Nick Stevenson and Kate Brooks, "Making Sense of Men's Lifestyle Magazines," *Society and Space* 17, no. 3 (1999): 253–368.
102 See *Society and Space* 17, no. 2 (1999).
103 David Livingstone, "The Spaces of Knowledge: Contribution Towards a Historical Geography of Science," *Society and Space* 13, no. 1 (February 1995): 5–34.
104 Ibid., 5.
105 *Society and Space* has played an important role in opening the field of spatial theory to competing approaches. The example set by the journal, as well as some of the criticisms presented in this chapter concerning its limitations in addressing the specificity of built form) have undoubtedly played a role in the founding of the innovative journal *Space and Culture. International Journal of Social Spaces*. This journal, founded by Canadian theorist and critic Rob Shields, shares similar theoretical ground with *Society and Space* but has been more successful in addressing space at the scale of buildings and urban space, both historically and in the present.

Chapter 7: Conclusion

Writing Spaces and the Spaces of Writing

In the case studies I have undertaken in the preceding chapters, I have explored writing and discourse as spatial practices. Each of the journals not only constructs an image of the world through the writing they publish; they are also social and institutional worlds in themselves. These practices of representation constitute diverse "spaces of knowledge" and communities of method whose readers and writers share research methods, vocabularies, theoretical sources, styles of writing (all of which are embedded with particular cultural assumptions). They also define, and are defined by, the shifting networks of cultural, educational, and political institutions, as well as metropolitan, national, and international contexts in which the participants (and objects studied) are located.

As the case studies have suggested, the social, representational, and spatial practices associated with journals play an important role in defining the boundaries of these spaces of knowledge. Each of the publications I have discussed began as part of a relatively unknown or (what their founders perceived to be) undervalued discourse. All began by constructing an oppositional relationship with an existing set of debates, methodologies, or even an entire discipline. What happened after the journals initially defined their areas of investigation varies dramatically between cases.

The way the journals and discourses examined here have changed, progressed, stagnated, fossilized or disappeared altogether, leads back to a consideration of the relationship between journals, discourse and the formation (and transformation) of fields of academic knowledge, as well as how this knowledge has helped to change education and professional practice. The "rise and fall" of discourse can be defined in many ways: in terms of the changing influence of a discourse within a scholarly community; in terms of the degree of critical reflexivity the participants possess about their techniques and agenda, and its political consequences; and (particularly in the case of the discourses examined here) in terms of the capacity of their writing to respond to the changing social and spatial practices of the built environment.

The cultural critic Cary Nelson associates what he calls the "decay" of scholarly discourse with its "normalization." He suggests that discourses become "normal" when they become "nontheoretical," a condition which he defines in the following way:

> In the wake of the poststructuralist revolution what probably most distinguishes theoretical from nontheoretical discourse is its tendency towards self-conscious and reflective, interpretive, methodological and rhetorical practices . . . when a body of theory ceases to be in crisis, when it no longer has to struggle to define its enterprise and mark its similarities and differences from other theories, when it imagines itself potentially co-extensive with the disciplines it addresses, when its assumptions come not to seem preferable but inevitable and automatic, when it is taken to be a given part of the natural world, when it can be entered into and applied almost without conscious decision, then it no longer counts as theory.[1]

The process of normalization cannot be reduced to a series of immutable and invariant causes; it is related to what Nelson calls "historical pressures" and is a complex process that varies from context to context.[2]

Although all the journals began with criticisms of existing fields as internally determined, self-enclosed, bounded conditions, some have turned into versions of what they criticized: they have become "worlds unto themselves," with secure walls around the spaces they have constructed. Others have been subject to continual change in their assumptions, languages, methodologies, objects of analysis, and participants. They are "leaky habitats" where new ideas seep in, and where disruptions are welcome. These are shaped as much by the connections they foster with "outside" worlds, as by their own debates. In other cases, ideas remain safely enclosed, and very dry.

Understanding how or why discourses change or remain fixed is a crucial step towards developing a model of interdisciplinarity that, to return to Deutsche's formulation takes account of the spatial relations between disciplines, and with other spheres outside the academy, including professional practice. All writing, academic or otherwise, constructs "spaces of knowledge": there can be no communication between writers and readers without common ideas and shared presuppositions. The issue is not whether such spaces exist, but how, for whom, and according to what terms.

In the sections that follow I do not suggest that such "change" is, in itself, a good thing. I do argue, however, that in order for scholarly research in the built environment disciplines to respond to what is happening in the world outside the academy, critical spatial theory needs to pursue forms of writing and research that are inherently interdisciplinary, because the city does not operate through discrete categeories, and has, perhaps more than at any other time, entered a "post-disciplinary" condition. On the one hand, this means developing an openness to theoretical positions and debates occurring in other disciplines in the academy. On the other, it means much more attention to the "scale politics" of scholarly research.

All the journals I have examined exhibit varying degrees of openness to debates in critical theory outside the built environment disciplines. With some notable exceptions, however, the research they have published has remained fixed at one scale of analysis: at the scale of the building, the settlement, the city, the region, or the world. Each of the discourses I have discussed has differentiated itself further within its own field through interdisciplinary combinations, while developing far fewer connections with other built environments disciplines.

As I suggest below, the journals also represent a second limitation, defined by the continuing opposition between theory and the professional practices they continue to uphold. While considerable attention has been directed towards the reflexive analysis of the academic as a professional, there has been almost no analysis of comparable depth and sophistication of the position of the practicing professional who is engaged in the "material spatial practices" of the city.[3] Yet precisely because all the discourses I have studied are produced within disciplines that span from professional practice to academic research, the theoretical knowledge they produce directly or indirectly shapes what happens to the built form of cities. The way in which these theory/practice connections have formed and changed over time is itself an important, but largely ignored area of study.

Despite these limitations, it is possible to examine the approaches I have studied here according to their different qualities as "worlds" of representation. I return to the five journals and the discourses they frame in the sections below in an effort to identify why some have become self-referential and internalized, and why others are more changeable, anti-foundational, and open-ended. I summarize some of the reasons why these different "spatial" conditions of discourse have emerged, and in doing so hope to identify possible alternative practices.

ON DRY GROUND

My discussion of these questions begins with the *IJURR* and the *JSAH* as examples of discourses that, after their initial formation, have remained relatively unchanged in their assumptions, methodologies, and forms of writing. In what follows, I consider how and why two journals with almost diametrically opposed views about the built environment ultimately define similar scholarly worlds. For most of their histories, both have operated according to predefined conceptions of historical time, elaborate systems of classification that extend from eighteenth century nails (*JSAH*) to world cities (*IJURR*), and a commitment to a "scientific" study of history or society through empirical research.

The *JSAH* and the *International Journal* represent opposite ends of the ideological spectrum. The former has seldom addressed the political economy of building and urban space. In the latter, the style and the aesthetics of built form are rarely, if ever, discussed; when they have been introduced, they appear as reflections of the economy, or ironically, are granted an independent existence as a "unique" and locally bounded force (as in the recent discussions of symbolic ecology). But because both journals are organized around large-scale forms of linear historical periodization (in the *JSAH*, through a Wolfflinian model of morphological change, and in the *IJURR*, through the progressive development of the mode of production) both become interiorized worlds with distinctive conceptions of historical time.

Though both employ linear models of periodization, their research is situated on opposite sides of the dividing line between past and present. The *JSAH* reconstructs the past and rarely examines contemporary conditions after 1945 (and how they shape representations of the past). The *International Journal* is primarily concerned with examining the contemporary city, with little consideration of historical conditions, not least those related to colonization and imperialism, which operate at an "international" scale. Each transition studied in the journal inaugurates a "new" mode of accumulation. In both cases the isolation of past from the present, and vice versa, removes consideration of their interrelationship. This conceptual and taxonomic separation contributes to the self-enclosed nature of these debates.

These two journals also construct very different networks of contributors and institutions. As such, they also differ in how they construct "international" spaces of knowledge. Yet, I would contend that for most of their histories, both have shared a fundamentally Eurocentric outlook that is expressed in different terms. Anxiety about "foreign" scholarship in the *JSAH* (which is less to do with topics than with methods and language) is one index of this Eurocentrism. Although the topics examined in the journal have expanded to include locations and histories outside of Europe and North America, those "other" places have to a great extent been understood through the methodologies, systems of classification and notions of periodization that emerged in relation to European modernity.

The *JSAH* continues to be overwhelmingly based in US academic institutions, both in terms of readership and contributors, though the recent and important "global inquiry" into the teaching of architectural history around the world suggests that this may be starting to change. It remains to be seen whether this attempt to move beyond the opposition between the "American" and the "Foreign," which has defined the journal for much of its history, has any substantive impact on its organization and direction.

The *International Journal*, though covering the most diverse geography of any of the journals in this study, has nevertheless become increasingly homogeneous in its representation of those places, so that their differences are effaced and they are ultimately represented as variations on a single global condition. Like the *JSAH*, diverse places are processed through a relatively fixed system of representation. In this case, it is clear that the journal's larger institutional connections have played a role in both disseminating its paradigm, and contributing to its homogeneity. The *International Journal* is an example of a total system, complete with its own institutional supports, conferences, books, symposia, and research foundation. The activities of Research Committee 21 and the International Sociological Association, as well as the now-extensive network of academics committed to urban political economy, means that it is possible not only to write within this paradigm, but to move within it internationally.

The *IJURR* is the only journal in this study to have published research submitted in other languages, and to present the author's argument in précis form in other languages. Language translation offers the possibility of interaction with scholarly communities outside the Anglo-American world. However, in this case, translation has diffused and consolidated the journal's paradigms, rather than disrupted them with alternate points of view. For the first three years of publication, the journal published articles in either English or French, underlining the strong connections the journal formed at the time between British and American scholars and the "French School" of urban sociology. This practice was abandoned after several years, and the journal was published in English until 1989, when it began including summaries of articles in three European languages: Spanish, French, and German, as part of its effort to become more "international." The addition of Spanish must be understood in the context of the *IJURR*'s growing base of readers and contributors in South America at the time, where Spanish and Portuguese are in wide use. Thus the journal's languages of translation followed the patterns of European colonization in South and Central America. The practice of publishing abstracts in German and Spanish lasted three years, and since 1990 they have appeared only in English and French, a more modest version of the journal's original language policy.

IJURR's experiments with translation demonstrated how the inclusion of "foreign" research, a source of concern at the *JSAH*, does not necessarily challenge the dominance of Euro-American scholarship. Rather, it may also produce the opposite result: its global diffusion.

Both journals began by defining, promoting, drawing attention to, and even leading, the discourses on US-based architectural history or international urban political economy. Both are now largely effects of these discourses. Their paradigms are securely established in the academy and their existence is not dependent upon the journals. To change the terms of these well-established discourses would require critical intervention at both textual and institutional levels, through changes in curricula, the organization of graduate education, and within the journals, in the editorial board, and/or the disciplinary background of writers.

This may be one of the reasons why Zeynep Çelik initiated the *JSAH*'s important "global inquiry" into how architectural history is taught around the world. The comparative survey implicitly recognizes that critical operations at the level of the text must be accompanied by parallel changes in the institutional contexts where knowledge is organized, produced, and disseminated. This requires a historical understanding of how such contexts are shaped by their affiliations with other sources of power. The *JSAH* is alone among the journals in this study in attempting to address these questions. Clearly, if the idea of what constitutes "architectural history" is redefined at the level of graduate and undergraduate education, the effects on subsequent published research – though gradual – would be immense.

Critical historiographies of architectural history that relate the writing of history to social forces such as colonialism, imperialism, and contemporary global capitalism are not only valuable documents of where things stand from a pedagogical point of view; they also reveal how institutions authorize some ideas while silencing others over time, and by implication, suggest possible strategies to transform them from within. Though the *JSAH* has started the first stage of this process (the micro-mapping of institutions in a global context), the second step (theorized speculation about how to act upon such knowledge once it becomes visible) is as yet unrealized, but just as crucial. Over fifty years ago the *JSAH* took an active role in leading discussions about the role of architectural history in nationally oriented models of architectural education. It now has the opportunity to do so again, this time by exploring the role of architectural history in creating a critical framework for architectural education in a global context.

STRATEGIES OF DISTURBANCE AND THEIR LIMITS

My criticisms of the *JSAH* and the *International Journal* outlined above are similar to those made of "conventional" architectural theory and criticism by the editors and contributors of *Assemblage*. The field of modernist criticism is described as a closed system of interpretation, where the architectural object is isolated in a purely "abstract and idealized realm." The critic enters into a "cycle of affirmation" that maintains rigidly defined disciplinary boundaries, dominant institutions, and "disengaged" modes of practice. From its inception the journal emphasized the importance of examining not only what was said, but also how it was said, and the "constitutive" role of writing in producing the object of analysis. Despite the journal's practice of "criticism through representations," by the time it ceased publication *Assemblage* had become as "self-affirming" as the critical writing it sought to challenge. How could this happen?

As I have suggested in my case study, part of the answer resides in the way the journal's critical program was related to architectural culture. The idea of dismantling the "apparatus" of modernist architectural thought (or even the more modest goal of "disturbing" it) is carried out at the level of representational practices, and even here, primarily at the level of the text. The journal can, therefore, be criticized for the narrow terms on which its deconstructive agenda was formulated. It did not, for example, examine the other "institutions" of architectural culture (such as the profession, education, or other levels of media practice) and their role in sustaining and producing architectural thought. Indeed, when viewed retrospectively, the institutional history of *Assemblage* looks remarkably conventional. It began, like the *International Journal*, as a project of a small group of academics based, in this case, in elite institutions on the East Coast of the United States. Yet *Assemblage* remained the project of a small group of academics (as the editors say in the closing issues, it published the work of over 100 scholars – a small figure when compared with, for example, *Society and Space* which has published at least twice that many over the same period).

Despite its claims to being a disruptive force, *Assemblage* positioned itself from the start as the continuation of a debate on architectural theory launched by *Oppositions*. Though many structuralist ideas are criticized in the journal, they nevertheless form the intellectual foundations of the debates in *Assemblage*. If it had not ceased publication when it did, *Assemblage* may well have been about to make the 1960s and "late modernism" the subject of the same form of radical canon revision its writers had previously directed towards the eminent figures of high modernism.[4] Indeed, one of the controversies in *Assemblage* concerned the perception that critics associated with the journal were positioned in a "generational" relationship with the senior figures involved in *Oppositions*. The flare-up demonstrates again that while there may be a direct connection between the rise of paradigms and the birth of journals, the end of a journal does not necessarily foretell the demise of a paradigm. Indeed, the end of *Assemblage* may instead have marked the wider institutionalization of the positions it sought to promote.

The situation is not unlike the ending of *Oppositions*, which ceased in part because the editors had become too busy and successful to continue the labor-intensive task of producing the journal.[5] Both *Assemblage* and *Oppositions* were also conceived as "projects" with beginning and end points, rather than as institutions that would evolve over time into something else. Their goals were to bring a certain point of view to their discipline. Once this had been achieved, the journals ceased. Yet, as I have argued from the beginning, this transformation cannot be viewed purely on the level of ideas. In obtaining institutional recognition for the paradigms they represented, both *Assemblage* and *Oppositions* participated in a wide range of other processes at the same time.

Assemblage was more than an intellectual project concerned with disrupting the fixed assumptions and practices of modernist criticism. It was also an active participant in the creation of intellectual territories: it continued to develop the space for US-based architectural theory that was opened up by *Oppositions* and a group of other smaller institutionally based publications.

Assemblage therefore operated in the contradictory space between two agendas: the first was conservative, and is defined by an acceptance of the academic system as it stands, adherence to the normative practices of professional self-definition, and the manipulation of knowledge as cultural capital. The second directly contradicted the first: the stated editorial program of the journal constructed "architecture" as an institution to be disrupted, and disturbed, and sought to reveal the complicity of the critic in the construction of the object analyzed. The tension between these two agendas – the first accepting the existing configuration of the academic hierarchy, and the second dismantling it at the level of textual practice – was never resolved in the journal, and perhaps was never intended to be.

LEAKY HABITATS

If *Assemblage*, the *JSAH*, and the *IJURR* all provide insights into some of the ways in which new intellectual territories are created and then become fixed, internalized, and self-referential, both the *TDSR* and *Society and Space* seem to suggest alternative possibilities. Though I want to resist the temptation to conclude this book by presenting them as the "solutions" to the issues I have identified above, both are strikingly different in their capacity to change and connect with issues that exist in the larger social world beyond the academy. Both began, like the other journals studied here, as the projects of a small group of academics, and both were responding to perceived deficiencies in their respective disciplines. Yet both have undergone a series of major changes that mark considerable departures from where they started. The first decade of publication in the *TDSR* was dominated by the arguments of the "ethnographic pastoral" which located "tradition" in an imaginary space that was isolated from the influences of large-scale social and historical forces. Writing on tradition in the journal was initially constructed through a series of dichotomies that opposed tradition to modernity, the past to the present, pre-industrial to post-industrial, first world to third. In as much as the terms of the traditional environments were defined through opposition with their dominant "first world" counterparts, they remained subordinate projections of the conditions they were defined against.

What permits the *TDSR* to move beyond these oppositions? The critical shift in the journal occurs when the term "tradition" itself is no longer understood as a received category, as something that exists naturally, outside cultural determination, but is in fact a social and historical construction, with an intellectual history closely intertwined with the emergence of industrial capitalism. Once tradition is "de-essentialized," it is no longer possible to understand it as something that can be discovered in exotic locations, and placed within given structures of classification (which are themselves increasingly understood as cultural artifacts). Thus tradition in the *TDSR* has moved from being a received category, to one that is produced in multiple ways, through the discourses of colonial power to the operation of a global tourist economy.

My comments suggest that the anti-idealist, anti-foundational orientation of post-structuralism that has become influential throughout the Anglo-American academy has had an influence on the journal. Yet, as the example of *Assemblage* suggests, the deconstruction of idealist categories can quickly devolve into a highly specialized, self-referential debate. One of the interesting differences between *Assemblage* and the *TDSR* concerns their respective relationship to academic discourses and disciplines (and in a broader sense) to the project of deconstruction. Though the *TDSR* was launched by forming a critique of conventional architectural history and theory, its response was to move "outside" that space, rather than deconstruct it from within. This has allowed the journal to form connections with other disciplines largely beyond the constraints of architectural culture. This is particularly noticeable in its policy of inviting regular contributions from scholars in disciplines relevant to its concerns – including anthropology, sociology, political science, Islamic studies, and geography.

The contrasting positions *Assemblage* and the *TDSR* define in relation to architectural culture are manifested in their practices of interdisciplinarity. Both draw on a wide range of theoretical debates from outside the built environment disciplines. Yet they do so in very different ways: in *Assemblage*, those who regard themselves as being part of the discipline of architectural theory use "borrowed materials" to transform it from within. As I have suggested, *Assemblage* was ultimately concerned with canon revision, where seminal works by "masters" such as Le Corbusier are re-examined in the light of contemporary critical theory. This can lead to profound alterations in the way their work is understood, but it does not fundamentally alter what is included in the canon; rather, it changes the terms through which it is understood. The *TDSR* is not concerned with transforming the canon of architectural theory "from within." Instead, the journal has examined the spaces and cultures in the vast domain of ideas excluded from this space.

Although the *TDSR* has a smaller circulation than *Assemblage* had, as a "little journal" it attracts a much broader range of contributions, both in terms of the location of topics and the nations and institutions the contributors are from. As I have suggested above, this is partly to do with the fact that "tradition" and even "traditional dwellings and settlements" are established areas of research not only in vernacular architectural studies, but in cultural anthropology, ethnography, archaelogy, and area studies. As a result, the journal and the Association have included academics from these fields from the start. This has certainly transformed the terms of debate in a way that has not occurred at *Assemblage*, where the object of analysis is architecture, including its discourses and professional products. While *Assemblage* transcoded critical paradigms from other disciplines, the "borrowing" of ideas was one directional: architectural theorists transcoded theoretical systems from other disciplines. The interdisciplinarity of the *TDSR* involves direct participation by scholars from a wide range of disciplines that share "tradition" and its contestation as an object of analysis. Their viewpoints, co-ordinated by the editors, and supplemented by a diverse editorial board, have stretched the intellectual and geographic boundaries of the journal.

THE POLITICS OF LOCATION

Society and Space has undergone more intellectual shifts than any of the other journals in this study. It began as a response to the opposition between the Marxist and "culturalist" approaches in the geography, one which stressed the influence of political economy in shaping space, and the other, ontological experience and perception. Yet the attempt to develop a unitary system that would bring these disparate interpretations together proved impossible to manage, and the journal splintered in two directions: the first is concerned with a wide range of Marxist-based research, particularly on issues connected to the social and spatial restructuring of global capitalism; the second, exploring embodied experience, the politics of position, and reflexive forms of knowledge, is further divided into numerous specializations, according to the identity of the critic, and the position from which the writing is produced.

It is perhaps an example of "unfixed" discourse that the founders of *Assemblage* might appreciate. Part of the reason for the highly differentiated and shifting perspectives offered by the journal can undoubtedly be traced to its editorial policy, which has involved inviting guest editors who hold diverse and often contradictory positions. The editorials in *Society and Space* are the most substantial of any in this study, and can be read as an ongoing dialogue about the impact and relevance of various theories on the analysis of space. The journal has also supported the most sustained and varied investigation into the politics of position of any of the journals. This has moved from criticisms of modernist objectivity, through debates about located scholarship, to hybrid positions that do not necessarily privilege the partial and located over the objective and general, but see them as "strategies" that can be mobilized, as required, in different situations.

In all the discussion about the potential and limitations of different theoretical positions, two critical points emerge. First, despite the enormous breadth of theory in the journal, the conception of physical space has remained largely unchanged, and rarely descends to the scale of individual buildings. Indeed, as the journal has become increasingly concerned with the politics of position and self-reflexivity, attention has shifted from the material "spatial practices" associated with the physical environments of cities, to imaginary "spaces of knowledge," their boundaries, foundations, and the viewpoints and positions they enable. Though this writing can sometimes retreat into narcissistic self-reference, it also considers the institutional contexts where writing is produced. This opens the history of the discipline and how it has been affected by larger historical forces (such as the state, the economy, and the changing structure of the academy itself), to analysis..

As an outsider to geography, I have found the social and cultural interpretations presented in *Society and Space* fascinating. At the same time, however, I have found it difficult to understand the role geographers play in the "production of space" in cities and urban regions. The history of the instrumental relationship between mapping and the organization of state power, through, for example, the surveillance operations of an expanding "military industrial complex," or more recently, through increasingly widespread "civilian" and military uses of global positioning systems, has not been fully examined as yet. This is ironic because the journal has published articles devoted to the question of "workplace ethics," and theoretical discussions of workplace ethnography.[6] Yet it has not connected these debates in any convincing way to geography as a field of professional knowledge. If the journal does not have an explicit critical relation to the professionalized practice of geography, and has also backed away from the analysis of physical space, what does this say about the status of critical theory in geography (where most of its contributors and subscribers are located)?

THEORY AND PRACTICE

The question is an important one because it leads back to the larger relationship between theory and professional practice that all these journals share. Given that each is based in a discipline that spans from professional training and practice to scholarly research, the question of how these critical debates relate to the world of the built environment professional seems crucial to ask. Where and how are the day-to-day (professional, regulatory, public policy) practices associated with the production of the built environment related to these discourses? All the journals reveal a growing awareness of the academic as a professional whose activities are both enabled and constrained by disciplinary convention. The self-conscious theorization of the writer as a "located" subject, and the reflexive critique of various disciplines and their histories consider the theory and practice of scholarly production. Everything from how the writer's identity is acknowledged or effaced in the writing, to the influence of gossip and "corridor talk" on research and careers is theorized and explored in detail.

These arguments tell us about the politics of professional identity in the academy, but reveal little about the professional identity of practicing architects, preservationists, planners, or geographers. The realms of material spatial practice in the city are an "absent presence" in these discourses. It is ironic, for example, that both *Assemblage* and *Society and Space* go to great lengths to analyze how the critic "constructs" the object of analysis s/he claims to merely describe, while the material, bureaucratic, regulatory, financial, and media practices (among others) involved in the construction of physical space are not discussed. What would happen, for example, if the writers at *Assemblage* employed the methods of the "post-occupancy" study to determine whether the rhizomatic claims of Deleuzian "blob" architecture produced any of its putative effects? Such analyses could also consider whether the so-called "Deleuzian moment" is manifested (or not) in the professional production of such buildings. Do the architects who seek the "proliferation of difference" through formal production invest their workplace practices with the same level of political analysis and transformative potential? This reflexive feedback loop, which would connect the claims of theory to the physical production that builds upon its foundations, would undoubtedly alter the assumptions of both spheres of activity.

Questions of "material spatial practice" are also deferred in the *TDSR*. Like the other journals in this study, it has also paid increasingly close attention to how critics construct their object of analyses. As I have suggested, this has led to a reformulation of the category of tradition in the journal. But in the shift from an idealist conception of tradition to one that makes its "social construction" the subject of research, there is arguably less concern with the physical production of built landscapes and the "traditions" of building. The narratives of the "ethnographic pastoral" were deeply concerned with how "traditional" communities "handed down" shared values through the process of construction. There is no comparable debate as yet that relates the anti-idealist version of tradition to the production of buildings by ordinary people. The journal has most recently been concerned with the appropriation of tradition by the commercial forces of global capitalism. Though there is attention to the practices of production and consumption, it is largely in relation to the spaces of "manufactured," postindustrial tradition. The question of how "non-professionals" construct alternative social worlds to those of hegemonic global capitalism by marshaling resources, evading or working within regulatory controls, creating alternative spaces of citizenship, remains a valid, if currently overlooked, area in the journal.

It is ironic that the two most inflexible journals from the standpoint of the critical positions they represent also articulate the most explicit, if opposed, relationships between theory and practice. The *JSAH*'s millennium issue suggests that architectural history is drifting away from a meaningful relationship with professional practice and towards an agenda that is determined largely by what is going on elsewhere in the academy. As I noted in my case study, while this may be true in other parts of the academy, it is not yet the case at the *JSAH*, where the predominant representation of the architect is that of the self-actualizing center of the building process, which is commanded from a position of autonomy. This image of professional practice continues to be one of the dominant mythologies used to market architectural services, and maintain architecture's fragile "monopoly of expertise" in a highly competitive arena for professional services. It thus remains closely, if uncritically, linked to the world of practice. The histories of architects and their work in the *JSAH* can be read as allegories of professional identity, and as such they constitute part of the staging ground where the "architect" is discursively produced and transmitted.

By contrast, the *International Journal* adopts a "structuralist" representation of the professional practitioner whose every action is determined by the capitalist mode of production. The planning profession is "dehumanized" and understood as part of the "state apparatus" which distributes social and spatial resources unequally in society. Planning is thus concerned primarily with either the distribution of space and the services and scarce resources they contain, or the zoning of space to enable the relations of production (and hence relations of domination and subordination) to function more smoothly. Changes in planning ideology reflect changes in processes of capitalist accumulation. The ideology of the planner is tied to the characteristics of the mode of production, as in "Fordist" or "post-Fordist" urban planning. Although planners engage in design, the aesthetics of urban planning is generally not examined. Nor is the role of personality or individual agency considered, even though some of the most influential planners in the United States, such as Robert Moses, were notorious for the careful manipulation of their public personas.

While providing a powerful critique of the planning profession as an instrument of capitalism, the journal does not propose alternative strategies for planners who work within the profession, but are opposed to its structural position within capitalism. The Marxist academic provides an analysis of the changing structure of capitalist oppression, but does not theorize how these insights might be used to inform a model of professional counter-practice. This has not always been the case. For a brief period when the *IJURR* began, the journal attempted to foster contact between planners, scholars and activist organizations who shared a similar "radical" consciousness. This is best illustrated by the Praxis section in the journal (published between 1977 and 1987), which contained reports about emerging protest movements, articles by activists and other non-academics concerned with the politics of the built environment. Writers such as Manuel Castells argued strongly in Praxis against the separation of academics from political movements outside the academy. Indeed, the thrust of the urban social movement discourse was based on the Gramscian model of the organic intellectual: researchers hoped to use the resources of the academy to develop forms of knowledge and practice that could be passed on to non-academic activists leading protest movements in the city. However, the withdrawal of state provision of collective consumption brought an end to attempts by the journal to foster links between political movements outside the academy. Indeed, an editorial statement published in the *IJURR* in 1998 to mark the change of editors underscored the journal's commitment to a purely analytic position in relation to social change.

My discussion of the relationship between theory and practice suggests that there has been a move away from engagement with the realm of professional practice across the built environment disciplines over the period I have studied. Attempts have been made to explain this shift in the journals I have discussed. In the *JSAH*, the reluctance on the part of historians, theorists and critics to find ways to engage with what is going on in the professional world, is presumed to have its origins in what are represented as the increasingly aimless distractions of interdisciplinary exchanges with other disciplines.

Yet I would suggest that if there is a fault in the model of interdisciplinarity that has developed until now, it is rooted in the reluctance of the "space" disciplines to communicate with each other, and hence reinforce the scale politics of spatial analysis that continues to divide the field as whole. If anything has emerged from the diverse analyses of the contemporary metropolis presented in the journals I have studied here, it is that the spatial categories that continue to separate the academic disciplines into neat compartments are rapidly dissolving in the worlds of material spatial practice. The dissolution begins with the city itself. The transformations in the world economy, the changing cultural demographies of large cities, the compression of time and space between national cultures, the juxtaposition of national cultures within cities, have not only altered the character of cities, they have also thrown into question the idea of the city as a self-enclosed object with its own "internal" economy and culture. The city now stretches across nations, just as migration and diasporic cultures extend nations beyond their geographical territories. The production of buildings, both in terms of the organization of professional knowledge, and in terms of the production of its component parts, is increasingly decentered and "transnational." Architectural practices are increasingly forming working relationships with advertising agencies, marketing consultants, and media strategies in a new form of "professional interdisciplinarity" geared towards developing architecture as an integrated part of product "theming." The very fact that these changes – which in many ways intensify or reactivate conditions associated with imperialist expansion – are sometimes regarded as "new," restates the urgent need to engage history with issues in contemporary practice.

If these examples suggest that the categories of "world," "territory," "nation," "city," "settlement," "architecture," "room," and "body" are increasingly difficult to separate, they nevertheless occur when the idea of the architect as a singular author is perhaps more popular and widespread than at any other time. The point here is that the "old" categories have not disappeared; they remain but are being mobilized in fundamentally new and sometimes contradictory relationships with each other. We will not even recognize these contradictions, let alone begin to address the issues they raise, until disciplinary categories are "opened up" to different scales and methods of analysis. This is not simply a matter of combining existing blocks of knowledge in "new" ways.

Rather, the very way the disciplines are constituted as such needs to be reconsidered, even as connections with other spheres of knowledge outside the academy are formed. Although I have sometimes been very critical of the discourses I have examined, they remain invaluable attempts to construct "worlds of representation" that begin to address the relational and interdependent character of spaces in the twenty-first century metropolis.

NOTES

1   Cary Nelson, *Manifesto of a Tenured Radical* (New York and London: New York University Press: 1997), 17.
2   Ibid.
3   I borrow this term from Henri Lefebvre, who used it to describe social practices in the city explicitly concerned with the production of buildings and urban space. See Henri Lefebvre, *The Production of Space*, trans. D. Nicholson Smith (Oxford: Basil Blackwell, 1991).
4   See, for example, *Assemblage* 39 (August 1999), which contains articles on Robert Smithson's architectural criticism, as well as contributions about Carl Andre and Jackson Pollack.
5   Joan Ockman, "Resurrecting the Avant Garde. The History and Program of *Oppositions*," in Beatriz Colomina (ed.), *Architectureproduction* (New York: Princeton Architectural Press, 1988), 198.
6   See, for example, the interesting discussion of the implications of writings of Bruno Latour for studies of the production of scientific research, by Nigel Thrift, Felix Driver and David Livingstone in "The Geography of Truth," in *Society and Space* 13 (1995): 1–4.

Selected Bibliography

BOOKS

Abbot, Andrew D. *The System of Professions: An Essay on the Expert Division of Labour.* Chicago: University of Chicago Press, 1988.

Abu-Lughod, Janet. *Cairo: 1001 Years of City Victorious.* Princeton, NJ: Princeton University Press, 1971.

Aglietta, M. *A Theory of Regulation.* London: Verso, 1979.

Altbach, P. (ed.). *Comparative Perspectives on the Academic Profession.* London and New York: Praeger, 1977.

——. *Higher Education in American Society.* Buffalo, NY: Prometheus Books, 1981.

——. *Higher Education in Perspective: A Survey and Bibliography.* London and New York: Mansell Publishing, 1985.

——. *The Knowledge Context: Comparative Perspectives on the Distribution of Knowledge.* Albany, NY: SUNY Press, 1987.

Anderson, Benedict. *Imagined Communities. Reflections on the Origin and Spread of Nationalism.* London and New York: Verso, 1991.

Anderson, Perry. *Considerations on Western Marxism.* London: New Left Books, 1976.

Apple, M. W. *Cultural and Economic Reproduction in Education: Essays on Class Ideology and the State.* London and Boston: Routledge and Kegan Paul, 1982.

——. *Education and Power.* Boston: Routledge and Kegan Paul, 1982.

Appadurai, Arjun. *Modernity at Large. Cultural Dimensions of Globalization.* Minneapolis: University of Minnesota Press, 1998.

Arac, Jonathan and Barbara Johnson (eds). *The Consequences of Theory.* Baltimore: Johns Hopkins University Press, 1991.

Aronowitz, S. *Postmodern Education: Politics, Culture, and Social Criticism.* Minneapolis: University of Minnesota Press, 1991.

Attridge, Derrick, Geoffrey Bennington, and Robert Young (eds). *Poststructuralism and the Question of History.* Cambridge: Cambridge University Press, 1987.

Barker, Francis, Peter Hulme, and Margaret Iverson (eds). *Colonial Discourse/ Postcolonial Theory.* New York: Manchester University Press, 1994.
Basu, Asoke. *Culture, Politics and Critical Academics.* Meerut, India: Archana, 1981.
Baudrillard, Jean. *Simulacra and Simulation.* Ann Arbor: University of Michigan Press, 1994.
Bauman, Zygmunt. *Legislators and Interpreters: On Modernity, Postmodernity and Intellectuals.* Cambridge: Polity Press, 1987.
Becher, Tony. *British Higher Education.* London and Boston: Unwin & Allen, 1987.
——. *Academic Tribes and Territories. Intellectual Enquiry and the Cultures of Disciplines.* New York: Taylor and Francis, 1989.
——. *Process and Structure in Higher Education.* London and New York: Routledge, 1991.
Bell, Daniel. *The Coming of the Postindustrial Society: A Venture in Social Forecasting.* New York: Basic Books, 1973.
Bell, David and Gill Valentine. *Mapping Desire. Geographies of Sexualities.* London and New York: Routledge, 1995.
Benda, Julian. *The Treason of the Intellectuals.* New York: Norton, 1956.
Benhabib, Seyla. *Situating the Self. Gender, Community and Postmodernism in Contemporary Ethics.* London and New York: Routledge, 1992.
Bhabha, Homi (ed.). *Nation and Narration.* London and New York: Routledge, 1990.
——. *The Location of Theory.* London and New York: Routledge, 1994.
Bledstein, Burton, J. *The Culture of Professionalism: The Middle Class and the Development of Higher Education in America.* New York: Norton, 1976.
Bourdier, Jean-Paul and Nezar AlSayyad (eds). *Dwellings, Settlements and Traditions. Cross-cultural Perspectives.* New York and London: University Press of America, 1989.
Bourdieu, Pierre. *Homo Academicus.* Trans. Peter Collier. Stanford: University of California Press, 1984.
——. *Outline of a Theory of Practice.* Cambridge: Cambridge University Press, 1991.
——. *Language and Symbolic Power.* Trans. by Gino Raymond and Matthew Adamson. Cambridge, MA: Harvard University Press, 1994.
——, Jean Claude Passeron, and Monique de St Martin. *Academic Discourse. Linguistic Understanding and Professorial Power.* Trans. Richard Teese. Stanford: Stanford University Press, 1965.
Bove, Paul. *Mastering Discourse. The Politics of Intellectual Culture.* Durham and London: Duke University Press, 1992.
Braudel, Fernand. *Civilization and Capitalism, 15th–18th Century. Vol. III. The Perspective of the World.* Trans. Sian Reynolds. London: Fontana Press, 1984.

Brown, Clara D. and Lynn S. Smith. *Serials: Past, Present and Future.* Birmingham, AL: Ebsco, 1980.

Cameron, Deborah and Thomas A. Markus. *The Words Between the Spaces.* New York and London: Routledge, 2002.

Caputo, John and Mark Yount. *Foucault and the Critique of Institutions.* University Park, PA: Pennsylvania State University Press, 1986.

Carapetian, Michael, Jonathan Moorehouse, and Leena Ahtola-Moorehouse. *Helsinki Jugendstil Architecture 1895–1915.* Helsinki: Otava Publishing Co., 1987.

Castells, M. *The Urban Question.* London: Edward Arnold, 1977.

——. *City Class and Power.* London and Basingstoke: Macmillan, 1987.

——. *The City and the Grassroots.* Berkeley: University of California Press, 1983.

——. *The Informational City.* Oxford: Basil Blackwell, 1989.

——. *The Rise of the Network Society.* Oxford and Maldon, MA: Blackwell Publishers, 2000.

de Certeau, Michel. *The Practice of Everyday Life.* Berkeley: University of California Press, 1984.

——. *Heterologies. Discourses on the Other.* Minneapolis: University of Minnesota Press, 1989.

Cheah, Pheng and Bruce Robbins. *Cosmopolitics. Thinking and Feeling Beyond the Nation.* Minneapolis: University of Minnesota Press, 1998.

Chomsky, Noam. *Problems of Knowledge and Freedom.* New York: Pantheon Books, 1971.

Chrisman, Laura and Patrick Williams. *Colonial Discourse and Post-Colonial Theory.* New York: Columbia University Press, 1994.

Clifford, James and George Marcus (eds). *Writing Culture. The Poetics and Politics of Ethnography.* Berkeley and London: University of California Press, 1986.

Cohen, Sande. *Academia and the Luster of Capital.* Minneapolis: University of Minnesota Press, 1993.

Colomina, Beatriz (ed.). *Sexuality and Space.* New York: Princeton Architectural Press, 1992.

—— (ed.). *Architecture Reproduction.* New York: Princeton Architectural Press, 1988.

Coward, Rosalind and John Ellis. *Language and Materialism: Developments in Semiology and the Theory of the Subject.* London: Routledge and Kegan Paul, 1977.

Cuff, Dana. *Architecture: The Story of Practice.* Cambridge, MA: The MIT Press, 1991.

Culler, Jonathan. *The Pursuit of Signs: Semiotics, Literature and Deconstruction.* Ithaca, NY: Cornell University Press, 1981.

——. *On Deconstruction. Theory and Criticism after Structuralism.* London: Routledge and Kegan Paul, 1985.

Dear, M. and A. Scott (eds). *Urbanization and Urban Planning in Capitalist Society.* London and New York: Methuen, 1981.
Debray, Regis. *Teachers, Writers, Celebrities: The Intellectuals of Modern France.* London: New Left Books, 1981.
Deleuze, Gilles and Felix Guatarri. *A Thousand Plateaus.* Trans. Brian Massumi. Minneapolis: University of Minnesota Press, 1987.
Derber, Charles. *Professionals as Workers: Mental Labour in Advanced Capitalism.* Cambridge, MA: G. K. Hall and Co., 1982.
Derrida, Jacques. *Positions.* (Trans. Alan Bass). Chicago: University of Chicago Press, 1981.
Deutsche, Rosalyn. *Evictions. Art and Spatial Politics.* Cambridge, MA: MIT Press, 1996.
Dingwall, Robert and Philip Lewis (eds). *The Sociology of the Professions. Lawyers, Doctors and Others.* New York: St Martin's Press, 1983.
Dreyfus, Herbert L. and Paul Rabinow. *Michel Foucault. Beyond Structuralism and Hermeneutics.* Chicago: University of Chicago Press, 1983.
Duncan, James. *The City as Text. The Politics of Landscape Interpretation in the Kandyan Kingdom.* Cambridge: Cambridge University Press, 1990.
—— and J. Agnew (eds). *The Power of Place: Bringing Together Geographical and Sociological Imaginations.* Winchester: Unwin Hyman, 1989.
—— and David Ley (eds). *Place/Culture/Representation.* London and New York: Routledge, 1983.
Duncombe, Stephen. *Notes from the Underground. Zines and the Politics of Alternative Culture.* London and New York: Verso, 1997.
Eagleton, Terry. *Literary Theory: An Introduction.* Oxford: Basil Blackwell, 1983.
——. *Marxism and Literary Criticism.* London: Methuen, 1976.
Edwards, R. *Contested Terrain: The Transformation of the Workplace in the 20th Century.* New York: Basic Books, 1980.
Eyerman, R., L. G. Svenson, and T. Sodergvist. *Intellectuals, Universities and the State in Western Societies.* Berkeley and London: University of California Press, 1987.
Fabian, Johannes. *Time and the Other. How Anthropology Makes its Object.* New York: Columbia University Press, 1983.
Fainstein, S., N. Fainstein, R. C. Hill, D. R. Judd, and M. P. Smith. *Restructuring the City.* New York: Longman, 1983.
Feagin, J. R. and M. P. Smith (eds). *The Capitalist City: Global Restructuring and Community Politics.* Oxford: Basil Blackwell, 1987.
Fish, Stanley. *There's No Such Thing as Free Speech.* New York and Oxford: Oxford University Press, 1994.
——. *Professional Correctness. Literary Studies and Political Change.* Oxford: Clarendon Press, 1995.

Forbes, D. and P. Rimmer (eds). *The Geographical Transfer of Value.* Canberra: The Australian National University Research School of Pacific Studies, Human Geography Monograph 16, 1984.

Foucault, Michel. *The Archeology of Knowledge.* Trans. A. M. Sheridan. New York: Pantheon Books, 1972.

——. *Order of Things. An Archaeology of the Human Sciences.* Ed. R. D. Laing. New York: Vintage Books, 1973.

——. *Power/Knowledge: Selected Interviews and Other Writings 1972–1977.* Ed. Gordon Campbell. New York: Pantheon, 1977.

——. *Discipline and Punish: The Birth of the Prison.* Trans. Alan Sheridan. New York: Vintage/Random House, 1979.

Fraser, Nancy. *Unruly Practices.* Minneapolis: University of Minnesota Press, 1989.

Freidson, Eliot. *Professional Powers: A Study of the Institutionalization of Formal Knowledge.* Chicago: University of Chicago Press, 1986.

Friedlander, Saul (ed.). *Probing the Limits of Representation.* Cambridge, MA: Harvard University Press, 1992.

Gale, Stephen and Gunnar Olsson (eds). *Philosophy in Geography.* Dordrecht: D. Reidel Publishing Co., 1974.

Gallop, Jane. *Around 1981. Academic Feminist Literary Theory.* New York: Chapman Hall Inc., 1992.

Gates, Henry Louis Jr. *The Signifying Monkey. A Theory of African American Literary Criticism.* New York and Oxford: Oxford University Press, 1988.

—— (ed.). *Race, Writing, and Difference.* Chicago: University of Chicago Press, 1987.

Geertz, Clifford. *Local Knowledge. Further Essays in Interpretive Anthropology.* New York: Basic Books, 1983.

Genette, Gerard. *Narrative Discourse. An Essay in Method.* Trans. Jane E. Lewin. Ithaca, NY: Cornell University Press, 1980.

Gershuny, Jonathan and Ian Miles. *The New Service Economy: The Transformation of Employment in Industrial Societies.* New York: Praeger, 1983.

Giddens, Anthony. *Central Problems in Social Theory: Action Structure and Contradiction in Social Analysis.* Macmillan: London, 1979.

——. *The Class Structure of Advanced Societies.* 2nd ed. London: Hutchinson, 1981.

—— and Anthony Held (eds). *Classes, Power and Conflict: Classical and Contemporary Debates.* Berkeley: University of California Press, 1982.

Gilbert, James. *Writers and Partisans: A History of Literary Radicalism in America.* New York: John Wiley and Sons, 1968.

Giroux, Henry. *Ideology, Culture and the Process of Schooling.* Philadelphia, PA: Temple University Press, 1981.

——. *Teachers as Intellectuals: Toward a Critical Pedagogy of Learning.* Granby, MA: Bergin and Garvey, 1988.

——. *Border Crossings: Cultural Politics and the Politics of Education*. New York: Routledge, 1992.
Goldberg, David Theo. *Racist Culture. Philosophy and the Politics of Meaning*. Oxford and Cambridge, MA: Blackwell, 1993.
Gombrich, Ernst H. *Norm and Form. Studies in the Art of the Renaissance*. London and New York: Phaidon, 1971.
Gordon, Avery F. and Christopher Newfield (eds). *Mapping Multiculturalism*. Minneapolis and London: University of Minnesota Press, 1996.
Gottdiener, M. *The Social Production of Urban Space*. Austin, TX: University of Texas Press, 1985.
——. *The Theming of America*. Boulder, CO: Westview Press, 2001.
Gouldner, Alvin. *The Future of Intellectuals and the Rise of the New Class: A Frame of Reference, Theses, Conjectures, Arguments, and an Historical Perspective on the Role of Intellectuals and Intelligentsia in the International Class Contest of the Modern Era*. New York: Oxford University Press, 1979.
Grafton, Anthony. *The Footnote. A Curious History*. Cambridge, MA: Harvard University Press, 1997.
Graham, Stephen and Simon Marvin. *Splintering Urbanism*. London and New York: Routledge, 2001.
Gregory, Derek. *Ideology, Science and Human Geography.* London: Hutchinson, 1978.
—— and John Urry (eds). *Social Relations and Spatial Structures*. London: Macmillan, 1985.
Guha, Ranajit and Gayatri Spivak (eds). *Selected Subaltern Studies*. New York and Oxford: Oxford University Press, 1988.
Gutman, Robert. *Architectural Practice: A Critical View*. New York: Princeton Architectural Press, 1988.
Haferkamp, H. and N. Smelser (eds). *Social Change and Modernity.* Berkeley: University of California Press, 1991.
Hardt, Michael. *Gilles Deleuze, An Apprenticeship in Philosophy*. Minneapolis: University of Minnesota Press, 1993.
Harloe, Michael (ed.). *Captive Cities: Studies in the Political Economy of Cities*. London and New York: Wiley, 1977.
Harvey, David. *Social Justice and the City.* London: Edward Arnold, 1973.
——. *The Urban Experience*. Oxford: Basil Blackwell, 1989.
——. *The Condition of Postmodernity. An Inquiry into the Origins of Cultural Change*. Cambridge, MA and Oxford: Blackwell, 1989.
Henderson, J. and Manuel Castells (eds). *Global Restructuring and Territorial Development*. London: Sage, 1987.
Heynen, Hilde. *Architecture and Modernity*. Cambridge, MA: The MIT Press, 1999.

Hoagland, Alison K. *Buildings of Alaska.* New York and Oxford: Oxford University Press, 1993.

Hoffman, Lily M. *The Politics of Knowledge: Activist Movements in Medicine and Planning.* Albany, NY: SUNY Press, 1989.

Holmes, Paul. *Professionalization and Social Change.* Keele: Keele University Press, 1973.

Jackson, Peter. *Maps of Meaning: An Introduction to Cultural Geography.* London and Winchester, MA: Unwin Hyman, 1989.

Jacoby, Russell. *The Last Intellectuals. American Culture in the Age of Academe.* New York: Basic Books, 1987.

Jameson, Frederic. *The Political Unconscious. Narrative as a Socially Symbolic Act.* London: Methuen, 1981.

——. *Late Marxism.* London and New York: Verso, 1990.

——. *Postmodernism or the Cultural Logic of Late Capitalism.* Durham, NC: Duke University Press, 1991.

——. *The Seeds of Time.* New York: Columbia University Press, 1994.

Johnson, Terrence J. *Professions and Power.* London: Macmillan, 1972.

Johnston, R. J. (ed.). *The Future of Geography.* London and New York: Methuen, 1985.

——. *Geographies and Geographers: Anglo-American Human Geography Since 1945.* London: Wiley, 1996.

King, A. D. *Colonial Urban Development. Culture, Social Power and Environment.* London: Routledge and Kegan Paul, 1976.

——. *Urbanism, Colonialism and the World-Economy. Cultural and Spatial Foundations of the World Urban System.* London and New York: Routledge, 1990.

—— (ed.). *Culture, Globalization and the World-System.* London: Macmillan, 1991.

—— (ed.). *Re-Presenting the City. Ethnicity, Capital and Culture in the 21st-Century Metropolis.* London and New York: Macmillan and New York University Press, 1996.

Knox, Paul and Peter J. Taylor (eds). *World Cities in a World System.* Cambridge: Cambridge University Press, 1995.

Kuhn, Thomas. *The Structure of Scientific Revolutions.* Chicago: University of Chicago Press, 1970.

Kumar, Amitava (ed.). *Poetics/Politics: Radical Aesthetics for the Classroom.* New York: St Martin's Press, 1999.

Laclau, Ernesto. *Hegemony and Socialist Strategy: Towards a Radical Democratic Politics.* London: Verso, 1985.

—— and Chantal Mouffe. *Capitalist Hegemony and Socialist Strategy: Towards a Radical Democratic Politics.* London: Verso, 1985.

Landry, Donn and Gerald Maclean. *The Spivak Reader.* New York and London: Routledge, 1996.

Larson, M. S. *The Rise of Professionalism.* Berkeley: University of California Press, 1977.

Lash, Scott and John Urry. *The End of Organized Capitalism.* Cambridge: Polity Press, 1987.

Leach, Neil. *Rethinking Architecture.* London and New York: Routledge, 1996.

Lebas, Elizabeth. "Introduction" in Michael Harloe (ed.), *Captive Cities: Studies in the Political Economy of Cities.* London and New York: Wiley, 1977.

Lefebvre, Henri. *The Production of Space.* Trans. D. Nicholson Smith. Oxford: Basil Blackwell, 1991.

Ley, David and Marwyn S. Samuels (eds). *Humanistic Geography. Prospects and Problems.* Chicago: Maaroufa Press, 1978.

Lipietz, A. *Mirages and Miracles: The Crisis of Global Fordism.* London: Verso, 1987.

Logan, J. R. and M. Molotch. *Urban Fortunes: Making Place in the City.* Berkeley: University of California Press, 1987.

Lowenthal, David. *The Past is a Foreign Country.* London and New York: Cambridge University Press, 1985.

Lynn, Greg. *Folds, Bodies & Blobs: Collected Essays.* Brussels: La Lettre Volée, 1998.

Lynn, Kenneth S. (ed.). *The Professions in America.* Boston, MA: Houghton Mifflin Co., 1965.

Lyotard, Jean Francois. *The Postmodern Condition: A Report on Knowledge.* Trans. Geoff Bennington and Brian Massumi. Manchester: Manchester University Press, 1986.

Macdonell, Diane. *Theories of Discourse.* Oxford: Blackwell, 1986.

MacDougal, Elizabeth Blair (ed.). *The Architectural Historian in America. Studies in the History of Art.* Washington, DC: The Smithsonian Institution, 1990.

MacLean, Ian, Alan Montefiore, and Peter Winch. *The Political Responsibility of Intellectuals.* Cambridge: Cambridge University Press, 1990.

Malchump, F. *The Production and Distribution of Knowledge in the United States.* Princeton: Princeton University Press, 1962.

Mandel, Ernst. *Late Capitalism.* London: New Left Review Books, 1980.

Marcuse, H. *Reason and Revolution: Hegel and the Rise of Social Theory.* 2nd ed. London: Routledge and Kegan Paul, 1960.

Marin, Louis. *Utopics: The Semiological Play of Textual Spaces.* Atlantic Highlands, NJ: Humanities Press, 1984.

Massey, Doreen. *Spatial Divisions of Labour: Social Structure and the Geography of Production.* London: Macmillan, 1984.

——. *Space, Place and Gender.* Minneapolis: University of Minnesota Press, 1994.

—— and J. Allen (eds). *Uneven Re-Development: Cities and Regions in Transition.* London: Hodder and Stoughton, 1988.

Merod, Jim. *The Political Responsibility of the Critic.* Ithaca, NY: Cornell University Press, 1989.

Mills, Sara. *Discourse.* New York and London: Routledge, 1997.

Mitchell, W. J. T. *Picture Theory.* Chicago: University of Chicago Press, 1990.

Nelson, Cary. *Manifesto of a Tenured Radical.* New York and London: New York University Press, 1997.

Oliver, Paul (ed.). *Shelter and Society.* London: Barrie and Rockliff Ltd, 1969.

——. *Shelter in Africa.* London: Barrie and Jenkins Ltd, 1971.

Oncu, Ayse and Petra Weyland (eds). *Space, Culture and Power. New Identities in Globalizing Cities.* London: Zed Books, 1997.

Ong, Aihwa. *Flexible Citizenship: The Cultural Logics of Transnationality.* Durham, NC: Duke University Press, 1999.

Palmer, Bryan D. *Descent into Discourse. The Reification of Language in the Writing of Social History.* Philadelphia: Temple University Press, 1990.

Parsons, Talcott and Gerald M. Platt. *The American University.* Cambridge, MA: Harvard University Press, 1975.

Peet, R. (ed.). *Radical Geography: Alternative Viewpoints on Contemporary Social Issues.* Chicago, Maaroufa and London: Methuen, 1977.

——. and N. Thrift (eds). *New Models in Geography.* London: Unwin Hyman, 1988.

Perkin, Howard. *The Rise of Professional Society: England Since 1880.* London and New York: Routledge, 1989.

Pile, Stephen and Nigel Thrift (eds.) *Mapping the Subject. Geographies of Cultural Transformation.* London and New York: Routledge, 1995.

Portes, Alejandro and John Walton. *Labour, Class, and the International System.* New York: Academic Press, 1981.

Pratt, Mary Louise. *The Imperial Eye/l. Writing and Transculturation.* London and New York: Routledge, 1992.

Pred, A. R. *City Systems in Advanced Economies.* London: Hutchinson, 1977.

Rabinow, Paul. *French Modern. Norms and Forms of the Social Environment.* Cambridge, MA: The MIT Press, 1989.

Rapoport, Amos. *House Form and Culture.* Englewood Cliffs, NJ: Prentice Hall, 1969.

Robbins, Bruce (ed.). *Intellectuals. Aesthetics, Politics, Academics.* Minneapolis: University of Minnesota Press, 1990.

——. *Secular Vocations. Intellectuals, Professionalism, Culture.* London and New York: Verso, 1993.

—— and Pheng Cheah. *Cosmopolitics. Thinking and Feeling Beyond the Nation.* Minneapolis: University of Minnesota Press, 1998.

Roberts, Brian, Ruth Finnegan, and Duncan Gallie (eds). *New Approaches to Economic Life/Economic Restructuring: Unemployment and the Social Division of Labour.* Manchester: Manchester University Press, 1985.
Robertson, Roland. *Globalization: Social Theory and Global Culture.* London and Newbury Park, CA: Sage Publications, 1992.
Rose, Gillian. *Feminism and Geography. The Limits of Geographical Knowledge.* Minneapolis: University of Minnesota Press, 1993.
Rudofsky, Bernard. *Architecture Without Architects.* New York: The Museum of Modern Art, 1964.
Ryan, Michael. *Marxism and Deconstruction.* Baltimore: Johns Hopkins University Press, 1982.
Sack, R. *Conceptions of Space in Social Thought.* Minneapolis: University of Minnesota Press, 1980.
Said, Edward. *Orientalism.* New York: Phaidon, 1977.
——. *The World, the Text and the Critic.* Cambridge, MA: Harvard University Press, 1983.
——. *Culture and Imperialism.* New York: Alfred A. Knopf, 1994.
——. *Representations of the Intellectual.* New York: Pantheon, 1994.
Saint, Andrew. *The Image of the Architect.* New Haven, CT and London: Yale University Press, 1983.
Sassen, Saskia. *The Mobility of Capital and Labour: A Study in International Investment and Labour Flow.* London: Cambridge University Press, 1988.
——. *The Global City: New York, London, Tokyo.* Princeton, NJ: Princeton University Press, 1991.
——. *Globalization and its Discontents. Essays on the New Mobility of People and Money.* New York: The New Press, 1998.
Scott, Allen J. and Michael Storper (eds). *Production, Work, Territory.* Boston: Unwin & Allen, 1986.
Sheets, R. G., S. Nord, and J. J. Philips. *The Impact of Service Industries on Underdevelopment in Metropolitan Economies.* Lexington, MA: D. C. Heath and Company, 1987.
Shelp, Ronald Kent. *Beyond Industrialization: Ascendency of the Global Service Economy.* New York: Praeger Books, 1981.
Shils, Edward. *Tradition.* Chicago: University of Chicago Press, 1981.
Silverman, Kaja. *The Subject of Semiotics.* New York and Oxford: Oxford University Press, 1983.
Singlemann, J. "The Sectoral Transformation of the Labor Forces in Seven Industrial Countries, 1920–60." PhD dissertation, University of Texas, 1974.
Smith, Dennis. *The Chicago School. A Liberal Critique of Capitalism.* London and Basingstoke: Macmillan, 1988.
Smith, M. P. *Nature, Capital and the Production of Space.* New York: Basil Blackwell, 1984.

———. *City State and Market: The Political Economy of Urban Society.* New York: Basil Blackwell, 1988.

———. *Transnational Urbanism. Locating Globalization.* Oxford: Blackwell, 2001.

Smith, N. and P. Williams. *Gentrification and the City.* Boston: Allen & Unwin, 1986.

Society of Architectural Historians. *Graduate Degree Programs in Architectural History.* Philadelphia: The Society of Architectural Historians, 1992.

Soja, Edward. *Postmodern Geographies: The Reassertion of Space in Critical Social Theory.* London: Verso, 1989.

———. and Allen J. Scott (eds). *The City. Los Angeles and Urban Theory at the End of the Twentieth Century.* Berkeley and London: University of California Press, 1996.

Spivak, Gayatri Chakravorty. *In Other Worlds. Essays in Cultural Politics.* New York and London: Methuen, 1988.

———. *The Post-Colonial Critic. Interviews, Strategies, Dialogues.* Edited by Sarah Harasym. New York and London: Routledge, 1990.

———. *Outside in the Teaching Machine.* New York and London: Routledge, 1993.

Stanbeck, Thomas M. Jr. *Understanding the Service Economy.* Baltimore: Johns Hopkins University Press, 1979.

Taylor, David Carson. *Managing the Serials Explosion.* New York: Knowledge Industry Publications Inc., 1982.

Thrift, N. and P. Williams (eds). *Class and Space.* London: Macmillan: 1987.

Thurlow, Lester C. *The Zero Sum Society.* New York: Basic Books, 1980.

Timberlake, Michael (ed.). *Urbanization and the World Economy.* Orlando, FL: Academic Press, 1985.

Torstendahl, R. (ed.). *The Formation of the Professions: Knowledge, State and Strategy.* London and Newbury Park, CA: Sage Publications, 1990.

Touraine, Alain. *The Post-Industrial Society.* Paris: Denoel, 1969.

———. *The Academic System in American Society.* New York: McGraw Hill, 1997.

Tuan, Yi-Fu. *Topophilia. A Study of Environmental Perception, Attitudes and Values.* Englewood Cliffs, NJ: Prentice-Hall, 1974.

Turner, Bryan S. *Orientalism, Postmodernism and Globalism.* New York and London: Routledge, 1994.

Vale, Lawrence J. *Architecture, Power and National Identity.* New Haven, CT: Yale University Press, 1992.

Walker, Pat (ed.). *Between Labour and Capital.* Boston, MA: South End Press, 1979.

Wallerstein, I. *The Modern World System III. The Second Era of Great Expansion of the Capitalist World-Economy 1730–1840s.* San Diego: Academic Press, 1989.

———. *The Capitalist World Economy.* 9th ed. Cambridge: Cambridge University Press, 1991.

Weatherhead, Clausen. *The History of Collegiate Architecture in the United States.* New York: The Association of Collegiate Schools of Architecture, 1942.

West, Cornel. *Keeping Faith. Philosophy and Race in America.* London and New York: Routledge, 1993.

White, Hayden. *Tropics of Discourse. Essays in Cultural Criticism.* Baltimore: The Johns Hopkins University Press, 1978.

———. *Narrative Discourse and Historical Representation.* Baltimore: The Johns Hopkins University Press, 1987.

———. "Historical Emplotment and the Problem of Truth" in Saul Friedlander (ed.), *Probing the Limits of Representation. Nazism and the Final Solution.* Cambridge, MA: Harvard University Press, 1992.

Whiteman, John. *Strategies in Architectural Thinking.* Chicago: The Chicago Institute for Architecture and Urbanism, 1992.

Wright, Gwendolyn and Janet Parke (eds). *The History of History in American Schools of Architecture, 1865–1975.* New York: The Temple Hoyne Buell Center and Princeton Architectural Press, 1990.

ARTICLES

Abu-Lughod, Janet. "Disappearing Dichotomies: First World–Third World; Traditional–Modern." *TDSR* 3, no. 2 (Spring 1992): 7–12.

Adams, Nicholas. "Architectural Touring American Style." *JSAH* 52, no. 3 (September 1993): 265–267.

———. "Celebrating Tradition and Change." *JSAH* 52, no. 2 (June 1993): 137–138.

Addiss, James and Steven Murray. "Plan and Space at Amiens Cathedral: With a New Plan Drawn by James Addiss." *JSAH* 49, no. 1 (March 1990): 44–66.

Addler, J. "The Dynamics of Transit Innovation in Los Angeles." *Society and Space* 4, no. 3 (September 1986): 321–336.

Adler, Sy and Johanner Brenner, "Gender and Space. Lesbians and Gay Men in the City." *IJURR* 16, no. 1 (March 1992): 24–34.

Allen, Anne E. Guernsey. "Architecture as Social Expression in Western Samoa. Axioms and Models." *TDSR* 5, no. 1 (Fall 1993): 33–46.

Allen, J. "Property Relations and Landlordism – A Realist Approach." *Society and Space* 1, no. 2 (June 1983): 191–203.

Allen, Stanley. "Leveraging Theory." *Assemblage* 17 (April 1992): 38–46.

Amerlinck, Marie Jose. "The Challenge of Change: Ethnic Identity and Built Form Amongst the Purepechas." *TDSR* 6, no. 2 (Spring 1995): 53–64.

Amin, A. and K. Robbins. "The Re-Emergence of Regional Economies? The Mythical Geography of Flexible Accumulation." *Society and Space* 8, no. 1 (1990): 7–34.

Anderson, K. J. "Cultural Hegemony and Race Definition Processes in Chinatown, Vancouver, 1880–1980." *Society and Space* 6, no. 2 (June 1988): 127–149.

Appiah, Anthony. "Is the Post- in Postmodernism the Post- in Postcolonial?" *Critical Inquiry* 17 (Winter 1991): 336–357.

Aranha, Joseph L. "A Comparison of Traditional Settlements in Nepal and Bali." *TDSR* 2, no. 2 (Spring 1991): 35–48.

Arets, Wiel. "Grid and Rhizome: Recent Work by Wiel Arets and Wim Van der Bergh." *AA Files* 21 (Spring 1991): 16–25.

Bagguley, P. and S. Walby. "Gender Restructuring: Five Labour Markets Compared." *Society and Space* 7, no. 3 (September 1989): 277–292.

Bal, Mieke. "De-disciplining the Eye." *Critical Inquiry* 16, no. 3 (Spring 1990): 506–531.

Bannister, Turpin. "Summary of Round Table Discussion on the Preservation of Historic Architectural Monuments." *JSAH* 1, no. 2 (April 1942): 22–24.

Barnes, T. J. and M. R. Curry. "Postmodernism in Economic Geography: Metaphor and the Construction of Alterity." *Society and Space* 10, no. 1 (February 1992): 57–68.

Barrage, M. "Nationalisation and the Professional Ideal." *Sociology* 7 (1973): 253–271.

Beauregard, Robert A. "Capital restructuring and the New Built Environment of Global Cities: New York and Los Angeles." *IJURR* 15, no. 1 (March 1991): 91–105.

Beckman, Richard M. and Dieter Ackerknecht. "Bern: A Traditional Settlement in Change." *TDSR* 5, no. 1 (Fall 1993): 47–57.

Bell, David J. "(screw)ING GEOGRAPHY (censor's version)." *Society and Space* 13, no. 2 (April 1995): 127–131.

Bhabha, Homi K. "DissemiNation: Time, Narrative, and the Margins of the Modern Nation" in Homi K. Bhabha (ed.), *Nation and Narration*. London and New York: Routledge, 1990, 291–322.

Bishop, P. "Rhetoric, Memory and Power: Depth Psychology and Postmodern Geography." *Society and Space* 10, no. 1 (February 1992): 5–22.

Bloomer, Jennifer. "In the Museyroom." *Assemblage* 5 (February 1988): 59–65.

———. "Abodes of Theory and Flesh: Tabbles of Bower." *Assemblage* 17 (April 1992): 6–30.

Bourdier, Jean-Paul and Nezar AlSayyad. "Editorial." *TDSR* 1, no. 1 (Fall 1989): 3.

Bowlby, S. R. "Planning for Women to Shop in Postwar Britain." *Society and Space* 2, no. 2 (June 1984): 179–200.

Bozdogogan, Sibel. "Vernacular Architecture and Oidentity Politics: The Case of the 'Turkish House'". *TDSR* 12, no. 11 (Spring 1998): 7–18.

Bromley, N. K. "Activism and the Academy." *Society and Space* 12, no. 4 (August 1994): 383–386.

Carrigan, Dennis P. "Publish or Perish: The Troubled State of Scholarly Communication." *Scholarly Publishing* (April 1991): 131–142.

——. "Research Libraries Evolving Response to the Serials Crisis." *Scholarly Publishing* (April 1992): 138–151.
Castells, Manuel. "Is there an Urban Sociology?" in Chris Pickvance (trans. and ed.) *Urban Sociology. Critical Essays*. London: Tavistock Press, 1976, 22–46.
——. "Les Conditions Sociales d'Émergence des Mouvements Sociaux et Urbains (à Partir d'une Enquete Explorations sur le Lutte Urbaines dans la Région Parisienne, 1968–73)." *IJURR* 1, no. 1 (Spring 1977): 45–75.
——. "High Technology, Economic Restructuring, and the Urban–Regional Process in the United States" in Manuel Castells (ed.), *High Technology, Space and Society*. Beverly Hills: Sage, 1985, 11–40.
Castrioti, Leonardo. "Living in a World Heritage Site: Preservation Politics and Local History in Ouro Preto, Brazil." *TDSR* 10, no. 2 (Spring 1999): 7–20.
Cataldi, Giancarlo, Rasid Abdelhamid, and Fabio Selva, "The Town of Ghardaia in M'zab, Algeria: Between Tradition and Modernity." *TDSR* 7, no. 2 (Spring 1996): 63–74.
Çelik, Zeynep, "Expanding Frameworks." *JSAH* 59, no. 2 (June 2000): 152–153.
——. "New Approaches to the 'Non-Western City'." *JSAH* 58, no. 3 (September 1999): 374.
Chewing, J. A. "The Teaching of Architectural History during the Advent of Modernism, 1920s–1950s" in Elizabeth Blair MacDougall (ed.), *The Architectural Historian in America. Studies in the History of Art 35*. Washington, DC: The Smithsonian Institution, 1990, 100–112.
Chivallon, Christine. "Space and Identity in Martinique: Towards a New Reading of the Spatial History of the Peasantry." *Society and Space* 13, no. 3 (August 1995): 289–310.
Christopherson, S. and M. Storper. "The City as Studio; The World as Backlot: The Impact of Vertical Disintegration on the Location of the Motion Picture Industry." *Society and Space* 14, no. 3 (September 1986): 305–320.
Clarke, David. "Consumption and the City, Modern and Postmodern," *IJURR* 21, no. 2 (June, 1997): 218–237.
Clement-Charpentier, Sophie. "New Towns in France and Thailand in the Middle Ages: A Comparative Analysis." *TDSR* 3, no. 1 (1991): 43–55.
Clifford, James. "On Ethnographic Allegory." James Clifford, and George E. Marcus (eds), in *Writing Culture. The Poetics and Politics of Ethnography*. Berkeley: University of California Press, 1986, 98–121.
Colomina, Beatriz. "At Home with his Parents." *Assemblage* 30 (August 1996): 108–111.
——. "Farewell to Assemblage." *Assemblage* 41 (April 2000): 19.
Connell, A. J. "Bali Revisited: Death, Rejuvination and the Tourist Cycle." *Society and Space* 11, no. 6 (February 1993): 641–661.
Cooke, P. "Regional Restructuring: Class, Politics, and Popular Protest in South Wales." *Society and Space* 1, no. 3 (August 1983): 265–280.

Cornell, Laurel L. "House Architecture and Family Form: On the Origin of Vernacular Traditions in Early Modern Japan." *TDSR* 13, no. 2 (Spring 1997): 21–32.

Crang, P. "The Politics of Polyphony: Reconfigurations in Geographical Authority." *Society and Space* 10, no. 2 (April 1992): 527–549.

Crews, Frederick. "Reductionism and its Discontents." *Critical Inquiry*, 1 (1975), 543–558.

Crow, Thomas. "Art Criticism in the Age of Incommensurable Values: On the Thirtieth Anniversary of Artforum" in *Modern Art in the Common Culture*. New Haven, CT: Yale University Press, 1996, 85–96.

Culler, Jonathan. "Criticism and its Institutions. The American University" in Derrick Attridge, Geoffrey Bennington, and Robert Young (eds), *Post-structuralism and the Question of History*. Cambridge: Cambridge University Press, 1987, 82–98.

Daher, Rami Farouk. "Gentrification and the Politics of Power, Capital and Culture in an Emerging Jordanian Heritage Industry." *TDSR* 10, no. 2 (Spring 1999): 33–47.

Davis, M. "The Political Economy of Late Imperial America." *New Left Review* 151 (1984): 6–38.

Dear, M. "Society and Space: An Introduction." *Society and Space* 1, no. 1 (March 1983): 1–2.

——. "Postmodernism and Planning." *Society and Space* 4, no. 3 (1986): 367–384.

—— and N. J. Thrift, "Unfinished Business: Ten Years of Society and Space, 1983–1992." *Society and Space* 6, no. 6 (December 1992): 715–720.

Denniston, Robin. "An Intellectual Explosion Without Precedent." *Scholarly Publishing* (October 1987): 3–17.

Deutsche, Rosalyne. "Boystown." *Society and Space* 9, no. 1 (March 1991): 5–30.

Douglass, Mike. "Transnational Capital and Urbanization in the Pacific Rim: An Introduction." *IJURR* 12, no. 3 (September 1988): 343–355.

——. "The Transnationalization of Urbanization in Japan." *IJURR* 12, no. 3 (September 1988): 425–454.

Driver, F. "Power, Space and the Body: A Critical Assessment of Foucault's *Discipline and Punish*." *Society and Space* 3, no. 4 (December 1985): 425–446.

Duncan, James. "Me(Trope)olis: Or Hayden White Amongst the Urbanists" in A. D. King (ed.), *Re-Presenting the City. Ethnicity, Capital and Culture in the 21st-Century Metropolis*. London and Basingstoke: Macmillan and New York University Press, 1996, 253–268.

—— and D. Ley. "Structural Marxism and Human Geography: A Critical Assessment." *Annals of the Association of Human Geographers* 72 (1982): 30–58.

Eckstein, Susan. "Poor People versus the State and Capital: Anatomy of a Successful Community Mobilization for Housing in Mexico City." *IJURR* 14, no. 3 (June 1990): 274–296.

Eden, J. A. "Race and the Reproduction of Factory Labor in Malaysia." *Society and Space* 8, no. 2 (June 1988): 175–190.

Ehrenreich, Barbara and John Ehrenreich. "The Professional Managerial Class" in Pat Walker (ed.), *Between Labour and Capital*. Boston: South End Press, 1979, 313–334.

Eisenman, Peter. "Post/El Cards: A Reply to Jacques Derrida." *Assemblage* 12 (August 1990): 14–18.

Esser, Josef and Joachim Hirsch. "The Crisis of Fordism and the Dimensions of a 'Postfordist' Regional and Urban Structure." *IJURR* 13, no. 3 (September 1989): 417–430.

Ettore, E. M. "Women, Urban Social Movements and the Lesbian Ghetto." *IJURR* 2, no. 3 (October 1978): 499–520.

Eyles, J. "Why Geography Cannot Be Marxist: Towards an Understanding of Lived Experience." *Environment and Planning A* 12 (1981): 1371–1378.

—— and M. Evans. "Popular Consciousness, Moral Ideology and Locality." *Society and Space* 2, no. 4 (December 1984): 397–405.

Feagin, J. R. "The Secondary Circuit of Capital: Office Construction in Houston, Texas." *IJURR* 11, no. 2 (June 1987): 172–192.

—— and Nestor P. Rodriguez. "Urban Specialization in the World System." *Urban Affairs Quarterly* 22, no. 2 (1986): 187–220.

Fleming, Marie. "The Geography of Freedom." *Urban Studies* 28 (August 1991): 658–660.

Forest, Benjamin. "West Hollywood as Symbol: The Significance of Place in the Construction of Gay Identity." *Society and Space* 13, no. 2 (April 1995): 133–157.

Forrest, Ray and Alan Murie. "Marginalization and Subsidized Individualism: The Sale of Council Housing in the Restructuring of the British Welfare State." *IJURR* 10, no. 1 (March 1986): 46–66.

Foucault, Michel. "The Political Function of the Intellectual." *Radical Philosophy* no. 17 (1977): 12–14.

Frampton, Kenneth and Alessandra Latour. "Notes on American Architectural Education from the End of the 19th Century to the 1970s." *Lotus International* 27, no. 2 (1980): 5–39.

Friedland, Roger. "Central Fiscal Strains: The Public Costs of Private Growth." *IJURR* 5, no. 3 (September 1981): 356–376.

Friedmann, John. "The World City Hypothesis." *Development and Change* 17, no. 1 (January 1986): 69–84.

——. "Where We Stand: A Decade of World City Research" in Paul L. Knox and Peter J. Taylor (eds), *World Cities in a World System*. Cambridge: Cambridge University Press, 1995, 22–47.

—— and Goetz Wolff. "World City Formation. An Agenda for Research and Action." *IJURR* 6, no. 3 (September 1982): 309–343.

Geltmaker, T. "The Queer Nation Acts Up: Health Care, Politics and Sexual Diversity in the County of Angels." *Society and Space* 10, no. 6 (December 1992): 609–650.

Georgalli, Maria-Christina. "The Morphology of Traditional Dwellings within an Insular Context: Amorgos, Greece." *TDSR* 2, no. 2 (Spring 1991): 49–64.

Giles, Wenona. "Class, gender and race struggles in a Portuguese neighborhood in London." *IJURR* 15, no. 3 (September 1991): 432–442.

Glasmeier, Amy K. "The Japanese Technopolis Programme: High-tech Development Strategy or Industrial Policy in Disguise?" *IJURR* 12, no. 3 (September 1988): 268–284.

Goodwin, M., S. Duncan, and S. Halford. "Regulation Theory, the Local State, and the Transitions of Urban Politics." *Society and Space* 11, no. 1 (1993): 67–88.

Goss, J. D. "Placing the Market and Marketing Place. Tourist Advertising of the Hawaiian Islands, 1972–1992." *Society and Space* 11, no. 6 (December 1993): 663–688.

Gouldner, Alvin Ward. "Cosmopolitans and Locals." *Administrative Science Quarterly* 2 (1957): 26–42.

Graburn, Nelson. "IASTE 1996: Retrospect and Prospect." *TDSR* 9, no. 1 (Fall 1997): 60–64.

Graham, J. "Post-Fordism as Politics: The Political Consequences of Narratives on the Left." *Society and Space* 10, no. 4 (1992): 393–410.

Green, William A. "Periodization and World History." *Journal of World History* 3, no. 1 (Spring 1992): 13–54.

Gregory, Derek. "Space, Time and Politics in Social Theory: An Interview with Anthony Giddens." *Society and Space* 2, no. 2 (June 1984): 123–132.

———. "Human Agency in Human Geography." *Transactions of the Institute of British Geographers* 6: 1–18.

Gross, David. "Symposium on Russell Jacoby's the Last Intellectuals. Hope Amongst the Ruins." *Telos* 73 (Fall 1987): 167–172.

Hadjimichalis, C. "The Geographical Transfer of Value: Notes on the Spatiality of Capitalism." *Society and Space* 2 (1984): 329–345.

Hall, P. R., D. C. Thorns, and W. E. Willmott. "Community, Class and Kinship – Bases for Collective Action within Localities." *Society and Space* 2, no. 2 (1984): 201–215.

Hannah, M. "Foucault on Theorizing Specificity." *Society and Space* 11, no. 3 (June 1993): 349–363.

Harloe, Michael. "Editorial." *IJURR* 1, no. 1 (Fall 1977): 3–4.

———. "Notes on Comparative Urban Research" in Michael Dear and Alan J. Scott (eds), *Urbanization and Urban Planning in Capitalist Society*. London and New York: Methuen, 1981, 179–195.

———. "In this Issue . . ." *IJURR* 11, no. 1 (March 1987): 1–4.

Harvey, David. "The Urban Processes under Capitalism: A Framework for Analysis." *IJURR* 2, no. 1 (March 1978): 101–132.

Hays, K. Michael. "About *Assemblage*." *Assemblage* 1 (October 1986): 4–5.

———. "Editorial." *Assemblage* 5 (February 1988): 4–5.

———. "The Displacement of Stucture and Ornament in the Frankfurt Projects. An Interview." *Assemblage* 5 (February 1988): 51–57.

———. "Architecture Theory, Media and the Question of Audience." *Assemblage* 27 (August 1995): 41–46.

———. "On Turning Thirty." *Assemblage* 30 (August 1996): 6–11.

——— and Alicia Kennedy. "Editorial." *Assemblage* 41 (April 2000): 3.

———, Catherine Ingraham, and Alicia Kennedy. "Reading Los Angeles: A Primitive Rebel's Account." *Assemblage* 14 (April 1991): 66–81.

Hays-Mitchell, Maureen. "Voices and Visions from the Streets: Gender Interests and Political Participation Amongst Women Informal Traders in Latin America." *Society and Space* 13, no. 4 (August 1995): 445–469.

Hegedus, Josef and Ivan Tosics. "Housing Classes and Housing Policy: Some Changes in the Budapest Housing Market."*IJURR* 7, no. 4 (December 1983): 467–495.

Henderson, Martha, L. "Duality in Modern Chiricahua Apache Settlement Patterns." *TDSR* 3, no. 2 (Spring 1991): 7–17.

Hill, Richard Child. "State Capitalism and the Urban Fiscal Crisis in the United States." *IJURR* 1, no. 1 (March 1977): 76–99.

———. "Two Divergent Theories of the State." *IJURR* 1, no. 1 (March 1977): 37–44.

Hosagrahar, Jyoti. "Fractured Plans: Real Estate, Moral Reform, and the Politics of Housing in New Delhi, 1936–1941." *TDSR* 11, no. 1 (Fall 1999): 37–48.

Hublin, Ann. "Analyzing Aerial Photographs of Traditional Maroon Settlements." *TDSR* 1, no. 1 (Fall 1989): 83–96.

Hudson, R. "National Industrial Policies and Regional Politics: The Role of the State in Capitalist Societies in the Deindustrialization and Reindustrialization of Regions." *Society and Space* 4, no. 1 (March 1986): 7–26.

Ingraham, Catherine. "The Faults of Architecture: Troping the Proper." *Assemblage* 7 (October 1988): 6–13.

International Sociological Association Research Committee on Sociology of Urban and Regional Development. "Active Members' Addresses and Research Interests at 01.07.1995," Essex, 1995.

Jameson, Frederic. "The Ideology of the Text." *Salmagundi*, nos. 31–32 (Fall 1975/Winter 1976): 204–246.

———. "The Politics of Theory: Ideological Positions in the Postmodern Debate." *New German Critique* 33 (1984): 53–65.

——— and Michael Speaks, "Envelopes and Enclaves: The Spaces of Post-Civil Society." *Assemblage* 17 (April 1992): 30–37.

Jarzombek, Mark. "The Disciplinary Dislocations of (Architectural) History." *JSAH* 58, no. 3 (September 1999): 488–493.

Johns, M. "The Urbanization of Peripheral Capital in Buenes Aires (1888–1920)." *IJURR* 16, no. 3 (September 1991): 352–374.

Johnston, R. J. and E. V. Black. "Appointment and Promotion in the British Academic Labour Market: A Preliminary Survey of British University Departments of Geography, 1933–1982." *Transactions. Journal of the Institute of British Geographers* 8 (1983): 100–111.

Jones, Andrew E. G. "The Scale Politics of Spatiality." *Society and Space* 12, no. 2 (June 1994): 257–264.

Kafkalas, Grigoris. "Location of production and forms of spatial integration: theoretical considerations and some examples from the non-fuels mineral sector." *IJURR* 9, no. 2 (June 1985): 233–253.

Kaufmann, Jean-Claude and Monique Laigneau. "The Crisis of French Urban Research." *IJURR* 9, no. 2 (June 1985): 155–163.

Keil, Roger. "Global Sprawl, Urban Form after Fordism." *Society and Space* 12, no. 2 (June 1994): 131–136.

Keith, M. "Angry Writing: Representing the Unethical World of the Ethnographer." *Society and Space* 10, no. 5 (October 1992): 551–568.

Kennedy, M. D. and A. D. Smith. "East Central European Urbanization. A Political Economy of the World System Perspective." *IJURR* 13, no. 4 (December 1991): 597–624.

Kester, Grant. "The Contamination of Discourse: Politics and Deleuzian Aesthetics." Unpublished Article (1998).

King, A. D. "Colonialism, Urbanism and the Capitalist World Economy." *IJURR* 13, no. 1 (March 1989).

———. "The Politics of Position: Inventing the Past; Constructing the Present; Imagining the Future." *TDSR* 4, no. 2 (Spring 1993): 9–18.

———. "The Politics of Traditional Settlements." *TDSR* 9, no. 1 (Fall 1997): 58–59.

Kipnis, Jeffrey. "/Twisting the Separatrix/." *Assemblage* 14 (April 1991): 31–61.

———. "Moonmark." *Assemblage* 16 (December 1991): 7–13.

Knopp, L. "Sexuality and the Spatial Dynamics of Capitalism." *Society and Space* 10, no. 6 (December 1992): 651–669.

Kwinter, Sandford. "Rem Koolhaas, OMA. Urbanism after Innocence: Four Projects." *Assemblage* 18 (August 1992): 83–85.

Lagana, Guido, Mario Pianta, and Anna Segre. "Urban Social Movements and Urban Restructuring in Turin 1969–1975." *IJURR* 6, no. 2 (June 1982): 223–245.

Lancaster, Clay. "The Philadelphia Centennial Towers." *JSAH* 19, no. 1 (March, 1960): 11–15.

Lazarus, Neil. "National Consciousness and the Specificity of (Post)colonial Intellectualism" in Francis Barker, Peter Hulme, and Margaret Iverson (eds), *Colonial Discourse/Postcolonial Theory*. New York: Manchester University Press, 1994, 197–220.

Lebas, Elizabeth. "Introduction. The New School of Urban and Regional Research: Into the Second Decade" in Michael Harloe (ed.), *Captive Cities. Studies in the Political Economy of Cities*. London and New York: Wiley, 1977, ix–xxxiii.

———. "Trend Report. Urban and Regional Sociology in Advanced Industrial Societies: A Decade of Marxist and Critical Perspectives." *Current Sociology* 30, no. 1 (Spring 1982): 1–271.

Le Gales, Patrick, Susan Fainstein, and Linda McDowell. "Policy Statement." *IJURR* 22, no. 1 (March 1998): v–viii.

Leontidou, Lila. "Urban Land Rights and Working-Class Consciousness in Peripheral Societies." *IJURR* 9, no. 4 (December 1985): 533–556.

———. "Alternatives to Modernism in Southern Urban Theory: Exploring In-Between Spaces." *IJURR* 20, no. 2 (June 1990): 178–195.

Ley, David and Marwyn S. Samuels. "Introduction" in David Ley and Marwyn S. Samuels (eds), *Humanistic Geography. Prospects and Problems*. Chicago: Maaroufa Press, 1978, 11–20.

Lipietz, Alain. "New Tendencies in the International Division of Labor: Regimes of Accumulation and Modes of Regulation" in A. Scott and M. Storper (eds), *Production, Work, Territory: The Geographical Anatomy of Industrial Capitalism*. Boston: Allen & Unwin, 1986, 16–40.

Livingstone, David. "The Spaces of Knowledge: Contribution Towards a Historical Geography of Science." *Society and Space* 13, no. 1 (February 1995): 5–34.

Logan, John. "A Note from the President." *International Sociological Association on the Sociology of Urban and Regional Development Newsletter* (November 1994): 3–4.

Lojkine, Jean. "L'Analyse Marxiste de l'Etat." *IJURR* 1, no. 1 (March 1977): 19–23.

Lovatt, David and Brian Ham. "Class Formation, Wage Formation, and Community Protest in a Metropolitan Control Center." *IJURR* 8, no. 3 (September 1984): 354–387.

Lu, Duanfang. "Ethnic Identity and Urban Form in Vancouver," *TDSR* 11, no. 2 (Spring 2000): 19–28.

Lubiano, Wahneema. "Like Being Mugged by a Metaphor: Multiculturalism and State Narratives" in Avery F. Gordon and Christopher Newfield (eds), *Mapping Multiculturalism*. Minneapolis and London: University of Minnesota Press, 1996, 64–75.

Lynn, Greg. "Multiplicitous and Inorganic Bodies." *Assemblage* 19 (December 1992): 32–50.

Maass, John. "Where Architectural Historians Fear to Tread." *JSAH* 28, no. 1 (March 1969): 3–8.

Machinura, Takashi. "The Urban Restructuring Process in Tokyo in the 1980s: Transforming Tokyo into a World City." *IJURR* 16, no. 1 (March 1992): 114–128.

McLeod, Mary. "Architecture and Politics in the Reagan Era: From Postmodernism to Deconstruction." *Assemblage* 8 (August 1989): 22–59.

Malaquais, Dominique. "You are What You Build: Architecture as Identity Amongst the Bamileke of West Cameroon." *TDSR* 5, no. 2 (Spring 1994): 22–36.

Marcus, George. "More Critically Reflexive than Thou." *Society and Space* 10, no. 5 (October 1992): 489–494.

Marder, Tod. "Note From the Editor." *JSAH* 49, no. 1 (March 1990): 5–6.

Markusen, Ann and Vicky Gwiasda. "Multipolarity, and the Layering of Functions in World Cities: New York's Struggle to Stay on Top." *IJURR* 18, no. 2 (June 1994): 167–193.

Marouli, Christina. "Women Resisting (in) the City: Struggles, Gender, Class and Space in Athens." IJURR 19, no. 4 (December 1995): 534–548.

Massey, Doreen. "New Directions in Space" in John Urry and Derek Gregory (eds), *Social Relations and Spatial Structures*. Basingstoke: Macmillan, 1985, 9–19.

——. "Flexible Sexism." *Society and Space* 9, no. 1 (March 1991): 31–57.

—— and D. Wield. "Science Parks: A Concept in Science Society and 'Space' (A Realist Tale)." *Society and Space* 10, no. 4 (August 1992): 411–422.

Matless, D. "An Occasion for Geography: Landscape, Representation, and Foucault's Corpus." *Society and Space* 10, no. 1 (February 1992): 41–56.

Maytsek, Eugene E. Jr. "Three Recent Literatures in Architectural Research: A Citation Analysis, 1986–1990." Unpublished student research paper, University of Maryland, 1–47.

Miller, Mike. "Community Organization USA: The View from the Movement." *IJURR* 5, no. 4 (December 1981): 565–573.

Miller, R. "The Hoover in the Garden: Middle-Class Women and Suburbanization, 1850–1920." *Society and Space* 1, no. 4 (September 1983): 73–87.

Mingione, Enzo. "Capitalist Crisis, Neo-Dualism, and Marginalization." *IJURR* 2, no. 2 (June 1978): 213–221.

——. "Informalization, Restructuring and the Survival Strategies of the Working Class." *IJURR* 7, no. 3 (September 1983): 311–339.

Mitchell, Kathryne. "Global Diasporas and Traditional Towns: Chinese Transnational Migration and the Redevelopment of Vancouver's Chinatown." *TDSR*, 11, no. 2 (Spring 2000): 7–18.

Mitchell, W. J. T. "Spatial Form in Literature: Towards a General Theory" in W. J. T. Mitchell (ed.), *The Language of Images*. Chicago: University of Chicago Press, 1980, 271–299.

Mohanty, Chandra Talpade. "On Race and Voice: Challenges for Liberal Education in the 1990s." *Cultural Critique* 14 (Winter 1989), 179–208.

Moholy-Nagy, Sibyl. "Maass for Measure." *JSAH* 29, no. 1 (March 1970): 60–61.

Momont, Marc. "The Emergence of Rural Struggles and their Ideological Effects." *IJURR* 7, no. 4 (December 1983): 559–572.

Morales, R. "The Los Angeles Automobile Industry in Historical Perspective." *Society and Space* 4, no. 3 (September 1986): 289–304.

Morris, J. L. "The State and Industrial Restructuring: Government Policies in Industrial Wales." *Society and Space* 5, no. 2 (1987): 195–213.

Mouffe, Chantal. "Post-Marxism, Democracy and Identity." *Society and Space* 13, no. 3 (1995): 259–265.

Mulhern Francis. "Teachers, Writers, Celebrities: Intelligentsia and their Histories". *New Left Review 126* (March/April 1981): 43–59.

Nichols, Stephen G. "Periodization and the Politics of Perception: A Romanesque Example." *Poetics Today* 10, no. 1 (Spring 1989): 127–155.

Oakes, T. S. "The Cultural Space of Modernity: Ethnic Tourism and Place Identity in China." *Society and Space* 11, no. 6 (December 1993): 47–66.

Ockman, J. "Resurrecting the Avant Garde: The History and Program of *Oppositions*" in Joan Ockman (ed.), *Architecture Reproduction*. New York: Princeton Architectural Press, 1988, 180–199.

Oliver, Paul. "Vernacular Studies: Objectives and Applications." Unpublished abstract of position paper presented to the IASTE 1996 Conference, 1–3.

Osburn, Charles E. "The Place of Journals in the Scholarly Communications System." *Library Resources and Technical Services* (October/December 1984): 315–325.

Overby, Osmund. "From 1947: The Society of Architectural Historians," *JSAH* 49, no. 1 (March 1990): 12–14.

Overton, J. D. "Social Control and Social Engineering: African Reserves in Kenya 1895–1920." *Society and Space* 8, no. 2 (June 1990): 163–174.

Pahl, R. E. "Employment, Work and the Domestic Division of Labour." *IJURR* 4, no. 1 March 1980: 1–21.

Peattie, Lisa. "Aesthetic Politics. Shantytown or New Vernacular?" *TDSR* 3, no. 2 (Spring 1992): 23–32.

Pecorra, Vincent. "Towers of Babel" in Diane Ghirardo (ed.), *Out of Site*. Seattle: Bay Press, 1990, 46–75.

Peet, R. "Spatial Dialectics in Marxist Geography." *Progress in Human Geography* 5 (1987): 105–110.

Pessar, Patricia R. "Sweatshop Workers and Domestic Ideologies: Dominican Women in New York's Apparel Industry." *IJURR* 14, no. 1 (March 1990): 127–142.

Petras, Elizabeth. "The Role of National Boundaries in a Cross-National Labour Market." *IJURR* 4, no. 2 (June 1980): 157–195.

Philo, C. "Foucault's Geography." *Society and Space* 10, no. 2 (April 1992): 137–161.

Pickvance, Chris. "The Rise and Fall of Urban Movements and the Role of Comparative Analysis." *Society and Space* 9, no. 1 (March 1985): 31–53.

———. "Introduction: Land and Housing Development in Middle Eastern and North African Cities." *IJURR* 12, no. 1 (March 1988): 1–3.

Pile, S. and G. Rose. "All or Nothing? Politics and Critique in the Modernism–Postmodernism Debate." *Society and Space* 10, no. 2 (April 1992): 123–136.

Portes, Alejandro and Jose Itzigsohn. "The Party or the Grassroots: A Comparative Analysis of Urban Political Participation in the Caribbean Basin." *IJURR* 18, no. 3 (September 1994): 491–509.

Pratt, Geraldine. "Class Analysis and Urban Domestic Property. A Critical Re-examination." *IJURR* 6, no. 4 (December 1982): 481–502.

Pratt, G. and S. Hanson. "Gender, Class and Space." *Society and Space* 6, no. 1 (March 1988): 15–36.

Pred, A. R. "The Interurban Transmission of Growth in Advanced Economies: Empirical Findings versus Regional Planning Assumptions." *Regional Studies* 10 (1976): 151–171.

———. "Structuration, Biography Formation and Knowledge: Observations in Port Growth during the Last Mercantile Period." *Society and Space* 2, no. 3 (September 1984): 251–276.

Priemus, Hugo. "Squatters in Amsterdam: Urban Social Movement, Urban Managers or Something Else?" *IJURR* 7, no. 3 (September 1983): 417–427.

Prussin, Labelle. "Non-Western Sacred Sites: African Models." *JSAH* 58, no. 3 (September 1999): 424–433.

Rabinow, Paul. "Representations are Social Facts" in James Clifford and George Marcus (eds), *Writing Culture. The Poetics and Politics of Ethnography*. Berkeley and London: University of California Press, 1986, 234–261.

———. "Governing Morocco: Modernity and Difference." *IJURR* 13, no. 1 (March 1989): 32–46.

Radcliffe, S. A. "Ethnicity, Patriarchy, and Incorporation into the Nation: Female Migrants as Domestic Servants in Peru." *Society and Space* 8, no. 3 (August 1990): 379–393.

Rakatansky, Mark. "Transformational Constructions (For Example: Adult Day)." *Assemblage* 9 (December 1992): 6–31

Rapoport, Amos. "On Cultural Landscapes." *TDSR* 3, no. 2 (Spring 1992), 33–48.

———. "A Retrospective and Prospective Look at IASTE." Unpublished abstract of position paper presented to the IASTE 1996 Conference: 1–3.

Rees, G. "Regional Restructuring, Class Change and Political Action: Preliminary Comments on the 1984–85 Miners' Strike in South Wales." *Society and Space* 3, no. 4 (December 1985): 389–406.

———. "'Coalfield Culture' and the 1984–1985 Miners' Strike: A Reply to Sunley." *Society and Space* 4, no. 4 (1986): 469–476.

Reichert, D. "Comedia Geographica: An Absurd One-Act Play." *Society and Space* 5, no. 3 (September 1987): 335–342.

———. "On Boundaries." *Society and Space* 10, no. 1 (February 1992): 87–98.
Reintges, Claudia M. "Urban Movements in South African Black Townships: A Case Study." *IJURR* 14, no. 1 (March 1990): 109–134.
Richter, Dagmar. "West Coast Gateway Competition, 1988." *Assemblage* 14 (April 1991): 67–82.
Rimmer, P. "Japanese Construction Contractors and the Australian States: Another Round of Interstate Rivalry." *IJURR* 12, no. 3 (September 1988): 404–424.
Robertson, Roland. "Mapping the Global Condition. Globalization as a Central Concept." *Theory, Culture and Society* 7, nos. 2–3 (1990): 15–30.
———. "Social Theory, Cultural Relativity and the Problem of Globality" in A. D. King (ed.), *Culture, Globalization and the World-System*. London: Macmillan, 1991, 69–90.
———. "Globality, Global Culture and Images of World Order" in H. Haferkamp and N. Smelser (eds), *Social Change and Modernity*. Berkeley: University of California Press, 1991, 395–411.
Robinson, J. "A Perfect System of Control? State Power and 'Native Locations' in South Africa." *Society and Space* 8, no. 2 (June 1990): 135–162.
Rose, D. "Rethinking Gentrification: Beyond the Uneven Development of Marxist Theory." *Society and Space* 2, no. 1 (March 1983): 47–74.
Rose, Gillian. "In Practice Supported, In Theory Denied: An Account of an Invisible Urban Movement." *IJURR* 2, no. 1 (March 1978): 521–537.
———. "Locality, Politics and Culture: Poplar in the 1920s." *Society and Space* 6, no. 2 (June 1988): 151–168.
———. "The Struggle for Political Democracy: Emancipation, Gender and Geography." *Society and Space* 8, no. 4 (December 1990): 395–408.
Roy, Ananya. "Traditions of the Modern." *TDSR* 12, no. 2 (Spring 2001): 7–20.
Rustin, Michael. "Postmodernism and Antimodernism in Contemporary British Architecture." *Assemblage* 8 (August 1989): 88–103.
Said, Edward. "Third World Intellectuals and Metropolitan Culture." *Raritan* 9 (Winter 1990): 27–50.
Saunders, Peter. "Beyond Housing Classes: The Sociological Significance of Private Property Rights in the Means of Consumption." *IJURR* 8, no. 2 (September 1984): 202–227.
——— and P. Williams. "For an Emancipated Social Science." *Society and Space* 5, no. 4 (December 1987): 427–430.
——— and ———. "The New Conservatism: Some Thoughts on Recent and Future Developments in Urban Studies." *Society and Space* 4, no. 4 (December 1986): 393–399.
Savage, Mike, Peter Dinckins, and Tony Fielding. "Some Social and Political Implications of Contemporary Fragmentation of the 'Service Class' in Britain." *IJURR* 12, no. 3 (1988): 455–476.

Savitch, H. "Post-Industrial Planning in New York, Paris and London." *Journal of the American Planning Association* 53, no. 1 (1987): 80–144.

Schoenberger, E. "From Fordism to Flexible Accumulation: Technology, Competitive Strategies, and International Location." *Society and Space* 6, no. 3 (1988): 245–262.

Schwarzer, Mitchell. "History and Theory in Architectural Periodicals: Assembling Oppositions." *JSAH* 58, no. 3 (September 1999): 342–349.

Scott, A. J. "Territorial Reproduction and Transformation in a Local Labor Market: The Animated Film Workers of Los Angeles." *Society and Space* 2, no. 3 (1984): 277–307.

———. "Flexible Production Systems and Regional Development: The Rise of New Industrial Spaces in North America and Western Europe." *IJURR* 12, no. 2 (June 1988): 171–186.

——— and E. W. Soja. "Los Angeles: Capital of the Late Twentieth Century." *Society and Space* 4, no. 3 (September 1986): 249–254.

Scott, Felicity. "Architecture without Architects: A Short Introduction to Non-pedigreed Architecture by Bernard Rudofsky." *Harvard Design Magazine*, (Fall 1998): 69–72.

Shields, R. "Social Spatialization and the Built Environment: The West Edmonton Mall." *Society and Space* 7, no. 2 (June 1989): 147–164.

———. "A Truant Proximity: Presence and Absence in the Space of Modernity." *Society and Space* 10, no. 2 (April 1992): 181–198.

Silver, Hilary. "A New Urban and Regional Hierarchy? Impacts of Modernization, Restructuring, and the End of Bipolarity: Conference, Los Angeles, April 1992." *IJURR* 16, no. 4 (December 1992): 651–653.

Singleman, J. and H. L. Browning. "Industrial Transformation and Occupational Change in the US 1960–70." *Social Forces* 59 (1980): 246–264.

Slymovics, Susan. "Discourses on the Pre-1948 Palestinian Village: The Case of Ein Hod/Ein Houd." *TDSR* 6, no. 2 (Spring 1995): 27–38.

Smith, Gavin. "Towards an Ethnography of Idiosyncratic Livelihood." *IJURR* 20, no. 1 (March 1994): 71–87.

Smith, Michael Peter, Bernadette Tarallo, and George Kagiwada. "Coloring California: New Asian Immigrant Households, Social Networks and the Local State." *IJURR* 15, no. 2 (June 1991): 276–287.

Smith, N. "Geography, Science and Post-Positivist Modes of Explanation." *Progress in Human Geography* 5 (1979): 356–383.

———. "Degeneracy in Theory and Practice: Spatial Interactionism and Radical Eclecticism." *Progress in Human Geography* 3 (1981): 111–118.

Soja, E. W. "Regions in Context: Spatiality, Periodicity and the Historical Geography of the Regional Question." *Society and Space* 3, no. 3 (June 1985): 175–190.

———. "Taking Los Angeles Apart." *Society and Space* 4, no. 3 (September 1986): 255–272.

Spivak, Gayatri Chakravorty. "Subaltern Studies: Deconstructing Historiography" in Ranajit Guha and Gayatri Spivak (eds), *Selected Subaltern Studies*. New York and Oxford: Oxford University Press, 1988, 3–32.

———. "How to Read a Culturally Different Book" in Francis Barker, Peter Hulme, and Margaret Iverson (eds), *Colonial Discourse/Postcolonial Theory*. New York: Manchester University Press, 1994, 126–150.

Steele, James. "The Translation of Tradition. A Comparative Dialectic." *TDSR* 7, no. 2 (Spring 1996): 19–34.

Stille, Alexander. "Invisible Cities." *Lingua Franca* (July/August 1998): 40–48.

Stoner, Jill. "Camp and Field: Notes on the Polish Landscape." *TDSR* 3, no. 1 (Fall 1991): 77–88.

Sunley, P. "Regional Restructuring, Class Change and Political Action: A Comment." *Society and Space* 4, no. 4 (1986): 465–468.

———. "Regional Restructuring, Class Change and Political Action: A Comment." *Society and Space* 4, no. 4 (December 1986): 465–468.

Taylor, Mark. "The Archetexture of Pyramids." *Assemblage* 5 (April 1990): 16–27.

Terasaka, Akinobu *et al*. "The Transformation of Regional Systems in an Information-Oriented Society." *Geographical Review of Japan* 61, no. 1 (January 1988): 36–53.

Testa, Peter. "Unity of the Discontinuous. Alvaro Siza's Works." *Assemblage* 2 (February 1987): 46–61.

Thorns, David C. "The Implications of Differential Rates of Capital Gain from Owner Occupation for the Formation and Development of Housing Classes." *IJURR* 5, no. 2 (June 1981): 205–217.

Thrift, Nigel. "The Politics of Context." *Society and Space* 1, no. 4 (December 1983): 371–375.

———. "On the Determination of Social Action in Space and Time." *Society and Space* 1, no. 1 (March 1983): 23–57.

———. "The Fixers: The Urban Geography of International Commercial Capital" in J. Henderson and M. Castells (eds), *Global Restructuring and Territorial Development*. London: Sage Books, 1987, 202–233.

Tigerman, Stanley. "Has Theory Displaced History as a Generator of Ideas in the Architectural Studio, or (More Importantly), Why Do Critics Continuously Displace Service Course Specialists?" *Journal of Architectural Education* (September 1992), 48–50.

Tofflin, Gerard. "Ecology and Anthropology of Traditional Dwellings." *TDSR* 5, no. 2 (Spring 1994): 9–20.

Topalov, Christian. "A History of Urban Research: The French Experience since 1965." *IJURR* 13, no. 4 (December 1989): 625–651.

Trachte, Kent and Robert Ross. "The Crisis of Detroit and the Emergence of Global Capitalism." *IJURR* 9, no. 2 (June 1985): 186–217.

Turgut, Huyla. "Normative Values and their Cultural Roots in the Traditional Turkish House." *TDSR* 6, no. 2 (Spring 1995): 65–74.

Ul-Haq, Saif. "Architecture within the Folk Tradition." *TDSR* 5, no. 2 (Spring 1994): 61–73.

Upton, Dell. "The Traditional House and its Enemies." *TDSR* 1, no. 2 (Spring 1990), 71–84.

———. "The Tradition of Change." *TDSR* 5, no. 2 (Fall 1993): 9–15.

Urry, John. "Localities, Regions and Social Class." *IJURR* 5, no. 4 (December 1981): 455–474.

———. "Survey 12: Society, Space and Locality." *Society and Space* 5, no. 4 (December 1987): 435–444.

Valentine, Gill. "Heterosexing Space: Lesbian Perceptions and Experiences of Everyday Spaces." *Society and Space* 11, no. 4 (August 1993), 395–413.

———. "Out and About: Geographies of Lesbian Landscapes." *IJURR* 19, no. 1 (March 1995): 96–111.

Viola, Eduardo J. "The Ecologist Movement in Brazil (1974–1986): From Environmentalism to Ecopolitics." *IJURR* 12, no. 3 (September 1988): 211–223.

Walton, John. "Urban Sociology: The Contributions and Limits of Political Economy." *Annual Review of Sociology* 19 (1993): 301–320.

Warde, Alan. "Industrial Restructuring, Local Politics and the Reproduction of Labor Power: Some Theoretical Considerations." *Society and Space* 6, no. 1 (1988): 75–95.

Wark, McKenzie. "From Fordism to Sonyism. Perverse Readings of the New World Order." *New Formations* no. 15 (Winter 1991): 43–54.

Water, Bronwyn. "Irishness, Gender and Place." *Society and Space* 13, no. 1 (February 1995): 35–50.

Watson, S. "Gilding the Smokestacks: The New Symbolic Representations of Deindustrialized Regions." *Society and Space* 9, no. 1 (1991): 59–70.

White, Hayden. "Historical Emplotment and the Problem of Truth" in Saul Friedlander (ed.), *Probing the Limits of Representation. Nazism and the Final Solution.* Cambridge, MA: Harvard University Press, 1992, 37–53.

Whiteman, John. "On Hegel's Definition of Architecture." *Assemblage* 2 (February 1987): 15–23.

———. "Divisible by Two." *Assemblage* 7 (October 1988): 42–55.

Wigley, Mark. "Story-Time." *Assemblage* 27 (August 1995): 81–94.

———. "The Displacement of Structure and Ornament." *Assemblage* 5 (February 1988): 51–57.

———. "The Translation of Architecture, The Production of Babel." *Assemblage* 8 (February 1989): 6–21.

Wilson, Stuart. "The 'Gifts' of Frederich Froebel." *JSAH* 26, no. 4 (December 1967): 238–241.

Woods, Mary. "The First American Architectural Journals: The Profession's Voice." *Journal of the Society of Architectural Historians* 58, no. 2 (June 1989): 117–138.

Wright, Gwendolyn. "History for Architects" in Gwendolyn Wright and Janet Parks (eds), *The History of History in American Schools of Architecture 1865–1975*. New York: Temple Hoyne Buell Center and Princeton Architectural Press, 1995, 13–52.

Zalewski, Daniel. "Inside Publishing. The Routledge Devolution." *Lingua Franca* (May/June 1995): 17–18.

——. "Inside Publishing. Can This Journal be Saved?" *Lingua Franca* (July/August 1995): 15–16.

Index

Note: page references in **bold type** indicate entries of major importance

AA Files 72
abstraction 15, 122, 153
Abu-Lughod, Janet 44, 103–4
academy 10–11, 45, 101, 107, 176–7, 199; authority 10, 17
Adami 64
Addams, Nicholas 41
Adler, Sy 125
aesthetics 65, 171, 192, 201
Africa 44; cities 123–4, 134
agency 15, 22, 156; and structure 23, 153–4, 157–8, 159
Aglietta, M. 127
Allen, Anne E. Guernsey 98–9, 100, 110n44
Allen, Stanley 71–3, 74
AlSayyad, Nezar 18, 87, 108n2
Althusser, Louis 20, 118, 120
American Indians 110n44
Amin, Samir 149n69
Amman, Jordan 100
Anderson, Kay 173–4
Anderson, Perry 144n17
Andre, Carl 203n4
Appadurai, Arjun 125
Aranha, Joseph 96, 98, 99, 100
a/r/c (*architecture/research/criticism*) vii, viii, ix
Architectural Association, Graduate Planning School 143n11
architectural education 10, 17, 61, 68, 80n8, 91, 101; architectural history in 16, 31–2, 33, 47–8, 57, 194

Architectural Review 54n65
architecture: canon revision 197; as category 1, 7, 202; history of 15, 16–17, 29–55, 57, 85, 194, 201; institutions 48, 76, 195; preservation of *see* preservation; *see also* architectural education; practice; research; theory
architecture/research/criticism *see* a/r/c
Architecture Today 54n65
Arets, Wiel 71–3
ARQ (*Architectural Research Quarterly*) 54n65
arts and crafts movement 89
Assemblage 2, 3, 8, 14, 15, 16, **17–18**, 19, 23, 48, **56–83**, 85, 86, 94, 103, 107, 115, 154, 155, 159, 168, 174, **194–6**, 197, 198, 200; Euro-American emphasis 79, 85–6, 107, 195; limits of disruptive strategies 75–80
Association of American Geographers 171, 175, 176–7; *Annals* 14
Association of Collegiate Schools of Architecture 50n11, 79
avant garde movements 89–90
Aysan, Yasemin 90, 93

Badran, Rasem 100–1
Bakhtin, Mikhail 172
Baird, George 79
Bali, traditional settlements 96, 100
Bamileke people 99–100
Bangladesh 90, 96

Bannister, Turpin 49n9, 50n11
Barnes, Carl F., Jr 36
Barthes, Roland 60, 61
base/superstructure model 153
Bataille, Georges 66
Baudrillard, Jean 128, 187n85
Beauregard, Robert 135–6
belief systems 97
Bell, David 171–2
Blau, Eve 43
"blob" architecture 71, 200
Bloom, Allan 6
Bloomer, Jennifer 65–6, 67
Blueprint 54n65
body 166–8, 170–2, 173, 174, 178, 198
Bonfil, Guillermo 110n45
Bourdier, Jean-Paul 18, 87
Bourdieu, Pierre 176
Bozdogan, Sibel 105, 134
Brazil 106, 134
Brenner, Johanner 125
Building Design 54n65
building(s): as category 1, 7; as signifying system 153, 180
built environment: disciplines 1–2; relationship to texts 4–5, 8–9

Cameron, D. 8–9
Cameroon, traditional environment 99
Canada vii–viii, 106, 163, 173
Canadian Architect viii
Capital and Class 143n12
capitalism 89, 160, 165–6, 194, 198, 200, 201; crises 2, 126–7, 137–8; and tradition 88, 95, 105, 197; urban processes 20–2, 115–41, 153
Castells, Manuel 116, 118–21, 124, 125, 145n38, 149n69, 202
Çelik, Zeynep 42, 43–4, 47, 48, 194
Center for Environmental Studies 119
Chandigarh 90
Chewing, J. A. 49n8
Chicago School of urban sociology 118, 135–6, 141, 162
Chinese culture 106, 133, 173
Chomsky, Noam 60
Christian architecture 43, 52n29

"Cities, Enterprises and Society on the Eve of the 21st Century" conference (1995) 148n57
city: as category 1, 153, 202; *see also* urban space
Clark, Gordon 156
Clarke, David 128–9
class *see* social class
Clifford, James 95
CNRS, Paris 120, 143n12, 148n58
collective assent (A. Rapoport) 93–4, 97
collective consumption 116, 117, 121, 122, 123, 151n98, 202
collective values 18, 19, 86, 93–5, 96, 97, 166
Colomina, Beatriz 78–9
colonialism 9, 48; socio/spatial relationship 156, 172, 173, 174, 175, 179, 192, 193, 194; tradition 89, 90, 105, 197; urban development 22, 134–5, 138, 151n96
commodification, of tradition 106, 107, 200
community studies 164
Conant, Kenneth J. 32
Conference of Socialist Economists (CSE) 143n12
Cornell, Laurel L. 105
Cornell University, holdings of journals in the Fine Art Library 14
Correa, Charles 197
critical cosmopolitanism (P. Rabinow) p26 n24
critical paradigms 5–8
Cultural Anthropology 27n35
cultural anthropology 86, 98, 156, 164, 197, 198
cultural capital 10–11, 176
cultural difference 6, 125, 140, 155
cultural identity 102, 123, 125, 177
cultural self-representation 42
cultural values 18, 19, 86, 93–5, 96, 97, 166
culture 202; socio/spatial relationship 154, 167, 170–1, 173, 177, 198; urban research 123–4, 133, 141–2, 153
culturescapes 179

Dal Co, Francesco 61
Davis, Mike 172
de Certeau, Michel 167–8, 172
Dear, Michael 124, 156, 179
deconstruction 16, 17, 23–4, 59, 62–5, 67, 68, 79, 177, 195, 197
Deleuze, Gilles 59, 60, 70–3, 74, 77, 187n85, 200
Della Seta, Piero 120
dependency theory 20
Derrida, Jacques 62, 64, 66, 172
descriptive discourse 39
Deutsche, Rosalyn 3–4, 167–8, 190
Deutsche Werkbund movement 89
Dhaka 90
diasporas 1, 202
dichotomies 103–4, 174–5, 178, 196
difference: proliferation of 65, 73, 74, 75, 76, 200; spaces of 22, 137–42; *see also* cultural difference
discourse 1–2, 3–4, 6–8, 9, 10, 189–91; journals as sites of 14–15; and literary theory 3–8; normalization 190
Douglass, Mike 132
Doxiadis, Constantinos 108n1

Eckstein, Susan 145n37
economic aid and development 90
economic migrants 127, 131
economic space *see* political economy
Eisenman, Peter 59, 60–1, 64, 65
Enlightenment culture 6
Environment and Planning D. Society and Space see Society and Space
Environments by Design 26n26
ethics, and tradition 93
ethnicity 21, 126–7, 151n98, 172–3
ethno-architecture (G. Toffin) 102
ethnocentrism 44, 172
ethnographic pastoral 20, 88, 95–8, 101, 105, 107, 166, 196, 200
ethnography 198
Ettorre, E. M. 121–2, 125
Eurocentrism 6, 15, 46, 48, 102, 162, 192–3
existentialism 156

Feagin, Joe 140
feminism 6, 12, 23, 24, 104, 125, 151n98, 159, 167, 168–70
Fletcher, Bannister 42
fold concept 60, 70
Forbes, Dean 156
Fordism 138, 201
formalism 60–1, 73, 75, 91–2
Forrest, Ray 145n29
Forty, Adrian 8, 9
Foucault, Michel 7–8, 9, 18, 172, 176
foundationalism 35
fragmentation 67, 73
France: theory 17, 60, 61; urban research 20, 119, 120, 123, 124, 193; urbanism 9, 110n44
Frank, André Gunder 149n69
Frankfurt School 115
Frankfurt science laboratories 64–5
Friedmann, John 130–1, 134, 135
functionalism 21, 61, 68–9, 70, 91

Gallop, Jane 12
Gandelsonas, Mario 60
gay movement 6, 125
Geertz, Clifford 164, 179
Geltmaker, T. 171
gender 21, 24, 142, 151n98, 166–8, 169, 170, 173, 174
generalization 15, 153, 176
geography 86, 116, 197; emphasis of *Society and Space* 22–4, 155–80 *passim*, 198–9
Georgalli, Maria-Christina 96–7
Giddens, Anthony 158–9, 160, 166
globalization 1, 87, 106, 107, 177, 197; research 86
Gombrich, E. H. 51n18
Gottdeiner, Mark 140
Graburn, Nelson 88–9
Gramsci, Antonio 201–2
grand narratives 7
Greece 110n45
Green, William A. 50n16
Gregory, Derek 157
grids 69, 72, 77
Gropius, Walter 32

Guatarri, Felix 71, 187n85
Gwiasda, Vicky 136

Habermas, Jürgen 187n85
Haggerstrand, Torsten 159–60
Hall, R. R. 165
Harloe, Michael 28n40, 119, 124, 141, 142
Harvard University 60; Design School 32
Harvey, David 118–19, 128, 149n69, 166–8, 170, 172
Hays, K. Michael 17, 57–8, 59, 61–2, 64, 78–9
Hays-Mitchell, Maureen 169
Henderson, Martha L. 110n44
heritage 105–6, 107, 173
heritage studies 86
Heynen, Hilde 90
Hill, Richard Child 120, 122, 146n43
history 3, 6–7, 85; return of 61; world cities debate 134–5
Hitchcock, Henry Russell 49n10, 52n25
Hobsbawm, Eric 2, 89
Hosagrahar, Jyoti 48, 105
housing 20, 21, 90, 98, 104, 105, 120, 121–2, 153
Huth, Hans 50n12
hybridity 20, 104–6, 107, 127
hyperconsumption 129

identity: cultural 102, 123, 125, 177; embodied 155, 166–8, 170, 174, 178; politics of 16, 103, 125, 142, 151n98, 167, 176, 175–7, 178, 200; professional 32, 35, 37, 41, 45, 200, 201
imagination 23
imperialism 22, 138, 156, 169, 179, 192, 194, 203
India 90, 105, 134
Indonesia 98
industrial capitalism *see* capitalism
informal economy 126
Institute for Architecture and Urban Studies, New York 60

interdisciplinarity 2–4, 24, 45, 86, 102, 190–1, 197, 198, 202–3
International Association for the Study of Traditional Environments (IASTE) 20, 86–7, 88, 101, 102, 103, 104, 107, 198
International Journal of Urban and Regional Research (IJURR) 2, 13, 15, **20–2**, 23, **113–51**, 153–4, 159, 162, 167, 177, 180n2, **191–4**, 195, 196, 201–2; definition of international 21–2, 116–17, 137–8, 140–1, 150n97, 193
International Sociological Association (ISA) 21–2; Research Committee 21, 20, 116, 119, 120, 136, 137, 140–1, 150n97, 193; World Congress (Varna, 1970) 119
interpretation 59, 62, 77
invented traditions (E. Hobsbawm and T. Ranger) 88
Islamic cities 44, 123
Islamic studies 197
Italy, housing 120
Itzigsohn, Jose 145n38

Jackson, Peter 175–6
Jacobs, Jane M. 175–6
Jameson, Frederic 74–5, 172
Japan 105, 133
Jarzombek, Mark 45–6
Jefferson, Thomas 52n30
Jordan 100, 106
Journal of Architecture 54n65
Journal of the American Institute of Planners 14
Journal of the Society of Architectural Historians (JSAH) ix, 2, 11, 13, 14, 15, **16–17, 29–55**, 76, 78, 85, 86, 94–5, 104, 107, 154, **191–4**, 196, 201, 202; Euro-American emphasis 31, 34–5, 41–2, 44, 46–7, 48, 85–6, 107, 192–3; sites of research at the millennium 42, 43–4
journals 2–5; and academic institutions 10–11; communities of method 11–13; format and organization 12–13, 35–6,

42, 88, 94, 103, 178, 198, 202; proliferation 13–14; publication protocols 12; relationship to formation of academic knowledge 24, 189–202; as resources for understanding critical discourse 11–12; sites of discourse 14–15; strategies of disturbance 57–83, 168, 194–6; *see also individual titles*

Kahn 90
Keith, M. 171, 177
Kennedy, Alicia 79
Kenya 173
Kester, Grant 70–1
Keynesianism 2, 117, 130
Kimball, Fiske 50n13
King, Anthony 134
Kipnis, Jeffrey 74
Knopp, Lawrence 125
Koolhaas, Rem 73–5
Kostof, Spiro 110n45
Krautheimer, Richard 40, 49n10
Kwinter, Sandford 73

labor issues 21, 126, 127–8, 131, 139, 151n96
Laclau, Ernesto 166
Lagana, Guido 122
Latin America, gender and politics 169
Latour, Bruno 203n6
Lebas, Elizabeth 118
Le Corbusier 37, 90, 196
Lee, David 157
Lefebvre, Henri 110n44, 149n69, 160, 161, 162, 163, 166, 172, 203n3
Le Galès, Patrick 151n103
lesbian politics 6, 121–2, 125
Lester, Doris 168, 169
Lévi-Strauss, Claude 60
linear space 39
linguistics 60
Liontidou, Lila 129
Lipietz, Alain 127–8
literary theory 5–8
Livingstone, David 179

locality 15, 106, 139, 154–5, 163–6, 177, 179; teaching of architectural history 47–8
located writing 16, 176, 178, 199, 200
Logan, John 140, 141
Lojkine, Jean 120
Loos, Adolph 89–90
Los Angeles 161–2, 163, 165
Los Angeles School 158, 161–2, 163, 165
Lu, Duanfang 104
Lynn, Greg 69, 71, 79
Lyotard, J. F. 172

Maass, John 34–5, 40, 48
Malaquais, Dominique 99, 100
Marcus, George 176
Markus, T. 8–9
Markusen, Ann 136
Marouli, Christina 147n48
Marx, Karl 118
Marxism 61, 115; regulation school 127, 177
Marxist geography 22–3, 156–8, 164–5, 198
Marxist social theory 157–8, 160–2, 164–5, 168, 176
Marxist urban research 20, 22, 113–51, 153, 166–7, 178, 201–2
masculinism 6, 167–8
Massachusetts Institute of Technology (MIT) 60
Massey, Doreen 157–8, 164–5, 167
Massotti, Louis 120
Matysek, Eugene E. 40
meaning 17, 62, 67, 151n98, 153, 154; multiplicity 77
Merleau Ponty, Maurice 66
metaphors 70–3
Mexico 110n44
migration 126–7, 202
mimesis 6, 38–9
Mingione, Enzo 120, 131
Mitchell, Kathryne 106, 173
Mitchell, W. J. T. 39
modernism 3, 8, 31, 32, 155, 156, 167–8, 199; *Assemblage* as challenge to 17, 58, 60, 61, 72, 75, 194–6; and

237

postmodernism 129, 172, 178; and tradition 20, 87–107 *passim*, 196
Molyneux 169
monumental architecture 52n29, 92
Morocco 89, 135
Moses, Robert 201
Mouffe, Chantal 166
multinational companies 116, 130, 133
multiple modernities 105
Murie, Alan 145n29

Nagy, Sibyl Moholy 35–6, 48
narrative(s) 6–7; of emancipation and redemption 21; in *JSAH* 36–8, 39, 95; of loss 20, 21, 95, 107, 166
nation 1, 15, 126–7, 132–3, 135, 202
nation-state 1, 35, 89, 132, 135
nationalism 35, 89, 105
naturalism, traditional environments 91
neighborhood 113
Nelson, Cary 190
neo-liberalism 116, 126
neo-Marxism *see* Marxism
Nepal 96, 100
New Criticism 5–6
New Delhi 105
new technology 130
newly industrializing countries 48, 87, 138
Nichols, Frederick D. 50n10
Nichols, Stephen G. 50n17
nodes 21, 130, 136

objectivity 34, 97–8, 103, 139, 141, 156, 175, 176, 178, 199
Office for Metropolitan Architecture (OMA) 73
Oliver, Paul 90, 91–2, 93
Olmsted, Frederick Law 40
Ong, Aihwa 132–3
Oppositions 60–1, 64, 195–6
Overby, Osmund 34, 52n31
Overton, J. D. 173

Pahl, Ray 122
Pankhurst, Sylvia 168, 169

patriarchy 168, 170
periodicals *see* journals
Perspecta 26n26
Pevsner, Nicholas 40
phenomenology 61, 156
Pianta, Mario 122
Pickvance, Chris 119, 120, 123–4
Pile, S. 172
planning 9, 36, 86, 116, 201–2
political economy 20–2, 113–51, 153, 154, 159–67, 177, 178, 192, 193, 198
political science 116, 197
politics 4, 6, 16, 68–9; Deleuze's philosophical language 70–5, 77–8; and interdisciplinarity 191, 202–3; of position 198–9; traditional environments 106, 107; urban space 121–5, 151n78, 164, 168–70, 179, 180, 202; *see also* identity
Pollock, Jackson 203n4
popular culture 61
Portes, Alejandro 120, 145n37, 149n69
positionality 98, 103, 137, 171–2, 176, 198, 199; *see also* located writing
positivist architectural history *see Journal of the Society of Architectural Historians*
post-civil society 74–5
post-colonial actor network theory 23
post-colonial contexts 90, 173
post-colonial studies 86, 175, 179
post-Fordism 21, 116, 126, 127–30, 138, 139, 151n98, 160, 161, 165, 166, 167, 180n2, 201
postmodernism 14, 45–6, 67, 73, 105, 128–9, 160–2, 167, 171, 172, 178
post-structuralism 17, 43, 61, 70, 85, 166, 176, 186n76, 197
Poulantzas, Nicos 20, 120
power relations 6, 8, 76, 98, 135, 139, 168, 169, 173
practice 17, 24, 31, 45, 61, 195; translation of tradition 98–103; *see also* theory, and practice
Pratt, Geraldine 180n4
praxis 107
preservation 32–4, 35, 36, 105–6

Preteceille, Edmond 120
primordialism, traditional environments 103, 106
Princeton University 60
privatization 21, 164, 165
professionalism 15, 17, 23, 67; identity 32, 35, 37, 41, 45, 200, 201; see also practice
protest movements see social movements
Prussin, Labelle 43, 44
psychoanalysis 59

queer space 171
queer studies 23, 125

Rabinow, Paul 8, 9, 51n18, 135
race 21, 24, 137, 142, 172–4, 175
Rakatansky, Mark 69, 75
Ranger, Terrence 89
Rapoport, Amos 91, 92–3, 94, 101–2
real/imaginary opposition 4, 6–7, 8–9, 97, 174–5
realism 22, 36, 38, 62, 183n35
reflexivity 16, 103, 107, 155–6, 173, 174–7, 178, 189, 191, 198, 200
region(s) 163, 179; restructuring 160, 161, 163, 165
regional economic systems 133
Reitgnes, Claudia N. 124
representation(s) 6, 8–9, 10, 38–40, 61–2, 67, 76, 78, 80, 85, 97, 106, 107, 155, 168–70, 174–6, 189, 193; of urban space 138–41; worlds of 203
research 9, 10–11, 13
rhizome concept 60, 70–1, 72, 75, 77, 200
Ribeiro 134
Richardson, H. H. 52n30
Rimmer, Peter 133
Robbins, Bruce 67, 112n76
Robertson, Roland 142n2
Robinson, J. 173
Rose, Gillian 121, 122, 159, 168–9, 172, 184n49
Rossi, Aldo 61, 110n44
Rowe, Colin 61
Roy, Ananya 104
Rudofsky, Bernard 90–2, 93, 101

Sack, Robert 110n44
Said, Edward 40
Saif-Ul-Haq 96
Samoa, traditional environment 98–9, 100, 110n44
Samuels, Marwyn S. 157
Saunders, Peter 122
schools of architecture see architectural education
Schwarzer, Mitchell 45
scientific method 141, 192; see also objectivity
Scott, Alan J. 124
Scott, Felicity 91–2
Segre, Anna 122
sexuality 21, 142, 166–8, 171–2, 173, 174
Shields, Rob 160, 162–3, 188n105
signification 17, 153, 180
Silver, Hilary 136–7
Sir John Soane's Museum, London 81n36
Smith, Michael Peter 126
Smithson, Robert 203n4
social anthropology see cultural anthropology
social class 21, 24, 121, 122, 126, 142, 166, 167, 170
social conditions 3
social construction 57, 105, 170, 173, 197, 200
social movements 2, 6, 20–1, 116, 118, 120, 121–5, 126, 137–8, 139, 151n96, 164, 166, 169, 180n2, 202
social organization: folk models 164; traditional environments as models 88–9, 99–100
social sciences 116, 154, 158–9; methodology 174–5
social stratification 20, 122
social theory, relationship to space 15, 22–4, 154–88, 198–9
Société Française de Sociologie 143n12
Society and Space 2, 11, 15, 16, **22–4**, 113, 115, **152–88**, 195, 196, **198–9**, 200; Euro-American emphasis 155, 156, 169, 172, 177, 179

Society of (American) Architectural Historians 16, 29, 31, 34, 46; *Newsletter* 33
socio-spatial dialectic 154–5, 160–2, 177
sociology 116, 197; Chicago School 118, 135–6, 141, 162
Soja, Edward 23, 158, 160–2, 163, 167, 168, 172
South Africa 173
South East Asia 132–3
space: interdependence 1, 153, 203; relationship to society 15, 22–4, 154–80, 198–9; relationship to writing 4, 189–204
Space and Culture. International Journal of Social Spaces 188n105
"spatial trialectics" (H. Lefebvre) 162
Speaks, Michael 74
specialization(s) 2, 4, 14, 40, 45, 113, 198; SS as bridge between 156–9, 179
specific intellectual concept 8, 18
state policy 20, 21, 116, 117, 118, 120–1, 124, 126, 138, 139, 151n98, 164, 165, 180n2, 201
Steele, James 100–1
structuralism 60, 61, 62, 141, 195, 201–2
structuration theory 159, 160
structure: and agency 23, 153–4, 157–8, 159; relation to ornament 64–5, 65–6, 75
Sullivan, Louis 37, 52n30, 64
symbolic ecology 141–2, 153, 162, 192
Szelenyi, Ivan 120

Tafuri, Manfredo 61
Taylor, Mark 63, 65, 66–7
tectonic space 39
text(s) 1; architecture as 17, 60, 62–5, 68–70; as architecture 59–60, 62–8; body as 170–2; relationship to built environment 4–5, 8–9; social as 61–2
Teymur, Necdut 90, 93
Thailand 110n45
theory 1, 11, 14–15, 57, 60, 190, 191, 196, 198; and practice 9, 17–18, 45, 48, 58, 59, 65, 67–8, 70, 75, 78, 79, 179, 191, 197, 199–203

third world 18, 19, 48, 87, 90, 91, 92, 93, 123–4, 126, 129–30, 138
Thrift, Nigel 156, 164
time-geography 159–60
time-space compression 167, 202
time-space interactionism 155, 159–60
Toffin, Gerard 102
Topolov, Christian 120
Toronto, Skydome Stadium vii–viii
Touraine, Alain 27n32
Town Planning Review 14
tradition 19–20, 70, 86, 87–8, 196–8, 200–1; architectural translation of 98–103; defining 88–95; hybridity and heritage 20, 104–6, 107; meaning 87–8, 106; transformation into "tradition" 103–4
Traditional Dwellings and Settlements Review 2, 13, 15, 16, **18–20**, 21, 44, 48, **84–112**, 113, 173, **196–8**, 200–1; Euro-American emphasis 99, 110n45; international frame of analysis 19, 85–7, 107
traditional environments 18–20, 48, 84–112, 196–8
transdisciplinary theory 4
transnational corporations 116, 130, 133
transnationalism 106, 117, 132–3
Tulane University 77
Turkish housing 105

United Kingdom: gender and space 167; journals 26n26, 45; locality studies 164–5; urban scholarship 119, 122, 124
universalism 19, 33, 47, 77
University of Birmingham, Centre for Urban and Regional Studies 143n12
University of California, Berkeley, College of Environmental Design 86, 198
University of Iowa 80n7
University of London, Bartlett School of Architecture and Planning 143n12
Upton, Dell 104
"Urban Change and Conflict" conferences 28n41, 119

Urban Design International 26n26
urban ecology 131, 141–2, 153, 162
urban "managerialism" 151n98
urban memory 142
urban planning *see* planning
urban research 113–51, 153, 158, 160–2
urban social movements *see* social movements
urban space 8, 15, 20–2, 23, 113–51, 153, 180, 192; application of Deleuzian narrative 73–5; politics 121–5, 151n98, 164, 168–70, 179, 180, 202; restructuring 135, 151n98, 180n2
urban voyeurism 167–8
Urry, John 157, 163–4

Valentine, Gill 125
Vancouver 106, 173
Venice School 61
Venturis, the 61
vernacular architecture 7, 33, 89, 90–4, 198
Vienna 90
Vint, Thomas 49n10

Wallerstein, Immanuel 149n69
Walton, John 119–20, 140, 141, 149n69
Weberian theory 20, 122
welfare state 117, 124
West Edmonton Mall, Canada 163
White, Hayden 6, 8, 36, 39
Whiteman, John 63, 67, 68–9, 75
Wigley, Mark 17, 62–4, 67, 68, 77–8
Williams, Peter 156
Williams, Raymond 172
Wirth, Louis 135–6
Wolff, Goetz 130–1, 134, 135
world city 21, 138, 139, 151n98, 154, 162; formation 117, 130–2; history 134–5; as ideal type 135–7
world economy 20, 107, 117, 130–1, 134, 138, 151n98, 202
world system approach 149n69
Wright, Frank Lloyd 29, 37, 40, 52n30
writing, relationship to space 4, 189–204

Zucker, Paul 49n10